BIRTHING MINISTRY

Leadership Essentials

BIRTHING MINISTRY
Leadership Essentials

DAISY S. DANIELS

THE WRITING ON THE WALL PUBLISHING SERVICES
ORLANDO, FL 32862, U.S.A.

THE WRITING ON THE WALL PUBLISHING SERVICES products are available at special quantity discounts for bulk purchases. For details, write The Writing on the Wall Publishing Services, P.O. Box 621194, Orlando, FL 32862, or telephone (708) 704-6117.

The Writing on the Wall Publishing Services
"...He sent the hand that wrote the inscription."

Birthing Ministry *Leadership Essentials*
Daisy S. Daniels
P.O. Box 621194
Orlando, Florida 32862 – 1433
Website: www.thewritingonthewal.wix.com/daisysdaniels
E-Mail address: thewritingonthewall@aol.com

Library of Congress Control Number: 2013951623

ISBN 978-0-9914002-0-1

Book production by:
The Writing on the Wall Publishing Services

Printed in the United States of America

Table of Contents

DEDICATION

This book is dedicated, first and foremost, to my Lord and Savior, Jesus Christ. It is because of His love, grace, mercy, and faithfulness that I'm able to offer this book as a sacrifice of praise unto Him. I am everything that I am because of Him; His love, grace, mercy, and faithfulness that have brought me this far. And to rest in His promise that He'll never leave nor forsake me is motivation enough to remain in Him no matter what challenges I may face. Clearly, the challenges in this life won't compare to the glory of being with Him. Jesus, I love you.

I also dedicate this book to my man of God, Pastor, Husband, and Friend, Randolph E. Daniels, Sr., who was right by my side through this experience. Undoubtedly, there wouldn't have been any way that I could've made it through this test, trial, and tribulation without you being there to help, teach, and encourage me. And for that, I am forever grateful. Thank you. I love you.

And to those of you who are longing to draw closer to God; whether you're a pastor, leader, or laymen in the Body of Christ:

It is a blessing, privilege, and an honor for me to share my experience with you: the tears, hurt, pain, betrayal, seeming defeat, and ultimate triumph. Therefore, it's my prayer that my experience will in some way allow you to see Christ in a way that you've never seen Him before; get to know Christ in a way that you've never known Him before, and experience Christ in a way that you've never experienced Him before. And as a result, He'll take you to higher levels and new dimensions in Him than you've ever experienced before.

I pray that this book, the transparency of my suffering and anguish, will cause you to be encouraged to remain faithful to Christ. And that it would be a testimony to His love, grace, mercy, and faithfulness.

To God be the glory for the things He has done.

Daisy S. Daniels

FOREWARD

After the birth of Jesus, during the reign of King Herod, the wise men of the east had seen the star and had come to worship the new born King. King Herod was disturbed to hear that the wise men had come to worship someone other than him. Feeling that the birth of this child was a threat to his kingdom, King Herod ordered the death of all boys in Bethlehem who were two years old and under. However, God exposed the enemy's demonic plot to kill the children, including baby Jesus, to Joseph, the guardian of His precious Son.

And with the writing of this book, Daisy allowed the Holy Spirit to work through her in order to expose the enemy's plot to kill the "baby" that God was birthing in her life. He has also exposed the enemy's plot to pastors, ministers, and leaders; the guardians of His precious church.

Daisy is such an anointed writer who is not afraid to invite the reader into the details of her life (we overcome by the Blood of the Lamb, and by the word of our testimony). Too often the members of the Body of Christ will provide a clean *Reader's Digest* version of their testimony, but Daisy has the courage to give every soiled detail of her experience.

In her first book *The Ties That Bind,* she chronicled how the enemy attempted to destroy her personal life. With her latest book, we get to see how the enemy orchestrated a strategic plan to destroy her ministry.

This book blows the trumpet in Zion and reminds us that the enemy has one purpose and that is to kill, steal, and destroy all that God is doing in the earth through us. *Birthing Ministry* will pull you into its pages and grip your attention until the final page has been read. You will be educated as well as entertained by the writing skills of the author. You'll experience emotions ranging from sadness to anger as you observe the lives of the individuals within this book.

This book is not only for pastors, ministers, and leaders – it is for anyone who believes God is birthing something extraordinary through them.

It would be wise not to take the devices of the enemy lightly – there will be opposition. Take your places on the wall and be on the lookout for the enemy because "these tigers are trained."

To the Glory of God

Randolph E. Daniels, Sr.
Senior Pastor
The Embassy of Grace
Orlando, Florida

ENDORSEMENTS

This book is written with such accuracy of what it takes to birth a ministry. The courage that it took for Daisy to be transparent is nothing short of ministry in itself. The way she tells her story is chronicled in such a way that makes it easy to relate to, whether you're a leader or not, in ministry or not. The step by step instructions allow you to see first-hand how you too can be successful with birthing ministry.

The way Daisy tells her story is done in a way that I've never heard before. She is very candid and open about the pain she experienced during this process, which is something she's never ashamed to do. Her ministry of healing and deliverance has prepared her and taught her that being open, honest, and transparent exposes the snares and traps of the enemy. So whatever it takes to expose Satan, she's willing to do – no matter the cost. And that's what you'll see in this book. You'll see the opposition that she faced as she gives you a realistic view and personal account of the challenges that she endured.

Ultimately, this book is such a great teaching tool that anyone in ministry or *before* starting a ministry needs to read this book. It is of the utmost importance that they learn and know what they'll encounter during each trimester of the birthing process. I have already started teaching from this book. This information has got to get into the hands of the people.

I'm so proud of my spiritual daughter. She continues to make me proud of her, the work she's done, and her ministry.

This book is so good that I couldn't put it down.

James E. Latimore, Sr.
Senior Pastor and Teacher
Kingdom Apostolic Church International
Chicago, Illinois

Hail the King of Glory for Pastor Daisy Daniels writing this book about what it takes to "Birth Ministry." This book is relevant to the world we live in. *Birthing Ministry: Leadership Essentials* is not only for leaders but, anyone who desires to be obedient to the voice of God and expose the enemy. Using the Word of God and the personal experiences she went through, Pastor Daniels teaches how to overcome the tricks of the enemy that are used to derail us.

Even when you think you have arrived, the wars of Canaan remind us we must obey God's instructions in order to be victorious. For me, HOLD YOUR PEACE helped me gain victory when I wanted to speak my mind. Don't read this book as just another book. This book is an

ENDORSEMENTS

instruction manual to make your ministry and life what God intended it to be. In this life-altering manual you will understand that Testing is in the middle of Vision and Birth. I pray as you read you will experience breakthroughs, deliverance and victory. Remember, everything you go through isn't the devil. God Almighty is preparing you to "Birth Ministry." As Pastor Daniels did, let God have full control until He says, "PUSH!!!"

Minister Michele Green
The Church of Healing and Prosperity
Orlando, Florida

Birthing Ministry is an amazing read for people at all stages of life and spiritual journey. *Birthing Ministry* engages, informs and inspires, as it relates to real issues concerning friendship, commitment, faith and spirituality. Daisy Daniels reveals her creative side as she uses the analogy of childbirth, from conception through delivery, to share the challenges and triumphs experienced while birthing her ministry. Thank you, Daisy, for giving me the opportunity to share your experience.

Deborah Wright Bell, BSBA, PHR
Orlando, Florida

As I began reading this book, I really did not know what to expect. However, as I proceeded to read the scriptures along with the detail of the realistic, personal experiences, the words captivated my mind, and I had the desire to read more. This diary provides eye-opening testimonies and revelation on how the ministry birthing process can become intensified; however, it also signifies how the delivery produces phenomenal victories. There is no way possible, after consuming this masterpiece, that your life will ever be the same. This book is a must read, especially for those who know for certain that they are pregnant with purpose. I am so very proud of the author, and how she allowed the Lord to use her to give birth in this season. I promise you that your life will be optimistically impacted and changed forever.

Prophetess Angie Williams
Co-Pastor
New Hope Church of the Living God
President, COLG State Youth Congress
Author
Orlando, Florida

ACKNOWLEDGEMENTS

To my husband, Randolph E. Daniels, Sr.: I cannot think of any words that can describe how indebted I am to you for all that you've done for me. In the twenty-three years of our marriage you've allowed me to be me, ministry and all. Your patience allows me to grow and develop at my own pace while always encouraging me to be all that I can be, and then enlightening me that I could be even more. Thank you for your love and for being there for me with each step I take on my journey. I love you.

To my children, Ronald, DaiSha, and Randolph Jr.: Each of you, in your own way, have been motivation for me. I am so proud of each of you and could not have asked for more loving children. There is absolutely no way I could be who I am without each of you. Your love has taught me what it means to love, and there is no greater lesson a mother can learn. I love you guys more than you'll ever know.

To my spiritual parents, James and Florence Latimore: Words cannot express how grateful I am to have you guys for my spiritual parents. You have always given me the freedom I needed to not only grow spiritually, but to cultivate, develop, and exercise my spiritual gifts. You are the best parents any daughter can have. If I had a choice of choosing the spiritual parents that would allow me to become the best spiritual daughter that I could become, I'd choose you. Thank you for all that you've been to me – my love to you.

To my brothers and sisters, the Dominguez family: You all represent the apostolic, five-fold ministry in your own rite: Apostle, Prophet, Evangelist, Pastor and Teacher. With me being the youngest of fourteen children, I've learned from the best. Each of you have demonstrated for me what it means to live for Christ. And you have taught me some valuable lessons as I've watched your lives model that of integrity, wisdom, strength, and endurance. I couldn't be who I am if you weren't who you are in my life. I love you with the love that has been woven by His blood.

To my prayer partners (you know who you are): I thank and praise God for each of you, for your diligence, faithfulness, and for standing in the gap tirelessly. There is no way I could've made it through this assignment or could even take any credit for it without giving credit where credit is due. There wouldn't have been a book or ministry to birth had you not answered when the Lord called. Your prayers not only moved God to open doors, but I have no doubt that they moved Him to have mercy on me and gave me the ultimate victory as I went through. I love you, my sistahs!

To Deborah Wright Bell: Words cannot express how thankful I am to have you to make sure that all the i's were dotted and all the t's were crossed. Not only do I thank you for your willingness to assist me with this assignment, but I thank God for your desire to work with a

ACKNOWLEDGEMENTS

spirit of excellence, and your eagerness to see me be successful. I'm so glad that our paths crossed, giving us the opportunity to do what we're both passionate about. I just want you to know, I couldn't have done this without you. I love you with the love of God.

PREFACE

Peace had finally come. I had gotten to a place where I could take a deep breath and my spirit could relax. It was over!

"Write a book," the Lord said. The spoken revelation caused me to be in awe of the Lord as I thought to myself, *all of that – for this.* "On leadership," He continued as if saying, 'Write a book' wasn't challenging enough.

I laughed to myself (as Sarah did when He told her she would have a son in her old age) as I questioned *leadership? What?*

"Leadership essentials," He said to be precise. Then suddenly the vision was before me:

> **The woman was in position to give birth, which was evident by the breaking of her water.**

And just as suddenly, the tears fell from my eyes as the pain rung out in my spirit and bore witness to the wound that had been birthed in my soul.

While the tears bore witness to me birthing the ministry, the pain bore witness to the ministry birthing me.

Immediately the contractions began; causing my womb to dilate – preparing the way for my spirit – to bring forth the delivery of what the Lord had deposited into my spirit. Anguish filled my heart at the thought of telling my story. And as if telling my story wasn't enough, the pain was induced as He made it clear, "I want all of the details."

I was silent.

As I struggled to write the details of my hurt and pain, I fought through the tears of transparency that exposed the vulnerability of my betrayal: exposed, naked, and uncovered; no hedge of protection.

The Holy Spirit penned my life in *Birthing Ministry.*

I received an abundance of powerful prophetic revelations that revealed the testing that was to come as well as a wealth of God's grace and love that carried me through the fire – taking me from levels of the prophetic to new dimensions of the prophetic.

"Lord, what are you birthing in the earth?" I questioned.

PREFACE

"Leaders," He said, "to lead my people; a covenant people, and obedience in the earth. Even as I was with Abraham, so shall I be with you – My will being done in the earth *not* your will."

Then the Lord prompted Psalms 39 in my spirit: ***I said to myself, "I will watch what I do***… and immediately, I was arrested in my spirit and detained by the command *watch*. Commanded to pay close attention; be on guard, look and wait attentively.

Then I was released to continue.

…and not sin in what I say. I will hold my tongue when the ungodly are around me.

Then the vision was before me:

I saw what appeared to be tongues of fire

The tongues of fire were to reveal *Himself, His Holy Spirit* to me; a demonstration of *His* purifying presence and *His* promise. To order the words of my mouth and baptize me with fire; empowering me to do His will. Immediately I was reminded of the book of Acts; the day of Pentecost. And the fulfillment of John the Baptist's words rang out in my spirit:

"…He will baptize you with the Holy Spirit and with fire."

Luke 3:16a NLT

Pregnant with the "word" of God, a prophetic burden conceived as a result of being intimate with Him to birth forth *obedience unto Him* and obtain *power over the promise.*

Equipped with prophetic visions and dreams, the demonstration of God's supernatural power and a divine visitation from God Himself; victory was imminent.

Then He said to the woman,

"I will sharpen the pain of your pregnancy,
   and in pain you will give birth."

Genesis 3:16a NLT

I was ready to deliver.

In a vision...

Heaven was open before me and I saw the manifestation of the Holy Spirit. In my spirit I heard, "You're sitting under an open heaven. God is trying to bless you."

The interpretation...

And the Spirit of the LORD will rest on him – the Spirit of wisdom and understanding, the Spirit of counsel and might, the Spirit of knowledge and the fear of the LORD.

Isaiah 11:2 NLT

PART

I

INTIMATE WITH GOD

~ INTRODUCTION ~

THE WARS OF CANAAN

As I sat before the Lord, in my spirit, I kept hearing, "The wars of Canaan." I knew the Lord was trying to reveal something to me, so I meditated on the passage of scriptures He revealed:

These are the nations that the LORD left in the land to test those Israelites who had not experienced the wars of Canaan. He did this to teach warfare to generations of Israelites who had no experience in battle. These people were left to test the Israelites – to see whether they would obey the commands the LORD had given to their ancestors through Moses.

Judges 3:1 – 2; 4 NLT

Needless to say, I had no idea what "the wars of Canaan" meant nor could I figure out how these wars had anything to do with me. But as I continued to meditate on the passage of scriptures, *He did this to teach warfare to the generations who had no experience in battle* seemed to demand my attention. *What?* I questioned. *How could this possibly have anything to do with me?* Undoubtedly, I figured the scriptures didn't pertain to me because I was experienced in warfare and obviously had experience in battle. So, I couldn't even begin to tell you how it was really throwing me for a loop. It made no sense to me, especially considering the ministry the Lord has entrusted me with; *deliverance.* All I've ever experienced was *warfare.* All I've ever done was *battle.*

Before I even knew I was called to the ministry of healing and deliverance, I was doing deliverance. Before I even knew what warfare was, I was doing warfare. Before I even knew what spiritual battles were, I was engaged in spiritual battles. So I was really confused.

As I continued to sit before the Lord, I was reminded of the ministry that I've been entrusted with. I was also reminded of how the Lord has so graciously used me to bring forth healing, deliverance and setting people free from demonic oppression that had them bound. The Lord has dealt with me, developed me at a young age through prophetic visions and dreams. And one thing I learned was when He revealed a dream or vision, it came to pass.

Consequently, I was reminded of some of the encounters that I had experienced during my ministry…

In a dream...

My mouth was open and what I had come to know as "deliverance" was coming out of my mouth.

The interpretation...

Immediately, I knew in my spirit, as the Lord had revealed, deliverance would come from my mouth.

When my son was about six years old, he took a hearing test at school. The specialist stated the test hadn't come back with the results that they hoped for, and suggested I follow up with another specialist. Now, I have to say, I had noticed that if his back was turned, he wouldn't always respond when I called him. So when the specialist advised me to take him for a follow up, I thought, okay, surely it wouldn't hurt.

Consequently, there were a series of tests conducted, and I awaited the outcome. Unfortunately, the initial results were confirmed.

However, for whatever reason, unbeknownst to me, I wasn't moved. Something within me remained calm as the specialist shared the information with me.

When I got home, I laid my hands on his ears and I began to pray; claiming his healing in the Name of Jesus! Amen? And I didn't think anything else about it.

The next morning, I noticed there was ear wax that had run out of both of his ears – giving me the impression that his ear drums had burst. As I was cleaning him up he said, "Momma, I had a dream last night. Do you want to hear it?"

"Yes, baby. I want to hear your dream," I said enthusiastically.

"I dreamed you kissed my lips and my lips came out through my ears," he said, as we both started laughing.

"You did?" I questioned excitedly. Of course he had no idea that what the Lord had revealed in his dream confirmed that the words from my lips brought healing to his ears.

And when I took him back to the specialist, they couldn't find anything wrong with his ears! Amen? Amen!

This is when I knew I operated in the ministry of healing.

There was a young lady at a women's conference that shared with me that she was struggling with a homosexual spirit and wanted to be delivered. However, she said, she wasn't sure if she "really" wanted to be delivered because she was afraid. During our conversation, I explained to the young lady that she had to make a choice and stick with her decision. It was clear to me that although she was saying with her mouth that she wanted to be delivered, she wasn't sure.

Consequently, I explained to her that the Lord was ready to deliver her and if she decided that she wanted to be delivered, He would set her free. She acknowledged that she understood. So I prayed for the young lady that the Lord would show up and show out on her behalf then we went our separate ways (because the conference was about to start). My heart went out to this young lady because I could see she was struggling with this decision. And while I could see she was struggling, I also knew the enemy had a hold on her that only the Lord could break by her making the decision that she wanted to be delivered.

After I preached the Word of God, the power of the Holy Spirit was manifested in that place and the Lord began to bring forth healing and deliverance. As the women came forth, and as the Lord dictated, I laid my hands on the women and one after the other they were being slain in the spirit; healed, delivered and set free.

The young lady that I had the privilege of ministering to earlier came forward.

"Are you ready to be set free?" I asked.

"Yes," she said with what sounded like uncertainty.

"Are you ready to be set free?" I asked again to cause her to declare that she had made a decision to be set free and she was ready.

"Yes, I'm ready," she said this time with assurance.

I laid my hands on the young lady. Immediately, the young lady began to cry out and instantly her face had become distorted. It changed into the appearance of a wolf as the spirit of lesbianism left her. She fell to the floor (weakened by the power of the Spirit as deliverance took place).

Therefore, I was very familiar with, and very acquainted with, warfare and spiritual battles. So for the Lord to say that He needed to *teach me warfare* because I had *no experience in battle,* confused me. And yet, in my spirit, I knew there was more to it than I realized. Whatever the Lord was trying to minister to me, concerning the wars of Canaan, I had yet to get the revelation.

I was baffled.

So I had to first find out what the scriptures meant, what "nations" in particular was the LORD referring to. So I allowed the Lord to take me deeper into the scriptures by starting at the beginning: The book of Genesis states, the LORD said to Abram, "Leave your native country, your relatives, and your father's family, and go to the land that I will show you."

And as we know, Abram departed as the LORD had instructed him, and Lot went with him. Abram was seventy-five years old when he left Haran. He took his wife, Sarai, his nephew, Lot, and all his wealth—his livestock and all the people he had taken into his household at Haran— and headed for the land of Canaan.

Then the LORD appeared to Abram and said, "I will give this land to your descendants."

Genesis 12:1; 4 – 5; 7 NLT

So the LORD made a covenant with Abram that day and said, "I have given this land to your descendants, all the way from the border of Egypt to the great Euphrates River—the land now occupied by the Kenites, Kenizzites, Kadmonites, Hittites, Perizzites, Rephaites, Amorites, Canaanites, Girgashites, and Jebusites."

Genesis 15:18 – 21 NLT

Then in the book of Exodus, the LORD told him [Moses], "I have certainly seen the oppression of my people in Egypt. I have heard their cries of distress because of their harsh slave drivers. Yes, I am aware of their suffering. So I have come down to rescue them from the power of the Egyptians and lead them out of Egypt into their own fertile and spacious land. It is a land flowing with milk and honey—the land where the Canaanites, Hittites, Amorites, Perizzites, Hivites, and Jebusites now live.

Exodus 3:7 – 8 NLT

And of course, that old familiar scripture in the book of Leviticus, "But I have promised you, 'You will possess their land because I will give it to you as your possession—a land flowing with milk and honey.' I am the LORD your God, who has set you apart from all other people."

Leviticus 20:24 NLT

Then in the book of Numbers, Moses had the men to go and spy out the land that had been given to them. After exploring the land for forty days, the men returned to Moses, Aaron, and the whole community of Israel at Kadesh in the wilderness of Paran. They reported to the whole community what they had seen and showed them the fruit they had taken from the land. This was their report to Moses:

"We entered the land you sent us to explore, and it is indeed a bountiful country—a land flowing with milk and honey. Here is the kind of fruit it produces. But the people living there are powerful, and their towns are large and fortified. We even saw giants there, the descendants of Anak! The Amalekites live in the Negev, and the Hittites, Jebusites, and Amorites live in the hill country. The Canaanites live along the coast of the Mediterranean Sea and along the Jordan Valley."

But Caleb tried to quiet the people as they stood before Moses. "Let's go at once to take the land," he said. "We can certainly conquer it!"

But the other men who had explored the land with him disagreed. "We can't go up against them! They are stronger than we are!" So they spread this bad report about the land among the Israelites: "The land we traveled through and explored will devour anyone who goes to live there. All the people we saw were huge. We even saw giants there, the descendants of Anak. Next to them we felt like grasshoppers, and that's what they thought, too!"

Numbers 13:25 – 33 NLT

Unfortunately, the Lord wasn't pleased with the report that they brought back and said, "But as surely as I [the LORD] live, and as surely as the earth is filled with the LORD's glory, not one of these people will ever enter that land. They have all seen my glorious presence and the miraculous signs I performed both in Egypt and in the wilderness, but again and again they have tested me by refusing to listen to my voice. They will never even see the land I swore to give their ancestors. None of those who have treated me with contempt will ever see it. But my servant Caleb has a different attitude than the others have. He has remained loyal to me, so I will bring him into the land he explored. His descendants will possess their full share of that land.

Then the LORD said to Moses and Aaron, "How long must I put up with this wicked community and its complaints about me? Yes, I have heard the complaints the Israelites are making against me. Now tell them this: 'As surely as I live, declares the LORD, I will do to you the very things I heard you say. You will all drop dead in this wilderness! Because you complained against me, every one of you who is twenty years old or older and was included in the registration will die. You will not enter and occupy the land I swore to give you. The only exceptions will be Caleb son of Jephunneh and Joshua son of Nun.

Numbers 14:21 – 24; 26 – 30 NLT

"Give the following instructions to the people of Israel: When you cross the Jordan River into the land of Canaan, you must drive out all the people living there. You must destroy all their carved and molten images and demolish all their pagan shrines. Take possession of the land and settle in it, because I have given it to you to occupy.

But if you fail to drive out the people who live in the land, those who remain will be like splinters in your eyes and thorns in your sides. They will harass you in the land where you live. And I will do to you what I had planned to do to them."

Numbers 33:51 – 53; 55 – 56 NLT

Okay, then in the book of Judges we see that after the death of Joshua, the Israelites asked the LORD, "Which tribe should go first to attack the Canaanites?" The LORD answered, "Judah, for I have given them victory over the land."

When the men of Judah attacked, the LORD gave them victory over the Canaanites and Perizzites, and they killed 10,000 enemy warriors at the town of Bezek.

Judges 1:1 – 2; 4 NLT

Now, how all of this pertained to me? I still didn't know. And again, I was reminded of the encounters that I had experienced during my ministry…

I was the guest speaker at a women's conference, and there was a young girl in particular that I was reminded of. While I was speaking, the Lord instructed me to blow into the microphone. As I blew into the microphone, it sounded like a mighty rushing wind. I continued to blow into the microphone knowing that the Spirit was moving in that place, and I continued to do so until the Lord said stop.

When I started to blow into the microphone, releasing the Holy Spirit in that place, this girl began to cry out in such a loud voice; she was heard above everyone else. And when the Holy Spirit prompted me to preach the Word of God, she continued to cry out during the entire time I ministered. When I finished ministering, I invited those who wanted to receive personal ministry to come forward. And needless to say, this girl came and stood before me (along with the other women) to allow ministry to go forth.

Sensitive to the prompting of the Holy Spirit, I ministered to the women as the Lord dictated in order to allow healing and deliverance to come forth. When I got to this girl, I stood there waiting for the Lord to say what He wanted to do for her.

As I stood there, the Lord said, "Blow on her." And just as I had blown into the microphone, I took a deep breath and slowly released the Spirit as the breath of God was blown on her chest.

Immediately, the Spirit had overpowered her and she fell backwards and was slain in the spirit. And instantly, she stopped crying.

That was when I knew I operated as a Spirit-Bearer.

Then I was reminded of yet another time when I was praying for a young lady and the Lord revealed to me that a spirit of rebellion was present.

While warring in the spirit, I began to call out the spirit of rebellion and commanded it to come out.

When I finished praying for the young lady, immediately, the spirit of rebellion manifested, which was evident as her face was distorted into that of a lion. As a result of the spirit's manifestation, her eyes were swollen; so much so, they were almost shut. The swelling lasted for several days.

Then, there was this young man that the Lord had me minister to. The young man had been telling me about his struggles. And of course, I prayed for the young man and wanted the Lord to do a mighty work regarding his situation.

As I stood ministering before the Lord, He revealed to me that this young man had seven demons. So, as the Lord dictated, I got my "oil" and asked the young man to come to me.

When he came, immediately, he fell at my feet. But when I got ready to anoint his head, he grabbed my hand and asked, "What are you doing?"

(Immediately, I recognized this was the demon talking and trying to stop me from anointing the young man).

"I'm getting ready to anoint your head," I said with authority, which I did. And I started to pray over the young man and called out the spirits as the Lord revealed them.

And the Lord delivered him in that place.

However, I continued to allow the Lord to minister to me:

Now as we pretty much have known from the many Sunday school lessons, bible studies, or history, the LORD was with the people of Judah, and they took possession of the hill country. But they failed to drive out the people living in the plains, who had iron chariots.

Judges 1:19 NLT

✓ The tribe of Benjamin, however, failed to drive out the Jebusites, who were living in Jerusalem. So to this day the Jebusites live in Jerusalem among the people of Benjamin.
✓ The tribe of Manasseh failed to drive out the people living in Beth-shan, Taanach, Dor, Ibleam, Megiddo, and all their surrounding settlements, because the Canaanites were determined to stay in that region. When the Israelites grew stronger, they forced the Canaanites to work as slaves, but they never did drive them completely out of the land.
✓ The tribe of Ephraim failed to drive out the Canaanites living in Gezer, so the Canaanites continued to live there among them.
✓ The tribe of Zebulun failed to drive out the residents of Kitron and Nahalol, so the Canaanites continued to live among them. But the Canaanites were forced to work as slaves for the people of Zebulun.
✓ The tribe of Asher failed to drive out the residents of Acco, Sidon, Ahlab, Aczib, Helbah, Aphik, and Rehob. Instead, the people of Asher moved in among the Canaanites, who controlled the land, for they failed to drive them out.
✓ Likewise, the tribe of Naphtali failed to drive out the residents of Beth-shemesh and Beth-anath. Instead, they moved in among the Canaanites, who controlled the land. Nevertheless, the people of Beth-shemesh and Beth-anath were forced to work as slaves for the people of Naphtali.
✓ As for the tribe of Dan, the Amorites forced them back into the hill country and would not let them come down into the plains. The Amorites were determined to stay in Mount Heres, Aijalon, and Shaalbim, but when the descendants of Joseph became stronger, they forced the Amorites to work as slaves.

Judges 1:21; 27 – 35 NLT

Oh, my God, I thought. I couldn't even imagine what was getting ready to happen as a result of them not driving the people out. Anyway, the angel of the LORD went up from Gilgal to Bokim and said to the Israelites, "I brought you out of Egypt into this land that I swore to give your ancestors, and I said I would never break my covenant with you. For your part, you were not to make any covenants with the people living in this land; instead, you were to destroy their altars. But you disobeyed my command. Why did you do this? So now I declare that I will no longer drive out the people living in your land. They will be thorns in your sides, and their gods will be a constant temptation to you."

Judges 2:1 – 3 NLT

However, get this: After that generation died, another generation grew up who did not acknowledge the LORD or remember the mighty things he had done for Israel.

Judges 2:10 NLT

Okay, I thought. I understood the passage of scriptures, but still couldn't figure out what the "wars" had to do with me. I couldn't even begin to tell you how difficult it was for me to comprehend – even though *test, warfare, no experience, wars of Canaan, and battle* kept ringing in my spirit.

Again, my mind was flooded with the memories of the ministry the Lord had entrusted me with….

I was reminded of another women's conference I attended. When the Woman of God finished speaking, she called me to come up and assist her with personal ministry as she ministered to the women.

"If anyone needs deliverance, come up and Pastor Daisy will pray for you. If anyone can bring forth deliverance, it's Pastor Daisy," she said.

And sure enough, I remembered this teenage girl in particular that came up. I began praying for the girl and the Lord revealed there was a spirit of fornication present.

Therefore, I laid my hand on the girl and began to war against the sexual sin in her life. Immediately, she screamed out, "Ohhh, it feels like fire."

And just as suddenly, she started vomiting as deliverance began to come forth.

And before I knew anything, the girl's mother ran up to try to help the girl. However, of course, I had to ask the mother not to interfere because demonic forces were present and the girl needed the deliverance to come forth.

"What's going on?" The mother asked. However, I continued to minister to the girl until her deliverance was complete.

Then I was reminded of the young lady who called me on the telephone because she was going through so much and just couldn't take it anymore.

She said, "The Lord told me to call you; I want to know if we could meet because I need deliverance."

However, when she shared with me what she was struggling with, immediately, I began to pray for her over the phone. And as the Lord dictated, I instructed her to lay her hand on her stomach as I continued to pray for her.

Immediately, the young lady started gagging, and just as suddenly, deliverance began to come forth as she started throwing up. I also instructed her to keep the phone to her ear as I continued to call out the spirits that were tormenting her.

Then deliverance came forth.

I was reminded of the time the Lord prompted me to pray and intercede on behalf of a young lady who was struggling with her husband being unfaithful.

And after praying and warring in the spirit, for what seemed like hours, I asked the Lord to "come down and see if the cry is as great as it sounds," as He told Abraham He'd do in Genesis, chapter eighteen.

After praying, I experienced my first encounter of seeing angels.

Now, according to the above-mentioned passage of scriptures, I understood and knew very well that Canaan was the "Promised Land," the land "flowing with milk and honey" that the Lord gave to the Israelites as an inheritance.

But "the wars of Canaan"?

Okay, let me see; *the wars of Canaan* represented the Israelites fighting against the *nations* that were living in the land of Canaan, which the Lord had promised them as their inheritance. Therefore, in order for the Israelites to possess the land or receive their inheritance that the Lord had given them, they had to *drive out the nations (Canaanites, Hittites, Amorites, Perizzites, Hivites, and Jebusites)* that were living there; by going to war against them and defeating them.

So, the Israelites had to fight in order to possess the "Promised Land." And while it is clear that the Lord had *given* them the land, they had to *fight* to *possess* the land – understood.

What did that have to do with me? I still wasn't getting it. What did *test, warfare, no experience, wars of Canaan, and battle* have to do with me?

Again, I was reminded of the Lord's ministry in my life….

I was reminded of a young man whose wife always talked about how he always praised and worshipped the Lord. So, it was good to meet him and fellowship together. She wanted him to experience God as she had experienced Him during our service.

During praise and worship, the young man began praising the Lord (as we had all done). However, to everyone's surprise, the young man had become so loud that it was very disturbing and distracting; so much so, that I became disturbed in my spirit.

"What's happening?" I asked the Lord. "Why am I disturbed if this man is worshiping You?"

The Lord revealed that the man wasn't praising Him; it was a spirit of divination; demonic influence; satanic power.

Therefore, I went over to the young man and commanded him to bow down and worship the True and Living God.

He kept "praising."

I laid my hand on the young man and began to call the spirit of divination out. And suddenly, the young man fell to his knees and started gagging and then throwing up as deliverance came forth.

Consequently, I continued to struggle with *no experience, warfare, battle*. Unfortunately, I wasn't getting it; therefore, I continued to seek the Lord regarding the passage of scriptures that He had ministered to me. He took me to the blackboard and began to teach me; giving me understanding. So, let me share with you what the Lord revealed to me:

These are the nations that the LORD left in the land to test those Israelites who had not experienced the wars of Canaan. He did this to teach warfare to generations of Israelites who had no experience in battle. These people were left to test the Israelites – to see whether they would obey the commands the LORD had given to their ancestors through Moses.

Judges 3:1 – 2; 4 NLT

Immediately, I was prompted to look up the word "battle," which I did. According to Dictionary.com, battle means *a hostile environment*. And according to the Webster's New World Dictionary, battle means *a large-scale fight between armed forces*.

"Oh, my God!" I said to myself as *fight between armed forces* rung out in my spirit. And immediately, I knew that the Lord was revealing *the fight between armed forces* was a battle between *Him and Satan*. And while I understood what a *hostile environment* was, I knew there was more to it than just a *hostile environment*.

"Lord, what does a *hostile environment* have to do with me?" I asked.

"You have no experience in a hostile environment," He answered.

And immediately, as I was reminded of the ministry that He had entrusted me with, He made it clear that just as He had *given* the victory to the Israelites, He had *given* the victory to me. So consequently, *I* had no experience in fighting against the enemy in *battle* where the demonic forces would *oppose me – come up against me – and fight back; creating a hostile environment*.

Oh, my God, I thought. I was stunned and perplexed because in my spirit I knew He wasn't just revealing this to me just to be revealing it to me. Immediately, I was weakened in my spirit at the thought of being in a "hostile environment." And I could not even imagine the intense warfare that would play the part in ***"teaching"*** or ***"testing"*** me to ***"prove my obedience unto Him"*** as the scripture states.

The tears welled up in my eyes as I prepared for the pain that I knew would come as a result of being in the hostile environment. The anticipation of the enemy coming up against me, opposing me, and fighting back pierced my spirit.

"I don't want to do it!" I cried out because I knew the pain that I'd encounter would be unlike anything I had encountered before, which solidified why I didn't want to go through it. Again, I cried out, "I don't want to do it," as the weight of the anticipated pain that I'd be challenged to endure surfaced. "I don't want to do it, Lord. Help me, Jesus," I pleaded as my spirit began to grow weaker and the tears surfaced to be released. And yet, I knew there was no other way. And this wasn't up for discussion. The Lord continued to minister to me in spite of my plea not to be faced with a *battle; a hostile environment.*

"You have no experience in driving the people out," He continued.

Consequently, I knew I was about to experience *the wars of Canaan.* I was going to have to *fight* against the opposing armed forces. Demonic attacks would come against me to **teach** and **test** me in order for me (like the Israelites) to "possess" the "promise" that He had given me.

There was no mistake. He had given me the promise; the promise was mine. However, He revealed, I, like the Israelites, had to **"possess"** the promise. "You have to have power over the promise," He said. In other words, when the enemy came up against me or opposed me, I had to have *"power over"* the enemy; thereby defeating the enemy and *"taking"* the promise.

Ultimately, revealing that while He had given the enemy into my hands during my ministry, just as with the Israelites, the time had come that *He* was no longer going to drive out the nations:

I will no longer drive out the nations that Joshua left unconquered when he died. I did this to test Israel—to see whether or not they would follow the ways of the Lord as their ancestors did."

Judges 2:21 – 22 NLT

I had to *fight*, *battle,* and *drive them out.*

So, while the Joshua generation had faithfully obeyed the Lord, the Lord led them to victory. But after Joshua's death, however, the Israelites failed to drive out the nations that remained. So the Lord withdrew His promise to drive the people out and bless the Israelites in battle *because* they had disobeyed His command: *For your part, you were not to make any covenants with the people living in this land; instead, you were to destroy their altars. But you disobeyed my command.*

Consequently, the new generation that remained had never experienced the wars of Canaan; therefore, the Lord was now going to use the *nations* that were in the land to "teach" and "test" the new generation who had never experienced battle – to see if they would obey the Lord.

And as I continued to sit before the Lord, He revealed that the *nations* that were left would *teach me* how to do battle in a hostile environment – *to see if I would obey Him.*

"Who are these *nations*?" I asked as the pain and tears surfaced.

He was silent.

~ THEY'RE TRAINED ~

In a dream...

I saw what appeared to be a circus; where the ring master and a tiger were in a cage. The ring master raised his whip to instruct the tiger to rise up. When the tiger rose, it appeared to be twelve – fifteen feet tall. I was astonished at how huge the tiger was.

Nonetheless, upon the tiger's rising, immediately, and on cue, three tigers were released and were coming towards me. All of them were white, with black stripes, and red eyes.

However, out of nowhere, the ring master appeared and intervened; coming in between me and two of the tigers. He commanded the two tigers away from me; commanding them to obey. And although I realized that I had just been saved by this gentleman, it didn't stop the fear that I felt of being attacked. I was disturbed in my spirit.

I turned and saw my house nearby and started to run towards the house. As I ran up the stairs, my husband, Randolph, opened the door and said, "I heard all the commotion going on outside."

And just as I made it to the door, from out of nowhere, the third tiger launched towards me to attack me.

Then I woke up.

The interpretation...

Immediately, I understood that the dream revealed the enemy's attack. I was disturbed in my spirit because the tigers weren't the usual demons (demonic forces) that I had contended with. But just as suddenly as I had seen the tigers, I knew I had been given another level of anointing, power, and authority. And yet, I knew this attack would be unlike any other that I had experienced. So I went before the Lord, "What are You revealing to me? What does the dream mean?" I asked, as I waited for the interpretation.

"The three tigers represent three different demonic attacks," He revealed. "The first two tigers (or the first two attacks) would come, but would be commanded in obedience to Me. But the third tiger (or the third attack) would come close to home."

Immediately, I was distressed in my spirit because the enemy had launched three attacks against me. And while they had been revealed in the spirit realm, they were about to manifest in the natural. And the fear of knowing the attacks were coming was crippling as it gripped me, and I started to cry. Therefore, I knew I had to prepare for battle.

"What shall I do, Lord?" I asked.

"Hold your peace." He responded.

I was about to come face to face with the enemy (not only to fight one battle, but three attacks would come). And I was reminded of the prophetic burden that I was carrying as a result of being intimate with the Lord. And the tears continued to roll down my face. I cried out; pleading for the Lord's mercy because I had anticipated the attacks would prove to be far too difficult for me to bear.

"Whyyy, Lord? Whyyy?" I cried out.

"They're trained," He said.

PART

II

CONCEPTION

~ CHAPTER 1 ~

PLANTING A SEED

The Lord prompted me to start having praise and worship and prayer in my home. So, I sent out an invitation to the women to join me and those who were appointed for this assignment responded.

At one of the gatherings in particular, my friends, Tiffany and Leah were present. The atmosphere had already been set to receive the Lord's presence. So, by the time the women of God showed up, He was already there; His glory filled the room. The women arrived pregnant with expectation (as had I). We expected the Lord to do something for us that we couldn't do ourselves. Therefore, we started to lift our voices in worship as we offered Him our sacrifices of praise.

Immediately, the Holy Spirit revealed Himself and demonstrated His power among His daughters. In labor for hours, and as if we had dilated to ten centimeters, it was time for the Lord to deliver.

As we were worshiping the Lord, Tiffany called me over and indicated that she felt like she was about to "throw up." The anointing was so heavy in the place that it prompted me to get in position to help the women of God push and birth the things of God in their life. With the cries of His daughters, the Lord demanded that I take the position of the midwife to assist the women, so that they could receive that which they came expecting to receive.

Immediately, I got the small garbage can and started to minister to Tiffany so that deliverance would come forth. I laid my hands on her and I called out the *spirit of fear* as the Lord had revealed. She continued to gag and vomit as the deliverance continued to come forth. After ministering to her for a while, I called Leah over to assist me by holding the garbage can, which allowed me to continue to assist Tiffany with her deliverance.

And deliverance came forth.

As the contractions of "letting go" prepared them to surrender their will to His will and trust Him, I encouraged the women to breathe. But instead of the usual "he, he, who" breathing technique, I encouraged them to respond to the Holy Spirit by saying, "Yes. Yes, Lord." And deliverance began to come forth: chains were broken, hearts mended, lives changed, struggles ended, faith released, fear defeated, and renewed commitments to the things of God as they submitted to the Lord.

As we continued to minister to the Lord, He prompted me to minister to Leah. I continued to encourage her to "let go" and let God direct her steps. And as I ministered to her, the Lord revealed that she was *tired; tired of struggling*, so I laid my hands on her. And with a loud wail, she screamed out – as *letting go* caused her deliverance to come forth. I continued to encourage her to allow the Lord to have His way. Streams of tears rolled down her face as surely, the Lord was delivering her.

I knew it was the first time she had ever experienced personal deliverance (or had been in the presence of deliverance; close and up front), and she had no clue of what was expected of her. However, I continued to minister God's love to her and encouraged her to live a life that was pleasing to the Lord. I knew this was not only the first step for her since re-establishing her relationship with Christ, but it was unfamiliar territory as well. As she continued to praise the Lord, I continued to minister to her.

And deliverance came forth.

"I knew this time and experience would be different," Leah said. "My heart was excited and filled with anticipation. As soon as I walked in, I felt an immediate comfort. Something filled the room; my heart and soul screamed 'Yes' louder than it has ever screamed before. My 'Yes' was that I was ready and no longer afraid. I felt the LORD's presence and it was unlike any other peace or calm I have ever felt. I underwent a change and I knew HE was there. I felt comfortable and knew it was time to let go of the hurt, shame, anger, struggle, pain and fear. I felt hands of comfort hold me and help me through. I desired to be in HIS calm, HIS peace, HIS place, and within HIS covering again."

The only thing that we had to do was receive, push, and rest in what the Lord had done.

To God be the glory for the things He has done.

Consequently, I put these things before the Lord to allow Him to continue to minister to me concerning the deliverance in their lives.

~ WORDS OF ENCOURAGEMENT ~

Woman of God, if you've been expecting the Lord to do something for you and have yet to see it manifest, if you're getting tired of holding on until the blessings come, or if you're just about to give up, I want to encourage you with the words of the Lord:

"He will do just what He said He would do."

"Get in position; a position of prayer," I heard in my spirit. Your due date is fast approaching. The Lord is about to birth some things into the earth and He's going to use you to do it.

You shall labor in prayer. But be encouraged because it won't be a long process. It may be intense, painful, and make you a little uncomfortable, but equally so is the extent of the promises of God.

And they shall come quickly!

Therefore, I pray that you are strengthened in your faith.

God is not a man, so he does not lie. He is not human, so he does not change his mind. Has he ever spoken and failed to act? Has he ever promised and not carried it through?

Numbers 23:19 NLT

~ CHAPTER 2 ~

LET US PRAY

Yet again, I was prompted by the Holy Spirit to pray during my lunch hour at work. Immediately, due to my excitement, I shared the information with Leah because we worked together. Excited that the Lord had prompted me to pray, I told her that I would be using my lunch hour to pray (instead of us hanging out). *Surely,* I thought, *she would be excited because we had been talking about how she wanted to establish a relationship with Christ.*

"Well," she responded. "I don't want to be obligated to attend because you're my friend. I use my lunch hour for me; to do the things that I want to do (run errands, pay bills, or whatever), and I don't want anyone dictating to me what I should be doing with my time."

I have to say, to say the least, I was flabbergasted. I did not see that coming. But I was reminded that just a few weeks ago she had shared a recurring dream with me:

She was on a ship and the ship was sinking.

I shared with her that the dream was a reflection of what was going on with her spiritually:

Revealing that water is a sign of the spirit realm and the ship was the vessel (her way of life) and of course, sinking was an indication that she was dying spiritually.

And consequently, I asked her about her relationship with Christ. She stated that she remembered someone had led her to Christ at summer camp, but she didn't really have a relationship with Him (and wasn't living the way she knew He would be pleased with). So I led her in the *prayer of salvation* and she re-dedicated her life to Christ.

But immediately, I understood and made it perfectly clear that the Lord had prompted *me* to pray – not her – and that she would, by no means, be under any obligation to attend. I just wanted to share the information with her and let her know that's how *I* would be spending my lunch hour, and I was excited about it. "However," she continued, "I'm not sure if it's a good idea or not because people like to use their lunch hour to eat and just take a break from work."

"It's really about me being prompted to pray and not really about anyone attending. I'll extend the invitation, and whoever shows up we'll pray together," I responded. And sure enough, the email invite went out to the people and with a great response those who were interested came, but Leah did not. So, for the first couple of weeks, I think Leah had only attended maybe once or twice. But I was being very careful not to impose on her (or her time), so that she didn't feel obligated to come (because this really wasn't about her, but rather it was about what the Lord had prompted me to do).

The prayer sessions continued to go well and it wasn't long before I realized, and to my amazement, all who had been in attendance were all in leadership positions in ministry: pastors, ministers, leaders, and prophetess. And immediately, I thought it was very odd that we were all in ministry. There was *something* going on in the spirit, but I couldn't put my finger on what was what. Anyway, the prayer continued regularly as we all came into agreement. And after a few weeks, Leah started coming on a regular basis. Of course, this did my heart good because she was my friend. She was the person who talked about wanting to get right with God.

After she started attending the prayer, Leah shared with me that she felt out of place because everyone else in attendance were so much more mature in the Lord than her. But I continued to encourage her that this would be an opportunity for her to learn some things, grow in her prayer life, and in her walk with Christ overall. However, with what appeared to be reluctance, she continued to come.

Then one day during my morning devotion with the Lord, I kept seeing a vision of an *open door.* I had no idea what the open door represented or what the Lord was revealing to me, so I stayed prayerful concerning the vision.

In a vision...

I see an open door.

The interpretation…

There is a wide-open door for a great work here, although many oppose me.

1 Corinthians 16:9 NLT

Immediately, I was excited about the open door because I thought, as a result of us praying, a great work could be done on the job even though the people opposed Him.

However, as I continued to seek the Lord regarding this revelation, it was revealed to me that there were some who opposed Him – within the prayer group.

And immediately, I was reminded of the Last Supper. And the Lord began to minister to me and revealed that just as Judas had betrayed Jesus, there was someone within the group who was going to betray me.

Immediately, the tears welled up in my eyes as the pain of betrayal surfaced.

However, I kept silent about the revelation as I continued to watch and pray.

With great disappointment, and reluctance, I cried out to the Lord as He made it clear that I had to open myself up to the betrayal; hurt and pain that would come as a result of this open door. I'd have to just allow one of them to betray me and just "deal with it" because *I was on an assignment.*

"I don't want to do it," I said as I cried before the Lord. "I don't want to be a fool and allow someone to hurt me or betray me *because* I'm on an assignment." And knowing the pain of betrayal would come proved to be too much as the Lord continued to minister to me.

"You have to open yourself up to be betrayed. The Son of Man was betrayed." And the tears rolled down my face as the pain of being betrayed came forth. Then the Lord asked, "Does it hurt?"

"Yes." I replied.

"Then you're not ready. It's only when it doesn't hurt that you'll be able to move forward," He revealed. Making known that I would have to be able to be betrayed and still love the person who betrays me. I continued to cry as I allowed the hurt to be released. I didn't want to do it! However, the Lord continued to minister to me and eventually, I gave in, but not without the reservation of knowing that going forward the betrayal would come.

By the time we came together for prayer, I shared the vision with the individuals who had attended the meeting, as well as what the Lord had revealed to me:

There is a wide-open door for a great work here, although many oppose me.

1 Corinthians 16:9 NLT

Consequently, we all continued to praise the Lord for the mighty work that He was about to do on behalf of His people. And I continued to ponder in my heart the revelation that *someone* within the group was going to betray me. My heart was troubled, but I prayed that it would fail me not.

After he had said this, Jesus was troubled in spirit and testified, "Very truly I tell you, one of you is going to betray me."

John 13:21 NIV

And yet, I continued to watch and pray as the Lord continued to minister His plan to me concerning this matter. However, with the revelation of betrayal, the *open door* took on a whole new meaning. I had come to the realization that the *open door* was the opportunity for the great work to be done concerning *me* as the now ever-present pain of my troubled spirit surfaced. And the Lord was going to use this opportunity to accomplish His will in my life.

One day while talking to Sandra, one of the prayer partners, she told me that she and Genevieve, another prayer partner, had decided that because all of our schedules were different they wanted to make sure that I would never be alone in prayer. Therefore, everyone would work out their lunch schedules so that someone would be with me at all times. First and foremost, they wanted to make sure that I was covered and secondly, to touch and agree – come against the attacks of the enemy as we prayed for God's people; His will.

Suddenly, and without warning, I started to cry. Because as soon as the words were released from her lips, the Lord revealed He had them in place to cover me as the attacks of the enemy began to unfold. Unable to restrain the tears, I just sat there and cried.

During this time, Leah's participation continued to be few and far in between. And when she did come, she didn't pray (for the most part she was just there). Surely, she might've felt obligated to come because the people had started to ask, "Why aren't you at prayer if Daisy's your friend?" So consequently, I'd say to her that she didn't have to feel obligated to come. But she indicated that she was coming because she wanted to come, not because of me or what the people had to say.

So, in an attempt to help her grow in her relationship with Christ, I asked about her personal time with the Lord to see how I could assist her. She indicated she prayed at night before going to bed and that was the extent of it. So one day, when it was just the two of us, I asked her to pray for me, so that I could see how she prayed. (I knew she felt intimidated when other people were in prayer, so since it was just the two of us, I thought she'd feel a little more comfortable.) But she struggled because she was afraid. She said she hadn't prayed out loud before and it, to say the least, was terrifying. But I encouraged her to do so. After all, I was her friend and I wanted to see her grow spiritually.

Then all of a sudden, I was reminded of a conversation we had about her praying out loud all the time at her previous place of employment. So it wasn't true that she had never prayed out loud before. And when I confronted her with this, she said she was afraid because it was *me*; her friend. Eventually, she gave in (after much convincing). Not only had I encouraged her to start praying consistently, even if they were short and simple prayers, but I also encouraged her to start reading her bible on a daily basis. Then, after finding out that she didn't have a daily devotional to assist her with her daily walk, I purchased one for her.

Unfortunately, a short time later, she said she felt like it was too much involved with being a Christian and she couldn't really find the time to pray and/or read her bible consistently, as I had suggested. She went on to say that she really wasn't comfortable praying out loud and she felt overwhelmed. However, I encouraged her to focus on one day at a time until she was comfortable and consistent.

So, after several weeks of prayer, and as the Lord continued to minister to me about the open door, Randolph and I were prompted to start our ministry. So, I shared the information with the prayer group and asked that they be in agreement with us.

Consequently, the Lord had prompted us to start with bible study in our home. And with much excitement, we prepared for ministry. Again, I couldn't wait to share the exciting information with Leah. When I shared it with her, she thought it was a great idea because she had always wanted to be a part of bible study; something she had never done before. So I extended an invitation to her to join the bible study and become a part of the ministry.

However, intimidated by the fact that she was a babe in Christ, the thought of really getting "involved" in a ministry was again, overwhelming.

By the time Randolph and I had decided to start bible study, the prayer group had started to dwindle down; causing me to believe that the group had specifically come together to open the door for us to start the ministry. It was just ironic that they were all leaders in the church and as soon as the Lord had opened the door for us to start the ministry, they started to disperse. Of course it wasn't by happenstance, but a clear indication that the purpose of the prayer meetings had been accomplished.

~ THREE VISIONS IN THE NIGHT ~

As I lie on my bed, a vision appeared before me:

I was drinking from a cup. There were three holes in the cup, and the water was coming out.

As I lie pondering the vision, the Lord began to give me a breakdown of the vision and immediately three visions appeared before me:

I was drinking from a cup. The cup was ½ empty – ½ full, it had a hole in it, and the water was coming out.

Then immediately a second vision appeared before me:

I was drinking from a cup. The cup was full, it had a hole in it, and the water was coming out.

Then just as suddenly, a third vision appeared before me:

I was drinking from a cup. The cup was empty, it had a hole in it, and yet, the water was coming out.

The interpretation…

I went before the Lord to allow Him to give me the interpretation of the visions.

He revealed to me:

The initial vision was an indication that I was about to drink from the cup of affliction – waters of afflictions and the three holes in the cup represented the three attacks that I'd endure and my spiritual state after each attack:

After the first attack, I'd be spiritually ½ empty – ½ full as the affliction would cause the anointing to be released.

After the second attack, I'd be spiritually full as the affliction would cause the anointing to be released.

After the third attack, I'd be spiritually empty as the affliction would cause the anointing to be released.

Though the Lord gave you adversity for food and suffering for drink, he will still be with you to teach you. You will see your teacher with your own eyes.

Isaiah 30:20 NLT

~ CHAPTER 3 ~

KNOW THOSE WHO LABOR AMONG YOU

Tiffany

My friend, Tiffany, was the first one who answered and accepted the invitation to join us for bible study. Tiffany and I used to work together. I remember she was someone who was seeking the Lord and how, on a few occasions, we had even prayed together.

When we first met, Tiffany mentioned she belonged to a church and the Pastor said she was a Prophetess. Tiffany also shared with me that she was going to attend the prophetic classes at her church, so she could grow in this area, to develop her gift. I remember one time in particular, she mentioned that, while attending the classes, she felt a strong force of *something* hit her spirit; some sort of demonic activity, but she didn't know what. And unfortunately, after that experience, she became concerned about being a part of the ministry because she wasn't able to bounce back from the devastating blow.

At the time Tiffany shared this information with me, I became concerned and wondered if anyone was praying for her (and the people) while taking these classes. She indicated that the Pastor was praying during class, but not specifically for her. Anyway, to help me understand the ministry that she was involved in, she brought me a couple of DVDs so I could see the Pastor minister. I was a little familiar with the Pastor's ministry from what I had seen on TV. However, I didn't necessarily see anything "wrong" or "alarming" with the ministry. There wasn't anything that prompted me in my spirit that the ministry was not of God. Yet, I continued to be concerned with what Tiffany experienced and with her growth.

I was concerned because it was clear to me that Tiffany wasn't mature in the spirit, but rather fairly new in Christ. I didn't know how long she had been in church, but it was clear that she wasn't mature in Christ. She hadn't really been *involved* in ministry, and for the most part, appeared to just be a member trying to grow. One of the many things that concerned me was the fact that almost every day after she had read the bible, she'd ask me, "What does this scripture mean?"

After doing that multiple times, it was an indication that while Tiffany *read* the bible, she wasn't *studying* the bible or spending time with Christ to really get *understanding.* She had become comfortable just looking for someone to explain the scriptures to her. So it was clear that she wasn't mature; therefore, I encouraged her to spend more time with Christ in prayer to get understanding – or have someone at church help her in that area.

Tiffany had two kids; she was a single parent. And at that time, she shared with me that she was living a life of celibacy. And of course, I encouraged her in that area. I remember a time in particular, she told me about a gentleman at church who was interested in her, romantically. However, I ministered to her and encouraged her not to get involved with this young man so that she wouldn't "fall into temptation."

Now, by the time my husband and I were starting the bible study, I had not talked to Tiffany – maybe a few times in about two years (if that) because I had left the place where we worked together. So we weren't really *friends* that hung out together or talked on the phone. She was just someone I worked with. However, by the time I reached out to share with her that we were starting bible study, to my surprise, she hadn't been in church in a year! Knowing that she didn't have a church home, I was excited to share with her that Randolph and I were starting bible study in our home. And since she didn't belong to a church, I asked if she would like to be a part of the ministry to help us get started and grow. And she said, "Yes," and of course we were all excited.

Now that Tiffany and I were back in contact with one another, I asked her, "Why haven't you been in church in a year, what happened?"

"I knew the church wasn't for me," she said abruptly. "But I'm okay with it because since I've been out of church, I've learned so much more on my own than I had in the years that I had been in church," she said.

"You're deceived if you think you've learned more on your own than you have since being in church." I responded. "You don't have the capacity to learn on your own the things that the Lord has imparted in the Pastor (and leaders) to teach you," I said emphatically, especially after I was reminded of her *habit* of just reading the bible.

"Ouch!" She said jokingly. "You cut me deep. But you're right."

Then I went on to share with her what we were trying to accomplish to get the ministry started. And sometime later, after thinking about Tiffany saying, "she knew the church wasn't for her" and "she hadn't been in church for a year" after leaving the church, my spirit was disturbed. Something wasn't right. And of course, she ended up sharing with me the reason she left the church.

"Girl, what happened at the church?" I asked again.

She said, "I would see a lot of demonic activity going on in that church and the Pastor wouldn't say anything about it."

"What kind of demonic activity?" I questioned.

"Well, like the Pastor's son was sleeping with all the women in the church."

"Well, maybe the Pastor didn't know anything about it."

"She knew," she said confidently.

"How do you know she knew?"

"Because I was sleeping with him and she knew about it. But she didn't say anything."

Oh, my God! I was speechless! Wait! Let me make sure I understood her rationale for leaving the church. You mean to tell me that she saw *demonic activity* that she was *involved in*, yet she didn't think the church was *for her,* because the Pastor knew she was living in sin, *fornicating with her son,* but didn't say anything about it?

"Are you serious?" I asked her. "You were sleeping with the Pastor's son? Last time we talked you were celibate."

"Well, I have been since then, which has been for the last year. But yeah, we were sleeping together. But he wouldn't commit – we were just sleeping together."

"What do you mean?"

"Well, after we'd been together, and I mean, "Sunday morning sleeping…""

"What is 'Sunday morning sleeping'?" I interrupted.

"Where he'd spend the night, we'd *'do the do'* and get up and go to church."

"Oh, Lord!" I said, hardly able to believe what I was hearing.

"Then one day," she continued. "He sent me a text saying that it was over."

"Are you serious?" Of course I couldn't believe what I was hearing; a text?

"Yes. He said that we couldn't continue to see each other because his wife would know her place in the church, and I wasn't the one."

I couldn't even imagine the hurt that Tiffany must've experienced as she expressed how painful it was receiving the text. So to change the subject, I asked about the prophetic class she was taking. "What happened with the prophetic class you were taking?"

"I didn't pass the class."

"What do you mean, 'I didn't pass the class'?" I questioned, while at the same time, tried to determine if the "breakup" and/or "not passing the class" was the *real* reason she left the church.

"You remember how I told you that the Pastor said that I was a Prophetess and I was taking the classes, right?"

"Yeah."

"Well, I don't know what happened, but when it came time for her to pass me in the class, she said she couldn't…"

"Why couldn't she pass you?" I interrupted.

"She said because I was too young."

"You were too young? Are you kidding me? That's not even possible! Wait! *She* said you have a gift, you completed the classes that *she* was teaching, and then, *she* told you that you were too young? No way – that's not possible!"

"Yeah, she said I was too young."

"That doesn't make any sense. You being too young wasn't the reason she didn't pass you," I said. "Do you think it was because you were sleeping with her son and not living a holy lifestyle?" I asked in an attempt to get her to see that her living in sin may have had more to do with it than she thought.

"Nah," she said. "I was too young. Now what that means? I don't know."

"Something isn't right. There's no way that you can't pass because you're too young. Did she mean you were immature spiritually?"

"I don't know what she meant. I just know she said I was too young. And I was so mad that I went through all of that."

"I bet you were," I said. Consequently, my spirit was uneasy concerning what she was saying. I was concerned because the Pastor is a well-respected woman of God and has a prophetic school.

Therefore, I kept this issue before the Lord so that He'd reveal to me the truth and how to minister to her.

Maria

Maria and I used to work together as well. As a matter of fact, Tiffany, Maria, and I all used to work together. When Maria received the email inviting her to come join us for bible study, she was very excited, and said she had to work out her schedule. She needed to speak with her supervisor and get back with me to let me know if she was going to be able to make it. But she was excited – and said this was just what she needed.

I didn't know much about Maria other than she was married and had a baby girl (at the time we started bible study, the baby wasn't even a year old). Maria was quiet. And for the most part, she came to work, did her job, and went home.

I remember one day when we were at work, we were having a conversation and somehow the topic of demons or demonic activity came up. And Maria stated that she knew demons were real. And she had in fact, witnessed the destruction that they had on a person; it was devastating. However, she never did go into any details as to what the demonic activity was or how the impact was devastating. But it was clear, she knew demons existed and were a force to be reckoned with.

After speaking with her supervisor, Maria had gotten the okay to change her schedule, and she was excited about coming.

She was hungry for God.

Leah

As I mentioned, Leah and I worked together and had been friends for about a year. We had become very close – when you saw me, you saw her; when you saw her, you saw me. We were always together. Prior to us becoming friends, my perception of her was that she was quiet, didn't really associate with a lot of people – mostly kept to herself. Anyway, we were only friends on the job; we didn't hang out together after work. But as we continued to become close, she started to open up to me; sharing that she was really struggling as a single parent. And there were times when we talked about past relationships she'd been involved in as well. However, one of the conversations that we had in particular, caused me to become concerned that her *friendship* was more than just a "friendship," but I didn't say anything. Nevertheless, she was now celibate (and had been for three or four years).

Consequently, due to my concern about this "friendship," I prayed and asked the Lord to reveal to me what was going on so that I would know how to pray and intercede on her behalf. I prayed for Leah concerning her struggle with parenting and the need for deliverance from her past relationships. The Lord revealed to me that not only did she need deliverance, but the deliverance wasn't concerning her parenting skills or the men she'd been involved with in the past. But rather, there was a *homosexual spirit* present that He wanted to deliver her from, which confirmed what I'd discerned during that "one conversation" we had. I was surprised because if the Lord hadn't revealed it to me, I wouldn't have ever guessed it. And yet, I didn't say anything to her about what the Lord had revealed.

Anyway, now that the spirit had been revealed, I continued to pray for her deliverance. In the meantime, I continued with the friendship – getting to know her and of course encouraging her to allow the Lord to bring forth deliverance in her life. And while I understood that she needed deliverance from the homosexual spirit, I was careful not to get ahead of the Lord, but allowed *her* to come to the realization that she needed deliverance.

Almost immediately after the Lord revealed the homosexual spirit, He set the stage for deliverance:

Just so happened, Leah's birthday was coming in a few weeks, and I'd asked her if she had any plans. And every time I asked, she said, "No." I thought, *at the absolute least, the guy she was "friends" with would take her to dinner or something.* But she kept saying, "No." The closer it got to her birthday, I continued to ask if she had anything planned and she continued to say, "No" – this went on for a few weeks. However, the day *of* her birthday she asked me to go with her to get her nails done. No big deal. This was something we always did together; either I was getting my nails done or she was. Yet, *that* visit to the nail shop was unlike any we've ever had.

While we were at the nail shop Leah said, with great hesitation I might add, "I have something to tell you, but it's very difficult to do. I'm afraid to tell you because I know what you're going to say. But most importantly," she continued, "I'm afraid of how you're going to respond."

Now, I have to admit that because it was so difficult for her to tell me, my first thought was that the guy she'd been "playing footsie" with had finally gotten her to sacrifice her celibacy, which she'd been challenged with. Therefore, I responded slowly in hopes that it wasn't so, "You sacrificed your celibacy?"

"No. That's not it. It's worse than that," she said, as she continued to struggle with telling me what was obviously very deeply distressing for her. "I want to tell you so bad," she continued, "but I can't." So we went back and forth with this for the duration of her getting her nails done – one hour. And of course, I continued to encourage her to just tell me – whatever it was. "I know that when I tell you," she said, "I'm sure that we won't be friends anymore and I don't want to lose your friendship. You've been such a blessing to my life and if it hadn't been for our friendship, I don't know where I would be or how I'd be able to make it. And I know you're going to have a different view point of our friendship once I tell you."

Anxious to know what she wanted so badly to tell me, but couldn't, I continued to encourage her that *whatever* she had to tell me wouldn't cause me to think differently about her or our friendship. But she wasn't able to bring herself to tell me before we left the nail shop. However, when we got in the car to go back to work, I continued to assure her that our friendship wouldn't change nor would I look at her any differently. *However,* I thought, *considering she hadn't sacrificed her celibacy, and she thought what she wanted to tell me was worse than sacrificing her celibacy, I really didn't know if our friendship would be affected or not (especially since she had such difficulty telling me).*

Anyway, by the time we made it back to work, she said, "I'm leaving work early today."

Immediately, I looked at her, surprised by what she said. "Why are you leaving early if you don't have any plans?" I asked.

"I know you've been asking me day after day if I had plans for my birthday, and I kept telling you that I didn't, but I deliberately deceived you."

"'You deliberately deceived me'?" I questioned. Immediately, I thought, w*ho says that; 'I deliberately deceived you.'* And just as suddenly, I was quickened in my spirit that this wasn't just her saying, *'I didn't tell you something,'* but rather it was a demon speaking. And immediately, I was reminded of what the Lord had revealed to me in prayer. That explained why it was so difficult for her to say what she wanted to say. The demon was trying to keep her from telling me so that he wouldn't be exposed.

"Yes," she said, as she continued to struggle to tell me what she'd been holding back for the last few weeks. "I wasn't going to say anything to you about it, but last night I talked to Dwayne and he convinced me that it was the right thing to do; especially since you're my friend. I didn't tell you before because I didn't want to hear what you had to say."

"What?" I said with astonishment. "You didn't want to hear what I had to say?" I repeated as I stood there amazed at what this demon was saying.

"I was invited to go somewhere with a friend," she continued, "and I didn't want to hear what you had to say."

"You didn't want to hear what I had to say?" I questioned again. This was a far cry from the conversation a few minutes ago when she said, "I know that when I tell you, I'm sure that we won't be friends anymore and I don't want to lose your friendship. You've been such a blessing to my life. If it hadn't been for our friendship, I don't know where I would be or how I'd be able to make it. And I know you're going to have a different view point of our friendship once I tell you."

"First of all," I said, while trying to be careful with my words since I knew demonic forces were present. "You don't owe me any explanations about what you do or who you do it with. Whatever you've decided to do and whomever you've decided to do it with, that's your decision. You don't have to worry about what I have to say. You can do whatever you want to do."

And yet, she continued to struggle with just saying what she had to say. But slowly, or should I say reluctantly, she continued. "About two weeks ago, Rachel invited me to go on a cruise with her, but I didn't want to tell you about it because I didn't want to hear what you had to say. I wanted to go; I decided that I was going, so that's why I'm leaving early. We're scheduled to meet up at my mother's house in a couple of hours. And by the way," she said, "I'll be gone for the week."

Wow! I thought. Let me make sure I understood what had just happened: I had been asking her for weeks about her birthday plans and for weeks she had known about her plans, and yet, she *deliberately deceived me* by continuing to deny that she had plans; *because* she didn't want to hear what I had to say. She had decided that that's what she wanted to do, so she was doing it. "Wow!" was all I could say as I stood there taken aback by *my friend*.

Rachel used to work with us, and it was no secret that she lived a homosexual lifestyle. And since Rachel had left the company, she and Leah had been hanging out together – quite often. But what Leah didn't know was that while she was making these plans (behind my back), the Lord had revealed the homosexual spirit to me. So I wasn't surprised that she had accepted Rachel's invitation to go on the cruise. Therefore, I saw this as an opportunity for me to see if she was *involved* in a relationship with Rachel, and I took advantage of the opportunity. "Is Rachel 'interested' in you?" I asked.

"She's not interested in me. She and her girlfriend broke up a few weeks ago and she didn't want to lose the tickets, so she asked if I wanted to go."

"And the cruise just so happened to be on your birthday," I said sarcastically.

"Yeah, it's just a coincidence," she said laughing. "Daisy, I'm serious. This wasn't planned."

As far as I was concerned, the conversation was over; she didn't owe me an explanation, and she left. Unfortunately, as a result of the conversation, I realized that not only was there a *homosexual spirit* present, but I was being confronted by the *spirit of manipulation, spirit of deception, and a lying spirit.* They're all associated spirits that work together.

In spite of the conversation we had, I understood the struggle of her wanting to tell me but not being able to tell me – she needed deliverance. I also understood that ultimately, as she said, 'she *wanted* to go and had *decided* that she *was* going,' and 'she didn't want to hear what I had to say.'

Unfortunately, unbeknownst to Leah, the demons that were present in her life were dictating to her the lifestyle that she would live. The demon, which was in authority, is what's known as a "strong man" in the area of deliverance (in the spirit realm). The strong man's name is Sexual Confusion. The *root* cause of homosexuality is the person is sexually confused. Sexual Confusion is a result of an individual being confused sexually by a number of factors: the environment that they grew up in (witnessing homosexual activity), individuals who may have been violated and overpowered by demonic oppression (rape, molestation), or a generational curse. The strong man is a demonic force that assigns associated spirits (demons with lesser power and authority) to accomplish the task of the strong man. And in this case, the task was to keep Leah in bondage by living the homosexual lifestyle. That way, she'd remain indebted or a slave to her flesh; fleshly desires. And, as a result of an individual being confused sexually, it "opens a door" or gives the enemy an opportunity to *influence* the person by having them engage in that demonic lifestyle.

Now, as I mentioned above, some of the associated spirits that were operating in Leah's life were the *spirit of homosexuality, spirit of manipulation, spirit of deception, and lying spirit.* They all work together and have similar functions in order to accomplish the goal of the strong man: keep her confused sexually, cover up the homosexual activity, and keep her in bondage. As long as the strong man could keep her confused, she'd remain demonically oppressed and living in sin. And the longer a person lives in sin, bondage, the stronger the demons become, which makes it that much more difficult for the person to break free and get delivered. So by keeping the individual wrapped up and tied up in the demonic activity, the spirits are able to continuously entice or tempt the person to remain active in the homosexual activity.

These demons deceive individuals by skillfully covering up their activity. They work together to make sure an individual would do or say anything necessary so that the strong man, the root cause of the demonic activity, won't be exposed. Not only do the spirits work together to lie, deceive, and manipulate other people, but they lie, deceive, and manipulate the *person* by making them *think* homosexuality is an "acceptable way of life" or "they were born that way." That way, the person doesn't become aware of the fact that they are in bondage and living in sin. And consequently, these spirits are present in the person's life because they've become too strong to be defeated without some sort of deliverance (or professional assistance) to set the person free. And lastly, but certainly not least, the function of the *spirit of homosexuality* is to cause the individual to trade **natural** sex between a man and a woman for **unnatural** sex between same sexes: a man and a man or a woman and a woman – hence *homo*sexual.

That is why God abandoned them to their shameful desires. Even the women turned against the natural way to have sex and instead indulged in sex with each other. And the men, instead of having normal sexual relations with women, burned with lust for each other. Men did shameful things with other men, and as a result of their sin, they suffered within themselves the penalty they deserved. Since they thought it foolish to acknowledge God, he abandoned them to their foolish thinking and let them do things that should never be done.

Romans 1:26 – 28 NLT

Another thing that I'd like to point out is that the spirits are able to identify one another (not to mention, they're territorial). So when it came to getting involved in the homosexual activity, it was foreseeable that Leah would become involved with Rachel because they had the same homosexual spirit; they identified with each other. It's no different than the phrase, *"Birds of a feather flock together,"* be it demonic or otherwise.

Now, on another note, the girls at work didn't make matters any better when they asked me why I hadn't mentioned Leah was going on a cruise with Rachel (after they'd seen the pictures posted on Facebook). My only response was, "Because *I* didn't know." So the pictures of Leah and Rachel pretty much solidified their suspicion that Leah was gay, which I had never confirmed when they asked me about it.

Unfortunately, Leah was right; I *did* have a different view point of our friendship, but not in the way that she thought. Immediately, the friendship shifted from *friends* to *ministry of deliverance.* The Lord (and I) wanted her to get delivered from the homosexual lifestyle. Although, I have to say, the situation with Rachel revealed to me that we weren't the "friends" that I thought we were – and not only that, but clearly, I wasn't going to continue to be friends with someone who *"deliberately deceives me."*

So when Leah came back from the cruise, I made a conscious effort to have very little, if anything, to do with her. I had to separate my so-called friendship from my, now, assignment.

PART

III

THE

FIRST

TIGER

❦

THE FIRST TRIMESTER

~ CHAPTER 1 ~

THE BABY BUMP IS STARTING TO SHOW

Once we started the ministry, I shared with Leah that we had our first member, Tiffany, and of course we were very excited. And she was also excited for us and expressed her sincere enthusiasm in supporting us. Then I extended the invitation to her to join and help us build and grow the ministry. "What does it mean to help you grow and build the ministry?" she asked.

"You'd be a member of our ministry, and once you've matured and we've increased in members, you'd be available to assist us in helping the others in the ministry grow in their relationship with Christ along with us," I responded.

Unfortunately, she thought taking on yet something else in her life would be too overwhelming; therefore, she declined. However, she made it clear that she'd come to *support us*, which I gladly accepted.

So we gathered for the first bible study and it was awesome. We started, of course, by welcoming the Holy Spirit with praise and worship and allowing Him to have His way with us. Then Pastor Randolph taught and dissected the Word of God. We studied the book of John to learn the foundation of our faith: Jesus Christ and His ministry. After bible study, we prayed and then fellowshipped with one another.

Although I continued to pray for Leah's deliverance to come forth, I still hadn't mentioned that I knew she lived a homosexual lifestyle or that the homosexual spirit was present. Not only that, but this was a topic that we had yet to really discuss in detail, and for the most part, I would follow her lead. Again, I had to be careful not to get ahead of the Lord, but wait for His timing to allow Him to bring forth the deliverance, not me.

However, one day Leah and I were talking and she mentioned she had some cruise tickets that she wasn't going to be able to use and wanted to see if she could get a refund or sell them. Immediately when she said, 'cruise tickets,' I was quickened in my spirit and knew *some how* these tickets were going to have something to do with Rachel (although I didn't know how). Then I was reminded that by this time, about six months had passed since the cruise incident with Rachel. So, when she mentioned she had cruise tickets that she was trying to get rid of, I was surprised, to say the least.

"What cruise tickets?" I asked surprised. "You never mentioned that you bought cruise tickets or that you were even *thinking* about taking a cruise."

"Since Rachel had taken me on a cruise," she said, "I purchased the cruise tickets for the following year to pay her back. The tickets were about $300.00."

"Wow!" I said. "That's funny! You never mentioned to me that you bought cruise tickets. How is that?"

"I just forgot," she said.

"You didn't *just forget*," I challenged her. "You are not going to spend $300.00 on cruise tickets for someone and then *just forget,* especially as often as we've talked about you and Rachel hanging out. You didn't 'just forget.'" It was clear that she was lying and said *"she forgot"* to cover it up. Immediately, I knew this was yet another one of her I *"deliberately deceived you"* instances. Just as she had known for a few weeks that she was going on the cruise with Rachel and didn't tell me, she had known for six months that she bought those tickets and had no intentions of telling me about *that,* either. But again, because she didn't know that I knew about her homosexual lifestyle and that I was praying and interceding for her, these "secret" things had already been revealed to me.

"I did. I did," she said trying to convince me that there was nothing more to her purchasing the tickets than to "pay Rachel back."

Immediately I thought, *How could you talk to someone every – single – day (and I mean every – single – day) for six months and not mention that you bought $300.00 cruise tickets for someone...* But my thought was immediately interrupted by being reminded of the demons she was dealing with. So needless to say, she had gotten good at "covering up."

I wanted desperately to tell her that I knew about her lifestyle, but I couldn't. I also wanted to tell her not to hang out with Rachel anymore because that only made the demons that much stronger. And I also knew I had to be careful because if she wasn't ready for deliverance, the demons would retaliate against me. Ultimately, they'd build an alliance with Rachel so that they couldn't be cast out; then there would be no chance for her deliverance. Again, because she didn't know that the demons were able to identify with one another, I used that as an opportunity to get her to open up. So to prepare the way for her deliverance I said, "Did you know that spirits are able to recognize one another?"

"No. What do you mean?"

"People that have the same spirit are able to recognize that in each other; let's just say, for example, the homosexual spirit in Rachel would be able to recognize the homosexual spirit in you – that's how it works, which is how the two are able to come together." Then I felt that it was an opportune time to ask her about her own struggle. "Have you ever been involved in a homosexual relationship?"

"No," she responded, even though *I* knew the truth. And I knew she bought the cruise tickets because she wanted to *be with* Rachel, intimately.

Unfortunately, she wasn't ready. Therefore, I didn't push.

It was sad to see her in that state and it broke my heart as the demons continued to influence, oppress, and keep her from getting deliverance. Again, if Jesus hadn't revealed it to me, I would've believed her. I mean, this girl fought tooth and nail that she did not need deliverance, and didn't even come close to admitting that she was *ever* involved in a homosexual relationship – not even the *"I tried it in college"* trick as some people would say.

The hard part for me was that I knew the Lord had come to deliver her from that lifestyle, but she wasn't ready. And while our conversations had gotten relaxed, they hadn't gotten *that* relaxed that she was ready to share that information with me. So I backed off, but I continued to pray and intercede. And little by little, as the Lord dictated, He'd open the door for us to talk about it. Then one day, when I asked her about it she said, "Well, I will say this, when the girls come on to me, it's flattering; it boosts my confidence."

The door had been opened and I walked right in.

"The girls were not just coming on to you, but they were drawn to you because you have the same spirit. You being flattered is an indication that their spirit was drawn to your spirit because they are the same kind of spirits. The spirits were familiar with each other. It's called a *homosexual spirit.* They recognize each other; attracted to each other. That's how you're able to tell who's homosexual and who's not; the person that has the same spirit is homosexual. So they are not just coming on to you just to be coming on to you, they know you have the same spirit."

"Wow! Are you serious?" she asked amazed.

"Absolutely!"

The next day, she came to me and said, "Okay, Daisy. I'm going to be completely honest with you. I'm going to be honest about everything and I'm not going to hold anything back." And she didn't – hold anything back. She shared everything in great detail. So much so, that I just stood there and listened to the homosexual demon as it boasted about all that *he* had influenced her to do while in that lifestyle. And almost as if to say, "And I'll do it again!"

"I already knew you were involved in that lifestyle; I've been waiting for you to be open and honest with me because the Lord wants to deliver you," I said. "And I want to help you."

"I don't need your help because I haven't been involved in that lifestyle for several years," the demon said as I stood there.

"Whether you know it or not," I said, "you *do* need my help because the demons are still present. As a matter of fact, that was the demon that just spoke. He stated proudly and boastfully about all that he had you involved in – while you were under his influence. It was a *haughty spirit* speaking *(a spirit of pride)* telling me how you enjoyed what you had done and would do it again. There was no remorse and you have not given the lifestyle up – the demons had been dormant. And while you thought you had done a great job of "covering up" your lifestyle, it has been the grace of God that has been covering you. Unfortunately," I continued, "the demons are now active again and you've been participating in that lifestyle. You haven't realized it, which explains your behavior over the last few months. You are blinded by their demonic activity."

Sadly, Leah vehemently disagreed with me as the demons once again tried to *deliberately deceive* me into thinking that they weren't present. "There's absolutely no way I'd ever go back to that lifestyle because I've spent the last few years making sure I'd never get involved in it again."

Then I started to point out to her the demonic activity that she had been involved in over the last few months – that she wasn't aware of. And of course, I started with the cruise she went on with Rachel:

"If the truth were told," I said, "you'd be in a relationship with Rachel. The only thing that kept you from getting involved with her was the fact that you knew the people at work would've found out – and you'd be exposed. If you thought you could have a relationship with her and no one knew about it, you'd be in a relationship with her; right back in that lifestyle. While you tried to get me to believe that it was "just a cruise," the homosexual spirit had already surfaced and it was your desire to be with Rachel intimately."

"Nah."

"If we looked back, that's why it was so difficult for you to tell me about the cruise, because that demon was trying to hide it from me – that's why you didn't want to *hear what I had to say.* Then, look at the activity that's been going on with you and Rachel over the last few months; hanging out a lot; texting all day, every day, and on a few occasions you've put yourself in some *compromising positions.* Not to mention, you told me that you have a set of keys to Rachel's apartment…"

"Oh, my gosh, Daiz!" she interrupted. "You are right! I didn't even realize that. Oh, man!" she said, as the realization of just how involved she'd gotten with that lifestyle and with Rachel hit her. She started to rejoice at the thought that the enemy almost got her, but hadn't. "I can't believe how close I came to getting back in that lifestyle. If it hadn't been for you, the enemy would've gotten me!" she said.

Her eyes had been opened. Deliverance was imminent.

And having disarmed the powers and authorities, he made a public spectacle of them, triumphing over them by the cross.

Colossians 2:15 NIV

~ CHAPTER 2 ~

WHAT'S MY POSITION?

We had been having bible study for about two weeks when I received an email from Tiffany:

Good Morning,

What do you think about a shut in? A group of women closed in for hours: fellowship, eat, praise, worship, read, minister, deliverance, laugh, cry, rebuke, cast out, and pray. YOU name it (anything that will cause attention to the Holy Spirit to show up and show out)! I was thinking that we can book a room at the resort for just one night – this way we will have room. I know some women who are hungry and need to be fed. I also know another woman of God that can and will be more than happy to assist you with the work you will have to do. Let me know what you think, just a thought.

I shared with her that while I thought a shut in at some point would be awesome, I would keep the idea before the Lord. However, I went on to explain to her the purpose of the ministry, which was to develop us first and mature in the things of God before the ministry was able to go forth. And that we had to first have people who were committed to the ministry, invested, and wanted to advance the vision that the Lord gave *us* to do. I also said that we had to get her and Leah involved in the ministry before we talked about going outside to minister. Then I encouraged her to bring the women of God that she knew to join us, so that we could help them develop in the things of God. And not only that, but I also expressed to her (as a reminder) that she had just been delivered herself a few days before. Ultimately, I challenged her to bring the women of God to the next gathering. Nevertheless, it wasn't long after that she then suggested being able to establish a praise dance team:

I was thinking (this is not a thus says the Lord...LOL) that Leah, Maria and I, as a form of worship and fellowship, could get together from time to time and put together a praise and worship dance. You know where we pick a song and use our temple (body) as a sacrifice unto the Lord for dance? What do you think?

Immediately, I shared with her that I thought it was a great idea. It was another way to worship the Lord while remaining focused on the ministry. Praise is always in season, and it would just be something that would be within the ministry. I was excited and surprised to hear that Leah and Maria would participate (considering their personalities). To be honest, I couldn't imagine either of them saying yes.

I just wanted to take the time to say that I THANK GOD for the both of you. It's a blessing to be a part of what God is doing in, and through the two of you! To God be the glory!!

Again, I thought it was a great idea. It was another vehicle to honor the Lord and it would be between us and Him. So I told Tiffany that I would inquire of the Lord to see what the Lord had to say about it. So Pastor Randolph and I went before the Lord to inquire about the praise team. And as we were praying, the Spirit of the Lord came upon me with great power. The anointing was so heavy as the vision was before me:

In a vision...

I saw Tiffany standing alone.

The interpretation...

It was clear, in my spirit I knew she was set apart to be the leader of the praise team as the voice of the Lord confirmed the vision.

"Tiffany is to be the Leader," I heard in my spirit as the vision before me confirmed what was spoken. His Hand was heavy upon me as His presence filled the room and the anointing rested on me; depositing a prophetic burden to birth this ministry. It was clear that the Lord was allowing the praise team to be established, and Tiffany was to be the leader. And consequently, we knew that they had to be "prepared" to minister to the Lord. Therefore, they had to be 'set apart' for holiness before they were able to come before Him as a ministry. However, before I was able to share the information with the girls, I received the following email from Tiffany:

...Now we got the preliminaries out of the way! When will the two of you share with Leah, Maria, and I what our position is in the church? I know we are supposed to learn, receive, participate, and serve, but we also have a position (a job) that God has called us to do as well. ...I am just waiting for the two of you to confirm what that is....

Immediately, it was revealed in my spirit that Tiffany was looking for Pastor Randolph and I to confirm what she thought was her spiritual gift; prophetess. And it was clear that she wanted a *position* in the church. Well, needless to say, that was not going to happen, especially since the Lord had revealed her gift, but it was *not* a prophetess. Not to mention, she hadn't been in church for a year (and when she was in church, she was sleeping with the Pastor's son). And now she had only been a part of our ministry for two weeks. So instead, I responded with the exciting news that the Lord had revealed to me; we could establish the praise team and she was to be the leader.

Nope that is not it. We are not gifted or anointed for that. We are doing it because we love the Lord and for fellowship and unity to bring honor to Him.

What?! I thought. Clearly, her response confirmed what was in my spirit. She wasn't really looking to *worship and fellowship, get together from time to time and put together a praise and worship dance. You know where we pick a song and use our temple (body) as a sacrifice unto the Lord for dance,* as she'd indicated, but rather she wanted us to confirm her *"gift"* – that's what that conversation was really about. But I went on to share with her that while she may have thought that it would've been something fun to do, it was the Lord who had prompted her to gather Leah and Maria and start the dance team. Ultimately, I explained to her *"that"* was her *"position"* in the church; *to praise the Lord.*

Praise Leader? Noooo way!!! What do you mean, Praise Leader? For what, to sing? Or to dance? Huh? My spirit is not in agreement with that. This was not a thus says the Lord! ...Thus says the Lord should be confirmation of what has already been spoken and this is not!!! ...The spirit is subject to the prophet!

Now, I have to say that, initially it baffled me why she wasn't open to taking ownership of the idea that *she* had suggested. It was *her* idea and for her not to take ownership of it, and be the leader, just didn't make any sense – but then again it did, that's not the *"position"* she wanted; she wanted to be the prophetess. Somehow this had turned from *"our sacrifice unto Him"* to *"Thus says the Lord should be confirmation of what the Lord has already spoken,"* and *"The spirit is subject to the prophet!"* So I asked her where she thought the idea had come from? And who did she think prompted her to get the praise dancers together; organize the team? While I understood she thought this was *her* idea and not God inspired, God inspired ideas are simply ideas or impressions that God has brought to an individual's mind. So, I explained to her that it was the Lord who had prompted her to do it. And He *confirmed* it with me. So in fact, the *"Thus says the Lord should be confirmation of what has already been spoken"* **had been confirmed.** He spoke it to her and confirmed it with me. While it was clear that she was "familiar" with the scriptures, she really didn't have any *understanding,* which spoke to her level of immaturity concerning prophecy.

She had been prompted by the Lord – whether she knew it or not – He inspired her to get the dance team together, and He confirmed it with me through prayer. Now, the confirmation that she was to be the *leader* simply spoke to the fact that He told *her* to gather the people; *lead,* which in fact is what she *had done* by getting Maria and Leah to participate.

Although the prophetic word had been spoken, she continued to express her concerns about being able to lead. Consequently, her being obedient to the "word" of the Lord would release the anointing to enable her to lead, but that would remain to be seen. And as a result of going back and forth, in spite of my encouragement, it was sad and my heart broke to see that she was about to *miss out* on how the Lord wanted to use her in this *position.* She was about to miss the Lord's anointing; the move of God in her life, which saddened me.

Our ministry, a prophetic ministry, was to help create a new beginning for her spiritual life. Surely, it would've allowed her to re-establish her relationship with Christ. Consequently, I shared with her that this was the *"position"* that He wanted her to have in this season, but certainly Pastor Randolph or I wouldn't force her to do it if she didn't want to. While at the same time, I tried to explain to her that it wasn't her will that was to be done in her life, but the Lord's will to be done in her life (just something for her to think about).

I will instruct you and teach you in the way you should go; I will counsel you with my loving eye on you.

Psalms 32:8 NIV

Anyone who is submitted to the Holy Spirit and led by His Spirit is also able to spiritually *discern* or determine if the message that is being spoken or prophesied is from the Spirit of God or from another spirit:

He gives one person the power to perform miracles, and another the ability to prophesy. He gives someone else the ability to discern whether a message is from the Spirit of God or from another spirit. Still another person is given the ability to speak in unknown languages, while another is given the ability to interpret what is being said.

1 Corinthians 12:10 NLT

The scripture is clear when operating in prophecy:

And the spirits of the prophets are subject to the prophets.

1 Corinthians 14:32 KJV

Now to give you a little more clarity and understanding of this scripture reference, let's take a look at the New Living Translation:

Let two or three people prophesy, and let the others evaluate what is said. But if someone is prophesying and another person receives a revelation from the Lord, the one who is speaking must stop. In this way, all who prophesy will have a turn to speak, one after the other, so that everyone will learn and be encouraged. Remember that people who prophesy are in control of their spirit and can take turns. For God is not a God of disorder but of peace, as in all the meetings of God's holy people.

1 Corinthians 14:29 – 33 NLT

Now according to this passage of scriptures, Paul gives instructions on prophesying when there's a group of people prophesying at the same time. Clearly, he's instructing the individuals to *"take turns"* in prophesying. By doing so, it would allow one person to speak at a time, and the others can evaluate what is being said (to determine if what's being spoken is of the Spirit; meaning, spoken by the Lord).

Consequently, the verse indicates that the prophet (or the person speaking prophetically) is in control of their own spirit; not only in control of *what* they say, but *when* they say it. And most importantly, this should be done because God is not a God of disorder or confusion, but He's a God of peace. Therefore, we're admonished to evaluate or *"test"* the spirit in which the person is speaking to know if the person is speaking on their own or if the Lord is speaking through that person.

So basically, Tiffany was saying that she didn't believe what I said came from the Lord. (Although, I have to say, I'm not sure if she *really* understood what the scripture meant.) Therefore, based on the interpretation of the scripture, she had the liberty to evaluate or *"test"* what I said to see if what I said was what the Lord said. Many of you may be familiar with *"try the spirit by the spirit"* or *"test the spirit by the spirit."* If not, that simply means to test what I've said by the Spirit of God to make sure that it lined up with what the Spirit of God says. If what I've said lines up with what God says, then it would confirm the "word" of the Lord.

John gives us the instructions concerning ***testing*** the spirit:

Dear friends, do not believe everyone who claims to speak by the Spirit. You must test them to see if the spirit they have comes from God. For there are many false prophets in this world. This is how we know if they have the Spirit of God: If a person claiming to be a prophet acknowledges that Jesus Christ came in a real body, that person has the Spirit of God. But if

someone claims to be a prophet and does not acknowledge the truth about Jesus, that person is not from God.

1 John 4:1 – 3 NLT

Now, the first thing I want to point out concerning this passage of scriptures is that John says, *test* them to see if the *spirit they have comes from God.* Secondly, he gives clear instructions on how we know if a person has the Spirit of God:

- ✓ If a person claiming to be a prophet acknowledges that Jesus Christ came in a real body, that person has the Spirit of God.
- ✓ If someone claims to be a prophet and does not acknowledge the truth about Jesus, that person is not from God.

Again, as the scripture mentioned above, God is not the author of confusion, but a God of peace. Therefore, anyone speaking on behalf of the Lord should not be afraid to be *"tested."* For that reason, listed below are some ways we can *test the spirit* to see if the spirit the individual has (or the prophetic words that they speak) comes from God:

- ✓ Does the "word" being spoken line up with what's said in the bible?
- ✓ What is the person's relationship with Jesus Christ?
- ✓ What about the fruit of their ministry?
- ✓ Does the prophecy promote Christ or the person?

...but test everything that is said. Hold on to what is good.

1 Thessalonians 5:21 NLT

So clearly, if Tiffany *understood* the scriptures, she would've known that all she had to do was *"test"* the spirit in which I spoke to determine if what I was saying was of God.

Then she responded:

...I really have to pray, Daisy, because I need to know what is required of me. Do you know that this whole time I thought I was called to do something totally different? Not one time did He reveal to me that this was one of them. So, that's why it is a shock to me. Love you.

So I went on to explain to her that this wasn't her "calling." This was a place in which the Lord would begin to restore her relationship with Him, draw her closer to Him, and take her to deeper levels in Him. Basically, preparing her for what she *was* "called" to do. Therefore, I encouraged her all the more and I shared with her that the praise dance was really just an *outward reflection of her relationship with Him in her secret place.*

Oh, okay. Not my calling, a place to draw me closer to Him. I understand that, my spirit bears witness to that. To prepare me for what I am called to do, but to lead???? ...When God told Moses to lead, he gave him a sign. Moses said, "How can I lead and speak on behalf of you?

God I stutter, I can't even talk." And God told him what to do and not to worry. God told him about his brother, Aaron, and he also went to his brother Aaron, so when his brother came to him, he was confident because it was confirmation of what God had already spoke over him.

Immediately, my spirit was quickened and the Lord revealed there was a bigger issue underlining our conversation; He revealed she wasn't open to receive what I was saying. She didn't trust me. Therefore, I wasn't going to going back and forth with her because she wasn't open to receive what I was saying – no matter how I tried to explain it. And as the Lord had revealed, I explained to her that it really came down to one or two things – no matter how many scriptures she used to look for a "confirmation." (1) Either she didn't trust me or (2) She didn't trust the Lord. Then I asked her, which was it?

Yes, its number 1. (Please don't be mad or offended.)

I understood. She wasn't open to receive from me nor was she submitted to the "word" of the Lord. Of course, her being the leader may not have been *reasonable* or *logical* to her because her only focus was on her *supposed gift* – prophetess. However, there was only one way that she'd be able to receive what the Lord had spoken, and that was if her mind, logic, and reason were submitted to the Spirit. Then the Lord revealed the *spirits of pride and rebellion* were present, so unless she chose to submit to Him, she was about to miss the move of God in her life.

The man without the Spirit does not accept the things that come from the Spirit of God, for they are foolishness to him, and he cannot understand them, because they are spiritually discerned.

1 Corinthians 2:14 NIV

I understood that since she hadn't been in church for a year, that she wasn't connected to the Lord; therefore, she wasn't able to spiritually discern, receive, or understand what the Lord was doing – not to mention the demons that were present – keeping her from becoming spiritually connected. Consequently, I went on to share with her that I wasn't mad or offended by what she said because it was the Lord who had prompted me to ask her if she trusted me. And her response really had nothing to do with me as much as it had revealed why she wouldn't submit: the *spirit of pride* and the *spirit of rebellion*. Hence, you have someone who's trying to tell me – your pastor how the "word" of the Lord is to be prophesied and confirmed; someone who's trying to tell me – your leader what her spirit was not in agreement with; not to mention, someone who's dealing with the *spirit of deception* that she came into the ministry with. Therefore, I shared with her that the spirits that had been revealed must be cast out! And I encouraged her to be prayerful concerning these things during our time of fasting and praying.

I also went on to explain and give her clarity regarding what she said about *God giving Moses a confirmation of what He had called Moses to do*:

When God told Moses to lead, He gave him a sign. Moses said, "How can I lead and speak on behalf of you? God I stutter, I can't even talk." And God told him what to do and not to worry. God told him about his brother, Aaron, and he also went to his brother Aaron, *so when his brother came to him, he was confident because it was confirmation of what God had already spoke over him.*

"Now go, for I am sending you to Pharaoh. You must lead my people Israel out of Egypt."

But Moses protested to God, "Who am I to appear before Pharaoh? Who am I to lead the people of Israel out of Egypt?"

Exodus 3:10 – 11 NLT

The first thing I want to point out is, when the Lord told Moses that He wanted him to *lead* His people out of Egypt, Moses had no clue – no idea that when he went to inquire of the burning bush, that the Lord would tell him to lead the people of Israel out of Egypt. In other words, what most people may not understand is that prophecy, the "word" of God that's spoken, also ***informs*** us of what God is getting ready to do in our lives; we don't always *know* the plans that He has for us. Do you think Moses knew God was going to ask him to lead the people out of Egypt? Absolutely not! Then, the Lord said to Moses:

"The elders of Israel will accept your message. Then you and the elders must go to the king of Egypt and tell him, 'The LORD, the God of the Hebrews, has met with us. So please let us take a three-day journey into the wilderness to offer sacrifices to the LORD, our God.'

Exodus 3:18 NLT

But Moses protested again according to Exodus, chapter four, verse one. Then, we see the Lord provides Moses with some miraculous signs of His power:

Moses' staff turns into a snake
Moses' hand has leprosy then is healed
The Lord instructs him to take some water from the Nile and turn it into blood
...if they don't believe the first two signs.

However, Moses continues to plead with the Lord to send someone else because he wasn't good with words; he gets tongue-tied and his words get tangled. And again, in verse twelve the Lord instructs Moses to go while assuring him that He'll be with him.

But in verse thirteen ***Moses protests yet again,*** "Lord, please! Send anyone else." So we see in the scriptures that not only did the Lord speak directly to Moses and instruct him to lead his people out of Israel, but He also told him to take the elders with him so that the people could offer sacrifices to the Lord. The Lord provided miraculous signs of His power for Moses; so His word was already confirmed, ***and it had nothing to do with his brother Aaron.***

And surely Tiffany hadn't remembered Exodus, chapter four, verse fourteen:

Then the LORD became angry with Moses. *"All right," He said. "What about your brother, Aaron the Levite? I know he speaks well. And look! He is on his way to meet you now. He will be delighted to see you."*

Exodus 4:14 NLT (emphasis added)

I continued by telling her to take notice that it had more to do with ***Moses making excuses*** for why he couldn't do what God called him to do, than God giving him a sign or *confirmation.* Because God is merciful and wanted His plan to go forward He did those things for Moses. However, in Tiffany's situation, the Lord had already revealed why she had yet to submit; she was prideful, rebellious, and deceived. Therefore, allow me to point out the difference between her and Moses: While Moses kept the focus on *him and his inadequacies*; her focus was trying to dictate to me, her spiritual leader, how to prophesy and confirm the word of God.

I also shared with Tiffany, when God wanted to set Aaron apart as Priest into a *leadership position*, He didn't speak to Aaron – He spoke to Moses, *the leader;* thereby, trying to assure her that the Lord speaks to the *leaders* concerning the church and the people. So, again, I told her that I wasn't at all offended that she didn't trust me. But I prayed that she'd submit not only to the things of God, but to the leadership that the Lord had placed over her to look after her soul.

He is the Holy Spirit, who leads into all truth. The world cannot receive him, because it isn't looking for him and doesn't recognize him.

John 14:17a NLT

Consequently, Tiffany wasn't able to *see* what the Lord was trying to do in her life because she was *looking* for a position. And when she was given a position, she wasn't able to recognize the move of the Spirit because it wasn't the position she wanted. Now what's most important when trying to "test" the spirit of someone is the person has to make sure *their* spirit is right; that they're in right standing with God to be able to spiritually discern properly. (This may very well be an indication of her "thinking" she learned more on her own than when she was in church.) You see, prophesying also reveals what's in a person's heart. As a result of the "word" being spoken, it revealed pride and rebellion was in Tiffany's heart. So now, this was about seeing if Tiffany was going to be obedient and submit to what she had been instructed to do and to see if she would submit to her leaders.

Then all of a sudden I couldn't help but wonder, *was this what she had a habit of doing: going from church to church to be confirmed as a prophetess or to get a position?* I wondered all the more as I was reminded of her telling me that she was involved in a long distance relationship with a *"Pastor"* and they were talking about marriage.

Anyone who prophesies – edifies, exhorts, and comforts. That includes: enlightens, informs, educates, instructs, improves, teaches, encourages, incites, advises, releases, breaks, and liberates others. That means, prophecy, the inspired word of God, informs or reveals the "work" that's inside of an individual that they may not be aware of; whether it's developing their character, gifts, or doing the work of the ministry. It makes them aware of the season they're in and the work that's to be done in that season. So, when the word is released and they believe it, it releases the anointing; God's power that enables them to do what the Lord has commissioned.

Unfortunately, this proved to be a very difficult task for Tiffany considering she was being influenced by the demonic spirits of pride, rebellion, and deception. And as a result of her drive and determination for her *own self-satisfaction,* she was opposed to the things of God.

But Samuel replied, "What is more pleasing to the LORD: your burnt offerings and sacrifices or your obedience to his voice? Listen! Obedience is better than sacrifice, and submission is better than offering the fat of rams." Rebellion is as sinful as witchcraft, and stubbornness as bad as worshipping idols. So because you have rejected the command of the LORD, he has rejected you as king."

1 Samuel 15:22 – 23 NLT

I was concerned about her spiritual well-being and wanted desperately for her to get delivered. But until the Lord instructed me to bring forth deliverance, the demons had a legal right to be there to influence her. Because of her lifestyle; "playing church" while having sex with the pastor's son, not being in church for a year, or not being connected to Jesus. She opened the door for the demonic forces to come in.

I continued to be prayerful concerning the matter.

In addition to my concern about her spiritual well-being, there was a red flag in my spirit. An ever so subtle wave of the banner; because she didn't trust me as her spiritual leader, then I knew this was *not* the ministry for her.

But I wondered *had she forgotten that I'm the same person the Lord used to bring forth deliverance in her life* as I was reminded of what she said:

I looked for the woman of God and reached for her to tell her that I had to throw up. She came right to my side and began to encourage me. I heard the woman of God call forth and call out a spirit that I asked God to release me from. When I heard that, it was confirmation that what I have been tormented with since I was a young girl was about to "loose" me. I could hear the woman of God comforting me and telling me to tell Him yes! Tell the Lord yes! The more I said yes the more I felt led to push, the more I pushed the harder my yes became, and then I began to throw up. The spirit of fear had no choice but to leave. I am free!

And now she was saying she didn't believe I heard from the Lord, she didn't trust me.

In my mind, I was like, *Come on, John, what have you seen and heard* (as Jesus had said to John the Baptist when he doubted if Jesus was the Messiah).

John the Baptist, who was in prison, heard about all the things the Messiah was doing. So he sent his disciples to ask Jesus, "Are you the Messiah we've been expecting, or should we keep looking for someone else?"

Jesus told them, "Go back to John and tell him what you have heard and seen – the blind see, the lame walk, the lepers are cured, the deaf hear, the dead are raised to life, and the Good News is being preached to the poor. And tell him, 'God blesses those who do not turn away because of me.'"

Matthew 11:2 – 5 NLT

And now she's talking about 'the spirit is subject to the prophet'?! Come on, John! I thought. *'Thus says the Lord should...'*

Then I realized…

THE TESTING HAD BEGUN

In a dream...

I was pregnant in the spirit.

The interpretation...

The Lord revealed to me that it would be four weeks until I was due to deliver that which He was birthing in my spirit.

As a result of knowing that I was pregnant in the spirit, I was prompted to fast and pray for twenty-one days. Consequently, the morning after completing the fast, I got up to pray at 3 a.m. (as I usually did); however, as soon as I entered the room, I was filled with a spirit of praise and worship. I was unable to pray or do anything else, so I continued to praise and worship the Lord. Then shortly after, I realized something was happening in the spirit. What? I didn't know, but there was a heavy anointing, a great demand, for praise and worship. And just as suddenly, in the midst of my praise, I realized I was in the midst of delivering that which the Lord had deposited in my spirit.

A birthing was taking place as I continued to praise the Lord.

I was amazed and astonished at the ease of the delivery and how quickly the birthing had taken place. So much so that it wasn't until the birthing process was over that I realized I hadn't pushed and there were no labor pains. It was then that the Lord said, "In the secret place."

In awe of His glory, I allowed Him to continue to minister to me as I continued to praise Him. I was honored to be in the presence of the Lord. 'In the secret place' kept ringing in my spirit. So I came to the realization that I was in the secret place, the Holy of Holies. I had been in the presence of the Lord – in His Holy place. Then the Lord said, "I shall hide thee."

HE THAT dwelleth in the secret place of the most High shall abide under the shadow of the Almighty.

Psalm 91:1 KJV

Then suddenly, I was reminded of the birthing of Christ (and how King Herod was out to kill Him in order to prevent the plan of God from going forward).

King Herod was deeply disturbed when he heard this, as was everyone in Jerusalem. He called a meeting of the leading priests and teachers of religious law and asked, "Where is the Messiah supposed to be born?"

Then he told them, "Go to Bethlehem and search carefully for the child. And when you find him, come back and tell me so that I can go and worship him, too!"

When it was time to leave, they returned to their own country by another route, for God had warned them in a dream not to return to Herod.

Matthew 2: 3; 8; 12 NLT

And immediately, it was impressed upon me that the birthing that had taken place *in the secret place, would be hidden until its due season* (so that the enemy wouldn't be able to kill it and stop the plan of God – the Will of God – in my life).

Then I cried out to the Lord with thanksgiving; knowing *that which He had promised – He had delivered.*

~ CHAPTER 3 ~

SET APART

One evening after bible study, I extended an invitation to Maria to join the ministry. However, while extending the invitation to Maria, Leah interrupted, "Why don't you just go ahead and ask me if I want to join." Everyone started laughing. However, I had no intentions of asking Leah again because she had already indicated that it would've been too much for her to handle. But, since she interrupted me, which reflected her interest in being a part of the ministry, I extended the invitation to her as well. As a result, she and Maria both joined the ministry.

Shortly after Leah became a part of the ministry, I encouraged her to spend time with her spiritual sisters (Tiffany and Maria), so that she could be encouraged and grow in her relationship with Christ. It did my heart good when they agreed to find a song and meet to practice for the praise dance. However, I asked them to hold off until they were "set apart" for ministry. Then I was prompted in my spirit that Maria wasn't a part of this ministry. I was taken aback by the revelation, which caused me to ponder this in my heart until the Lord revealed why.

To prepare ourselves for ministering to the Lord, we were to consecrate ourselves so that everyone would be on one accord. Then Pastor Randolph would anoint them; setting them apart for the Lord's use and glory. Consequently, we fasted and prayed for three days leading up to the day of the service.

Then he [Moses] poured some of the anointing oil on Aaron's head, anointing him and making him holy for his work.

Leviticus 8:12 NLT (emphasis added)

During the three days of fasting and praying, I have to say that my spirit was troubled about the situation with Tiffany. I desperately wanted the Lord to deliver her. I prayed that as we were fasting, He'd move mightily on her behalf. The concern weighed heavily on me and I couldn't seem to shake it. Of course, the more I thought about it, the more I became troubled in my spirit. She had been out of church for a year, she was operating under the influence of demonic forces, and at that point, she'd only been connected with our ministry for a month. And in that month, she was going against what I said; she didn't trust me. My heart was burdened for her. As the tears rolled down my face, I pleaded with the Lord to deliver her.

In addition to my heart being burdened for Tiffany, I was also *concerned* about the revelation of her being the praise leader. The revelation went against what I knew to be "protocol" of putting someone in a leadership position, not to mention she said she didn't trust me; her spiritual leader. *How is it that she's being set apart?* I wondered. *What's going on?* So I continued to go before the Lord so He would reveal His plan to me. And while in His presence, He responded:

"Expose the spirit of deception!"

"Oh, my God!" I exclaimed. I was astounded at what He said. I sat there and waited for understanding; for Him to reveal His plan to me, which was about to unfold before my very eyes.

"When you lay hands on her," He said, "it's going to cause her to either worship or leave. She will not be able to stay in the presence of *Truth.*"

"Oh, my God!" I was speechless at what the Lord was about to accomplish. And I could hardly wait for it to come to pass.

We all came together the night of the service, which was held in place of the bible study. We started with praise and worship. And as if the Lord had been waiting for us to get started, His presence filled the room immediately. Pastor Randolph ministered to them; anointing them as vessels unto Him. And they were open to receive, well, some of them.

Timothy, my son, here are my instructions for you, based on the prophetic words spoken about you earlier. May they help you fight well in the Lord's battles.

1 Timothy 1:18 NLT

Then Pastor Randolph ministered to Tiffany; he explained to her the importance of being in the leadership position. Then he asked her if she was willing to accept her position, which she responded, "Yes." However, I discerned that she was reluctant, *she wasn't willing,* but she stood there. And immediately, the power of God came upon me, and I laid hands on her and began to pray in the spirit; calling out, exposing the spirits that were present.

Consequently, as I was calling out the spirits, I noticed Maria was visibly shaken and frightened (as she anxiously asked if we could open the door in order to let the demons out). I shook my head to indicate yes to help combat her fear, which she did. Then Tiffany began speaking in tongues; however, I discerned that she was speaking with *false tongues.* She wasn't speaking *in the Spirit* or *by the Spirit,* but rather by demonic forces; satanic powers.

We can't forget that tongues, signs and wonders also come from satanic powers; by deceitful workers disguising themselves as servants of God. Any time someone is perceived to be speaking in tongues but isn't committed to Jesus' authority (or the Word of God), whatever manifestations (or gifts) they may have *aren't* from the Holy Spirit. Therefore, after she wouldn't submit, the Lord advised me to minister to the other ladies as He dictated.

As I ministered to Leah, I shared with her that God was going to do for her what she'd asked Him to do; all she had to do was allow Him to have His way. Then the Lord prompted me to minister to her concerning *purity,* so I laid hands on her and commanded purity (holiness, righteousness, and wholeness) to come forth. I rebuked impure thoughts, behaviors, and words, and asked the Lord to cleanse her from all unrighteousness. Then I released the Spirit of the Lord over her life and called her unto submission to the Lord.

While I was ministering, someone's cell phone kept ringing, but no one answered it; therefore, it continued to ring. When I started ministering to Maria, I discerned that she wasn't open to receive ministry. So I asked her if she wanted the Lord to move in her life?

"Yes," she said. "But I'm just distracted because my husband keeps calling."

"Oh, okay. Answer the phone."

She answered the phone and then said she had to leave because she had to go get her baby. And shortly after, we ended the service.

A short time later, after everyone left, my cell phone rang; it was Leah calling. My initial thought was *she was calling to let me know that she had made it home.* But then again, I was a little concerned because she never called – she always texted. Then I thought, *Okay. She's calling to say she was blessed by the service (as she always did).* But when I answered the call, I answered to a voice that was distressed and crying. Immediately, my heart went out to her (even though I had no idea what was going on). Anxiously, I asked, "What's wrong?"

As she spoke through her tears she said, "Daisy, this is too hard."

"What's too hard? What's happening?" I asked anxiously, but also taking into consideration that she was crying. Her silence prompted me to allow her time to answer, so I waited for her response.

"This walk!" she said. "It's too much for me to handle. I can't do it."

"Leah. You *can* do it," I encouraged her as my heart broke, even though I had no idea *what* she was referring to. "You've got to hold on; it's a process. You'll get through this." And immediately, I thought she was struggling because she didn't understand what took place during the service. So I asked her, "What are you experiencing?" (Surely, the Lord was still ministering to her.)

"It's too difficult for me; I'm overwhelmed," she said as she continued to cry.

"Why are you overwhelmed? What are you experiencing?" She was barely able to talk. So I encouraged her to calm down and get herself together; it was okay because the Lord was with her.

"Daiz, you don't understand. It's more to it than that," she interrupted.

"What do you mean? What '*more*' are you talking about? What's going on?" I was concerned that this "more" had nothing to do with what happened in the service. But even so, *whatever it was,* I was confident in my spirit that the Lord was delivering her from it, which is why she was expressing her concern of being able to "walk this walk."

"Because I want to please the Lord," she started, "I know that there are some things that I can and cannot do, as well as, there are some people that I can and cannot continue to hang out with. So I called Rachel to let her know that since she's not trying to live the life that I'm trying to live, then we can't hang out anymore." The breaths that she took between every few words indicated she desperately needed some relief, but she continued. "I was telling her that we couldn't hang out anymore and I didn't want to hear about her relationship with her girlfriend anymore because that's not building me up. And she just went off on me; telling me that I was just like everyone else; that I turned my back on her because I don't understand the lifestyle that she lives, and that she's no different than anybody else. Then she went on to say how she goes to church and does everything anybody else would do, but if I wanted to turn my back on her, then just go right ahead – she's use to it." She took in a deep breath and let it out as she continued, "Daiz, this is too much. I didn't know that it was going to be this hard."

"You did the right thing," I encouraged her. "What you're experiencing is separation anxiety as a result of the Lord calling you to holiness, so that you can live a life that's pleasing to Him. The worst part is over (taking the first step). Just let Him continue to have His way with you, and you'll be okay," I said. She understood and after she'd been comforted, we hung up.

I knew Leah wasn't in a position for me to explain to her exactly what was going on, so I waited until the next day to explain it to her. So when I saw her the next day, I explained to her that the separation she was experiencing was not just from people that she didn't want to have contact with, but the Spirit was preparing her for deliverance from the spirit of homosexuality. And that it was difficult because her flesh didn't want to separate. "So what you experienced was you submitting to the will of God; you brought your flesh under subjection. You did an awesome job of taking that first step of defeating that demon, and I'm so proud of you!"

"Daiz, are you serious?!"

"Yes. So what you experienced last night was a '*tearing away*' of your soul. But you weren't in a position to understand what was happening, so I waited until today to tell you."

However, as a result of her taking that first step, the enemy launched an all-out attack against her: She later came to me and told me that one of the girls at work asked her, "What's going on with you and Rachel?"

And she asked her, "Why do you ask that?"

"Obviously, you haven't seen what she posted on Facebook."

"Nah, I haven't."

"You have to see it."

"Okay," Leah said, but walked away instead.

So I asked her if she was going to look at what was posted. And she said she wasn't sure (she didn't think so, but she wasn't sure). Careful not to dictate to her what she should do, I said, "Let me know what's what."

"Okay. But really, I don't think I'm going to get involved with that. I already know what she posted, so what's the point. I just don't want to deal with that."

And of course, I understood. So I encouraged her not to look because it was apparent that what was posted wasn't in a positive light, and I didn't want her to be exposed to the enemy's attack. Still, I asked her if she *cared* about what Rachel had to say? She said, "No. Because I know it's in response to me telling her that we couldn't be friends anymore, and I don't care what she has to say." So I encouraged her to just let it go. Then, as a result of what Rachel had posted, Leah decided to just delete herself from Facebook altogether. She'd come to the realization that Facebook wasn't building her up either, and that the only thing that people were posting was who did what to who and who said what to who. She thought it was best that she wasn't on it at all. And she could use the time that she'd been spending on Facebook to be with Jesus.

"That's a good move," I said.

After talking to Leah, I sent Maria an email expressing how sorry I was if we had caused her to be inconvenienced in any way by last night's service.

She said, "That's alright, but my husband and I have decided that we'll go to a church where we can go as a family."

Immediately, my heart sank. I was devastated! And as if the enemy had punched me in my stomach with the hardest blow that he had, the wind had been knocked out of me, and her words left me gasping for air. Devastated, I sat there, unable to respond. Then, as I tried to get myself together, I anxiously tried to keep her from leaving; I extended an invitation for her husband to come and join us. But, it was to no avail, she insisted; *he* thought going to a "church" would be best for them.

It was distressing to see her go because I knew how much she enjoyed coming together: studying the bible, fellowshipping, and getting so much out of it. Unfortunately, I knew there wasn't anything that I could do. So, I encouraged her to honor her husband's decision. I said, "It's our prayer that at some point, the Lord will allow us to come together again in His name."

THE BLOW THAT WAS DELIVERED WAS THE BLOW THAT WAS RECEIVED

I sat there. Struggling in my spirit – I wasn't able to grasp what had just happened. How was this possible? *Whhyyyy?* I cried out in my spirit. I was baffled! How could this be? She was hungry for God and wanted desperately to get to know Him. *She* was serious about sitting at the feet of Jesus and taking in everything that He had for her. And with much disappointment, I sent the email to Pastor Randolph to inform him that Maria wouldn't be coming back.

I couldn't understand how the enemy was able to come in and take her from this ministry. I was distraught! Then I was reminded of when the Lord had revealed to me that she wasn't going to be a part of this ministry. And as the tears began to well up in my eyes, I became sorrowful and distressed. Then the Lord began to minister to me:

"It's not about the numbers," He said.

What? I thought. *What numbers, it's only three people.* Then I was reminded of Gideon:

The LORD said to Gideon, "You have too many for me to deliver Midian into their hands. In order that Israel may not boast against me that her own strength has saved her, announce now to the people, 'Anyone who trembles with fear may turn back and leave Mount Gilead.'" So twenty-two thousand men left, while ten thousand remained.

But the LORD said to Gideon, "There are still too many men. Take them down to the water, and I will sift them for you there. If I say, 'This one shall go with you,' he shall go; but if I say, 'This one shall not go with you,' he shall not go."

So Gideon took the men down to the water. There the LORD told him, "Separate those who lap the water with their tongues like a dog laps from those who kneel down to drink." Three hundred men lapped with their hands to their mouths. All the rest got down on their knees to drink.

The LORD said to Gideon, "With the three hundred men that lapped I will save you and give the Midianites into your hands. Let all the others go, each to his own place." So Gideon sent the rest of the Israelites to their tents but kept the three hundred, who took over the provisions and trumpets of the others.

Judges 7:2 – 8 NIV

The following week at bible study, Pastor Randolph shared with everyone that Maria would no longer be joining us. However, because the blow was so devastating, I can't begin to tell you how deeply we all were affected; her leaving was felt throughout the ministry. *Everyone* in the ministry felt the pain of that blow – it went throughout the body. And it was so devastating that the only thing I could do was cry out to God. It was so painful that it took everything that I had in me to keep going. My soul was exceedingly distressed. Then I was reminded of the first vision....

I was drinking from a cup. The cup was ½ empty – ½ full, it had a hole in it, and the water was coming out.

The interpretation...

After the first attack, I'd be spiritually ½ empty – ½ full as the affliction would cause the anointing to be released.

He went on a little farther and bowed with his face to the ground, praying, "My Father! If it is possible, let this cup of suffering be taken away from me. Yet I want your will to be done, not mine."

Matthew 26:39 NLT

LEADERSHIP ESSENTIAL

~ YOUR FAITH WILL BE TESTED ~

I know most of you may already be familiar with the story of Gideon defeating the Midianites:

The LORD said to Gideon, "You have too many for me to deliver Midian into their hands. In order that Israel may not boast against me that her own strength has saved her, announce now to the people, 'Anyone who trembles with fear may turn back and leave Mount Gilead.'" So twenty-two thousand men left, while ten thousand remained.

But the LORD said to Gideon, "There are still too many men. Take them down to the water, and I will sift them for you there. If I say, 'This one shall go with you,' he shall go; but if I say, 'This one shall not go with you,' he shall not go."

So Gideon took the men down to the water. There the LORD told him, "Separate those who lap the water with their tongues like a dog laps from those who kneel down to drink." Three hundred men lapped with their hands to their mouths. All the rest got down on their knees to drink.

The LORD said to Gideon, "With the three hundred men that lapped I will save you and give the Midianites into your hands. Let all the others go, each to his own place." So Gideon sent the rest of the Israelites to their tents but kept the three hundred, who took over the provisions and trumpets of the others.

Judges 7:2 – 8 NIV

However, I'd have to say that unlike Gideon, our ministry didn't have a vast army that would accommodate the Lord separating the strong from the weak or the fearless from the fearful. We were barely able to get our footing in the ministry before the enemy had delivered such a devastating blow. And the impact of the spiritual damage that resulted from that blow was powerful; to say the least. We were impacted so intensely that it was as if the blow was received to *the head*, and the pain reverberated throughout *the body*; *everyone* in the ministry felt it!

But none more than I; I was completely devastated. And the tears proved to be evidence that the blow shook me to my core. And consequently, I struggled to move forward. As I sat before the Lord, shattered, I desperately needed Him to explain to me how He had *called us* to start this ministry, and then allowed the enemy to come in and *take* one of the members.

As I sat, I was reminded of how fearful Maria was during the service, and the thought played over and over in my mind, then I heard the Lord saying,

'Anyone who trembles with fear may leave…'

Then He prompted in my spirit:

If I say, 'This one shall go with you,' he shall go; but if I say, 'This one shall not go with you,' he shall not go."

And then He made it clear, "The *enemy* didn't *take* anyone who *belonged* to this ministry."

Oh, my God, I thought. I was baffled. I knew I had to be careful not to look at (or depend on) the number of people that were in the ministry. Clearly, I knew it didn't matter how big the ministry was, but rather if the ministry was submitted to the Lord's authority. Was His presence there, the Anointing, the *power* of the Holy Spirit? Were we submitted, obedient to His instructions? I knew that! I knew that I couldn't be self-reliant, but instead to keep my eyes on Him, trust Him, and let Him do the work *through me*. I knew that! But I couldn't understand why He would say, 'It's not about the numbers' when there were only three people in the ministry. Not only that, but what weighed heavily on my heart and I often pondered, *if you've called us to start this ministry, why is she leaving (before we even have a chance to get started)?*

Immediately, the pain of my own insecurities surfaced, and the tears rolled down my face. *Had I prayed enough? Was I faithful enough? Was I committed enough? How could this have happened? How could the enemy have come into this ministry – broken through our defenses?* Then I was challenged, *Am I ready for this? The pain?* And my heart responded, *I'm done; there is no way I can do this. The blow was too devastating.*

Then, as if answering my heart's apprehension, the Lord began to minister to me. And as I continued to ponder my thoughts, He continued to give me understanding. Consequently, I noticed the ever slightest impression of *fear* began to surface. So I continued to be open to the Spirit as He continued to minister. And ever so subtly the fear made itself known (almost as if it knew its presence wasn't welcomed). *But that can't be possible*, I told myself. Every day I struggled with coming to terms with the uneasiness. I knew it was there, but had chosen not to acknowledge it; I struggled with it being there, but it wouldn't leave. Then after coming to the understanding of it all, I acknowledged it; I was afraid of losing the people – letting them go.

I couldn't help but be reminded of Gideon and how he must've felt when the Lord told him he had too many people. I imagined he wondered and had some trepidation of letting go **twenty-two**

thousand men while ten thousand remained; and still, that was too many. I'm sure he himself was trembling with fear as he wondered, *how do I fight a vast, overpowering army with only three hundred people?* Consequently, I had reasoned with my heart and mind; *if there are no people, there is no ministry.* And the fear gave way to the tears that questioned if "the ministry" was ever going to happen. The comfort of Pastor Randolph's words rang out in my spirit, "David was king, but he didn't have a kingdom." But wasn't enough to satisfy my heart's cry.

"It's not about the numbers," the Lord said, again.

"What?" I questioned.

"*This* is not about the numbers," He reiterated. "This is not about having only three members – this is not about Maria – this is about *you.*"

I sat there, silently; searching desperately in my spirit for clarity. Then immediately I was confronted with my own insecurity.

"Do you believe I called you?"

I couldn't answer because I was choked by the tears as they spoke for me. And the pain challenged my inadequacies. All of a sudden, 'It's not about the numbers' had become, like Gideon, about my insecurities – not about the number of people.

Then I was devastated for a different reason.

But unmoved by the tears or the pain, He confronted me again; "Do you believe I've called you to lead my people?" *I can't do this,* I thought as the tears continued to fall from my eyes. His words deliberately spoke to the frailties of Gideon's fleece and my faith. They weighed my belief and exposed the fear.

And immediately, I felt as though I was in the middle of an ocean being overtaken by its waves; tossed to and fro. My fears were as vast as the ocean. The fear of drowning, going under, was present and real. But His presence gave me the assurance that the waves wouldn't overpower me as He calmed me – and the waters. But not without me first realizing the call *is* as one in the middle of the ocean; *it* is nothing compared to *Him.*

And yet, I kept hearing,

…**"Go with the strength you have…I am sending you!"**

Judges 6:14 NLT

And while I hadn't asked for a sign, as Gideon had, my unspoken uncertainties were heard and He answered by making it known…

MY FAITH WOULD BE TESTED.

PART

IV

THE

SECOND

TIGER

❧

THE SECOND TRIMESTER

~ CHAPTER 1 ~

THE SPIRIT OF DIVINATION

In an attempt to assist Tiffany with the praise team, she came to bible study early. The preparation consisted of prayer, praise and worship; playing a praise and worship CD to set the atmosphere. As I had shared with her before, the praise and worship was only going to be an outward expression of whatever she did in her private time. By doing so, the Lord would be present when we came together for bible study. Therefore, the first time she came to prepare, I instructed her, and then I continued doing what I was doing; however, she didn't know that I was *watching her to discern her spirit.*

The following week, she came early again and prepared to go before the Lord, and again I watched. When we started, she put the CD on and we all began to worship. She put the song on repeat, got a spot on the floor off by herself, and as if she was worshiping the Lord, she remained there for the duration of the praise and worship time. However, I was prompted in my spirit that she wasn't *worshiping* the Lord – it was all for show, which ultimately reflected she still wasn't submitted. Tiffany was operating in a *spirit of divination,* and I couldn't help but be reminded of the demon-possessed girl who had taunted Paul and Silas:

One day as we were going down to the place of prayer, we met a demon-possessed slave girl. She was a fortune-teller who earned a lot of money for her masters. She followed Paul and the rest of us, shouting, "These men are servants of the Most High God, and they have come to tell you how to be saved."

This went on day after day until Paul got so exasperated that he turned and said to the demon within her, "I command you in the name of Jesus Christ to come out of her." And instantly it left her.

Acts 16:16 – 18 NLT

Allow me to point out the fact that although the slave girl had the ability to speak the *truth* concerning Paul and the men of God, the spirit in which she spoke was discerned by Paul to be a *spirit of divination.* Consequently, the person who's under the influence of divination has the ability to speak the truth by demonic, supernatural means. In other words, they are influenced by *a* spirit, but not the *Holy Spirit.*

Now what may be confusing is the fact that the slave girl was able to speak the truth concerning the men of God. But she wasn't speaking by the Holy Spirit, but rather she spoke by way of satanic powers. The Word of God is clear that people who *divine* are controlled or possessed by demonic spirits. So while it *appeared* that Tiffany was "worshiping" the Lord, she was not. And if you don't have the ability to discern the spirit in which she operated, you wouldn't be able to determine that she wasn't worshiping the True and Living God.

And do not let your people practice fortune-telling, or use sorcery, or interpret omens, or engage in witchcraft, or cast spells, or function as mediums or psychics, or call forth the spirits of the dead.

Deuteronomy 18:10b – 11 NLT

Practicing fortune-telling, using sorcery, interpreting omens, engaging in witchcraft, casting spells, functioning as mediums or psychics, or calling forth the spirits of the dead are all a part of satanic / demonic powers, which Satan controls. Ultimately, as it is reflected in the above scripture reference, the slave girl's source of knowledge was a demon.

Therefore, as Paul became more and more grieved in his spirit, the Holy Spirit revealed what was going on then he rebuked the spirit of divination. You see, if Paul would've allowed the demon to continue to speak, it would've appeared that he was okay with the demonic activity (fortune-telling), which went against his message about Jesus Christ. Consequently, it becomes our responsibility to discern the spirit in which a person is operating.

Some demonic activity can easily be mistaken for godly activity, but it will lead God's people astray. The message can't go against or contradict the Word of God, which brings me back to Tiffany, who was still not submitted to God.

But Samuel replied, "What is more pleasing to the LORD:
    your burnt offerings and sacrifices
    or your obedience to his voice?
Listen! Obedience is better than sacrifice,
    and submission is better than offering the fat of rams.
Rebellion is as sinful as witchcraft,
    and stubbornness as bad as worshiping idols.

1 Samuel 15:22 – 23a NLT

As the Lord had already revealed, Tiffany was operating in a spirit of rebellion. Therefore, it is only befitting that I share with you according to the above scripture reference, *rebellion is as sinful as witchcraft and stubbornness as bad as worshiping idols;* so what she was doing was no different than witchcraft; a *witch* operating within our ministry.

Clearly, if her heart wasn't towards submitting to the Lord or to the leadership, then she was, in essence, rebellious; walking in disobedience. She was *religious* – she didn't have a real relationship with Christ; coming to every bible study, praise and worship gatherings, prayer, paying her tithe, and yet, not submitted to the leadership or the Lord. And the longer she rebelled, the longer it would take for the Lord to forgive her and restore her back to right standing with Him.

A few days later, Leah confirmed what the Lord had revealed:

"Tiffany really doesn't want to do praise and worship; she's having a hard time submitting to this role," Leah said.

"Why do you say that?" I asked.

"When Tiffany and I were praying the other morning, she said, 'I don't really think this is what I'm supposed to do because this is *not my gift*.'"

Here we go again, I thought, *not her gift.*

Consequently, he who rebels against the authority is rebelling against what God has instituted, and those who do so will bring judgment on themselves.

Romans 13:2 NIV

Therefore, I remained prayerful concerning this matter.

~ CHAPTER 2 ~

I FELT THE BABY MOVE

Tiffany called and said she had some friends that she wanted to bring to the praise and worship gathering; however, she didn't have money for gas to go and pick them up. "They don't have a car?" I asked.

"Well, yeah, but I didn't want to give them any excuses why they couldn't come, so I'm going to go and pick them up," she said. So I gave her some gas money and she went to pick them up. In the meantime, I prepared the atmosphere and began welcoming the Lord into the place. Surely, when they arrived, the Lord would be there waiting for them to bring deliverance forth.

When they arrived, they came into the house but just stood at the front door. For some reason, it seemed very odd to me. It wasn't just a "stood there" because they didn't know who I was; it was different, but I didn't know why. Anyway, I encouraged them to come in and worship the Lord and allow Him to have His way, and they came in slowly as Tiffany introduced everyone.

The atmosphere had already been set so they came in and started to worship. And immediately the power of God was manifested. I don't think Viola had even gotten in the house good before the Lord had me minister to her. I went over to her and immediately, I noticed she was crying, so I laid my hand on her and began to pray in the spirit. Instantly, when I laid my hand on her, she cried out; as if she'd been given permission to release the tears – she began to wail. I continued to lay my hand on her, and the Lord revealed to me the spirits that were present. I called out the spirit of hurt, and without any warning, she screamed out in a loud voice. And before I knew anything, she was screaming and crying as it appeared that she was trying to get away from me. She continued to cry out and the hurt continued to come forth. Clearly, the wall had become the only thing that was keeping her from getting away from me, but I wouldn't take my hand off of her.

Back and forth she went up against the wall – that demon wanted out of there, but the Lord had come to deliver. Then I called out the spirit of pain. Instantly, she fell to the floor – doubled over in a fetal position – clearly the pain began to manifest itself and come forth. And I continued to minister to her as the Lord dictated, and she continued to cry out. The Lord began to command her to submit as He was calling her to obedience. After she was delivered, I ministered to the other ladies that were there as well.

After the gathering, a couple of the ladies stayed to fellowship and so did Leah. As we sat and talked, they started talking about their experience during the gathering:

"When I first walked in the door, I knew the power of God was in this place. The anointing was so heavy, I couldn't move," Dillia said.

"Are you serious?" I asked in amazement.

"Yeah. I don't know if you noticed it or not, but that's why when I came in, I just stood there."

"Yes. I noticed that and I wondered why you guys were just standing there, which caused me to encourage you guys to come in."

"Well, that's why. I could feel the anointing as soon as I walked in the door, and I knew I was in the right place."

"Well, Amen to that!" I responded.

We sat for about an hour just talking about ministry and how good God has been in our lives – then they left.

"I am not sending you to a foreign people whose language you cannot understand. No, I am not sending you to people with strange and difficult speech. If I did, they would listen! But the people of Israel won't listen to you any more than they listen to me! For the whole lot of them are hard-hearted and stubborn. But look, I have made you as obstinate and hard-hearted as they are. I have made your forehead as hard as the hardest rock! So don't be afraid of them or fear their angry looks, even though they are rebels."

Ezekiel 3:5 – 9 NLT

~ CHAPTER 3 ~

PROPHETIC DELIVERANCE

Consequently, the enemy was mad that Leah had decided to live her life to please the Lord. So as a result of her decision, and the now conflict between her and Rachel, the enemy was pulling out all stops. One of the guys at work, Henry, who also lived a homosexual lifestyle, didn't think that Leah was right for what she had done. So then, she was engaged in an all-out war with Henry. *Every day* (and I mean *every day*) he would confront her about how she didn't handle the situation properly. And even went so far as to say, "You're only doing this to please Daisy." (Of course he had no idea that Leah was struggling with the homosexual lifestyle.) His only concern was that Rachel was being done wrong because she lived a homosexual lifestyle as well.

Consequently, I continuously explained to her that Henry's attacks were a result of the enemy because she decided to live her life for Jesus. I also continuously encouraged her not to give in to Henry's accusations because clearly the enemy was using him to attack her. And therefore, we were in **constant** prayer. However, I guess at some point, Leah had become concerned and wondered if she *had* handled the situation properly. Therefore, she shared with me that she had talked to one of her friends, Lucia, who used to work with us. And she stated that Lucia didn't think she handled it appropriately either and thought that she should still be friends with Rachel.

"Does Lucia know that you're struggling with a homosexual lifestyle?" I asked her.

"No," she said.

"So, how do you think Lucia is in position to give you an intelligent answer to your situation if she doesn't have all of the information?"

"Well, I guess you're right."

Anyway, she had had enough with trying to deal with Henry. And one day, she just exploded and went completely off – on just about everyone that seemed to have offended her in any way. By the time our co-workers had come to get me, things had already seemed to have calmed down. When I asked her about what happened, she said, "I have had it!"

Anyway, Leah and I continued to talk about her deliverance; however, she decided that she didn't really want to know all that was involved, so that she wouldn't have an opportunity to back out. Therefore, I just gave her an "overview" of what would take place: We'd pray, the Holy Spirit would reveal the root of the demonic oppression, I'd cast the demons out, and then deliverance would come forth.

In a dream...

I saw the Lord delivering Leah.

The interpretation...

Immediately, I knew the Lord was revealing she was ready.

Excited about the revelation, I told Leah that the Lord had revealed to me that she was ready. So, whenever she wanted to get started, we could. And she was just as excited. So we made plans to meet at my house to conduct the deliverance session. And needless to say, her anticipation mounted as the day approached.

"I'm thinking of fasting (if we are going to do deliverance)," she said. "What do you think?"

"I think that's great! How long? Are we meeting Tuesday?"

"Daisy, Tuesday? Sure. Do you think I'm ready? I know, crazy question."

"Is Tuesday not okay? Yes, I think you're ready."

"Okay then, I'm ready. Tuesday is okay. Could you not have on your priest collar that freaked me out!"

"LEAH! You are crazy! Why are you freaked out?"

"Because it's like I don't recognize you in it. The comfort, trust thing goes right out the window then I tense up!" she said laughing.

"Okay, my Love."

"OMG! Thank goodness I said something. I think you were going to pull it out of the closet on me for Tuesday!" she said. Then she went on to share with me how she was reminded of all the things she'd been through, all the people she'd hurt, and mentioned how ashamed she was. "Daiz, okay, I'm fasting starting tomorrow," she continued.

"Okay. How many days? Sunday through Tuesday?"

"You got it!"

"Okay. From 6 a.m. – 6 p.m.?"

"I'm thinking of a full fast. I wonder if I can do it! I've never done it before – just liquids Sunday through Tuesday. I want deliverance so bad!"

"My Love, deliverance *will* come. Considering you're new to fasting, commit to 6 – 6 then, if you feel like you can continue, it'll be an added sacrifice."

"I keep hearing doors shut in my head."

"AAAmen!!!" I explained to her that *deliverance had already begun.* And the Lord was closing the doors that allowed the enemy to come in and oppress her. "Praise God as He continues to do a mighty work on your behalf!"

Prophetic deliverance is more than likely unlike the usual deliverance that most people may be familiar with. The purpose of prophetic deliverance is to get to the ***root*** of the issue that has prevented an individual from moving forward in their lives. Therefore, it goes far deeper than just laying hands on someone and rebuking the enemy. ***It requires prophetic activation.***

The prophetic activation would cause the *prophetic anointing* to become activated in her life. It would allow her to experience God's presence and start communicating with God prophetically. She'd be able to operate in the *gift of prophecy:* she'd be able to hear the voice of the Lord, see visions, dream prophetic dreams, feel His presence, and speak prophetically as the Spirit prompts her to do so. So I started the session by activating the prophetic; the gift of prophecy in her life.

Prophetic deliverance consists of me praying and asking the Lord to reveal to me the root cause of the specific area(s) that she needed deliverance in. Now what's also important in this form of ministry is that she'd be responsible for communicating *with* me to bring forth deliverance (hence the prophetic activation, so she could hear, see, feel by impression, and/or say what needed to be said).

During this time, the Lord would minister to both of us in several ways: *vision (anything He showed us), hearing (anything we heard), memory (anything that was brought to her remembrance), and/or touch (anything that we felt as an impression – in our spirits).* In which, I explained to her that it was important for her to share with me anything she saw, heard, remembered, or felt. As she shared these things with me, the Lord would give me the interpretation of what was revealed then I'd explain it to her, which would give her understanding of what happen, why it happened, how it happened, so she could move past this point in her life.

Ultimately, the Lord would reveal how and when the doors were opened that allowed the demons access, which allowed us to get to the root of her demonic oppression. And consequently, as He revealed the demonic activity, He'd allow me to cast the demons out, which would result in her deliverance.

So, how does an individual get to this point of prophetic deliverance? Let's take a look in Genesis, chapter three, starting at verse six:

When the woman saw that the fruit of the tree was good for food and pleasing to the eye, and also desirable for gaining wisdom, she took some and ate it. She also gave some to her husband, who was with her, and he ate it.

We desire what is out of the will of God. We sin.

Then the eyes of both of them were opened, and they realized they were naked; so they sewed fig leaves together and made coverings for themselves.

We're made aware of our sin; our eyes are opened to see the wrong we've done, but we try to cover it up (we try to hide it, keep it a secret).

Then the man and his wife heard the sound of the LORD God as he was walking in the garden in the cool of the day, and they hid from the LORD God among the trees of the garden.

The spirit of conviction is released to get us to repent, but we hide from God.

But the LORD God called to the man, "Where are you?"

This is a rhetorical question. Clearly, the Lord knows where he is and where we are. He's asking Adam, "Where are you *spiritually*?" Once we've sinned, we need to take a look at how we've been affected spiritually. Sin separates us from God. When we sin, it's an indication that we're not in fellowship with the Lord.

He answered, "I heard you in the garden, and I was afraid because I was naked; so I hid."

Sin opens the door for the *spirit of fear* to enter in and consequently, we try to hide from God. We're *not* afraid because we've sinned against God, but we're afraid because *someone will find out.* So we try to hide what we've done; cover it up, keep it a secret. However, when there's sin that hasn't been confessed, it gives the enemy power to rule over us, which results in bondage.

And he said, "Who told you that you were naked? Have you eaten from the tree that I commanded you not to eat from?"

Once we've sinned, the Lord confronts us, just as He confronted Adam and Eve. Again, He asks a rhetorical question, 'who told you that you were naked,' which is to get us to realize that Satan is at the root of our sin. Then our spirit is pricked by the spirit of conviction. And we come to the realization that we've sinned and were walking in disobedience to the Lord's commands. The spirit of conviction also allows our eyes to be opened; to become aware of our sin, aware of the demonic activity that resulted in us sinning, and allows us to confess our sin. Then, guess what?

We must give an account of what we've done – as we'll see in these next verses of scripture.

The man said, "The woman you put here with me – she gave me some fruit from the tree, and I ate it."

Then the LORD God said to the woman, "What have you done?"

"The serpent deceived me," she replied. "That's why I ate it."

So the LORD God said to the serpent, "Because you have done this, "Cursed are you above all the livestock and all the wild animals! You will crawl on your belly and you will eat dust all the days of your life.

Ultimately, we understand that the woman was deceived by Satan; however, I'd like to point out a number of things:

(1) She's responsible for her own actions

(2) She must give an account of what she did

(3) She must be punished for her disobedience and suffer the consequences of her actions

We see this in verse sixteen:

To the woman he said, "I will greatly increase your pains in childbearing; with pain you will give birth to children. Your desire will be for your husband, and he will rule over you.

We also know that everyone involved was punished:

And I will put enmity between you and the woman, and between your offspring and hers; he will crush your head, and you will strike his heel."

To Adam he said, "Because you listened to your wife and ate from the tree about which I commanded you, 'You must not eat of it,' "Cursed is the ground because of you; through painful toil you will eat of it all the days of your life.

It will produce thorns and thistles for you, and you will eat the plants of the field.

By the sweat of your brow you will eat your food until you return to the ground, since from it you were taken; for dust you are and to dust you will return."

Genesis 3:6 – 15; 17 – 19 NIV

However, if you notice, even though she had confessed her sin (or had given an account of what she had done), she was still punished. I pointed this out so that you'll know that even though we confess our sins and are forgiven of our sins, **we still have to suffer the consequences of our actions.** Consequently, the Lord's mercy is shown to us just as it was shown to Adam and Eve in verse twenty-one.

The LORD God made garments of skin for Adam and his wife and clothed them.

This, you see, is the Lord providing the sacrifice for our sin and covering us – setting us free from the consequences of sin, death, and hell, which is *deliverance.* Yes, Christ was the ultimate sacrifice, but I said all of this to show you the process of deliverance and our need to be set free.

So this is the same deliverance process that was used during the prophetic deliverance session:

The Lord revealed the areas of sin, she gave an account of what she'd done, came into agreement with the Lord and acknowledged that she sinned, repented, and deliverance came forth.

When Leah arrived at my house, she was on the phone talking to a young lady that she had an intimate relationship with in the past. She felt the need to call her to apologize for any hurt she caused her and took responsibility for contributing to the dissolution of the woman's marriage.

When the deliverance process started, I prayed for the Lord to reveal to Leah the root cause of her need for deliverance. Then the Lord began to reveal the areas in need of deliverance. And immediately, she started to cry. There was a constant stream of tears that flowed from her eyes as the Lord brought these things to her remembrance. She continued to cry as the areas of deliverance were continuously revealed. She shared with me what the Lord was revealing to her; how she'd gotten involved in this lifestyle. And when the Lord dictated, I advised her that it was time for deliverance to come forth. Therefore, I started calling out the demons that the Lord revealed were present that had her entangled in homosexual bondage.

And all of a sudden, *before* I could even lay my hands on her, her whole body went limp and she fell to the floor. Consequently, I continued to call out the demons as the Lord continued to reveal them. As she laid helplessly on the floor, I instructed her to stand up. (By doing so, it revealed to me when the demons were leaving her body.) But she had no strength to stand, so I helped her up. Time and time again, as the demons were called out, her body went limp. And as we continued, I explained to her that every time her body went limp, a demon was leaving her body.

And I continued to war in the spirit, calling the demons out.

Then, all of a sudden, she cried out, "Oooh, my stomach!"

"What's happening with your stomach?" I asked. Although I knew it was the strong man, because he didn't want to be cast out, I wanted to know what she was experiencing.

"Ooohhh, it hurts so badly; oh, my stomach!"

"What's happening?" I asked again. "I want to know what you're feeling. What's going on?"

"Ooohhhh!" she continued to cry out as she doubled over in what was apparent pain.

The demon was retaliating.

"What does it feel like?" I asked in an attempt to get her to explain what she was feeling.

"Oh, my God; it hurts so badly."

"Leah, you have to tell me what you're experiencing."

"It just hurts really badly. Oh, my gosh! It feels like my stomach is bleeding inside," she said as she remained doubled over.

The strong man, the root, had been entrenched (deeply-rooted) for years and it was apparent that he wasn't going to be cast out without a fight.

"You're okay," I assured her. "Your stomach is not bleeding. It just feels that way. It's the demon leaving. He's leaving, but not without a fight. This is the strong man; he's retaliating. Once he leaves, it'll be all over. You're okay. Don't worry. You're okay. Do you hear me? You're okay," I assured her.

"Yes. Oh, it hurts so badly. Are you sure it's not bleeding?"

"Yes. I'm sure. It's almost over." And I commanded the strong man to come out. And just as the Lord had promised, the demon came out. Again, her body went limp as the demon left, and I held on to her as tight as I could to keep her from falling to the floor. I couldn't help but be reminded of the violent behavior of these demons (evil spirits) as it was in the case with Leah.

- ✓ *One of the men in the crowd spoke up and said, "Teacher, I brought my son so you could heal him. He is possessed by an evil spirit that won't let him talk. And whenever this spirit seizes him, <u>it throws him violently to the ground. Then he foams at the mouth and grinds his teeth and becomes rigid (weak).</u>*

- ✓ *But when the evil spirit <u>saw</u> Jesus, it threw the child into a <u>violent convulsion, and he fell to the ground,</u> writhing and foaming at the mouth.*

- ✓ *<u>The spirit often throws him into the fire or into the water, trying to kill him.</u>*

- ✓ *"Listen, you spirit that makes this boy unable to hear and speak," he [Jesus] said. "I command you to come out of this child and never enter him again!" <u>Then the spirit screamed and threw the boy into another violent convulsion and left him.</u>*

    Mark 9:17 – 18b; 20b; 22; 25b – 26 NLT (emphasis added)

- ✓ *Suddenly, a man in the synagogue who was possessed by an evil spirit began shouting, "Why are you interfering with us, Jesus of Nazareth? Have you come to destroy us? I know who you are – the Holy One sent from God!" Jesus cut him short. "Be quiet! Come out of the man," he ordered. <u>At that, the evil spirit screamed, threw the man into a convulsion, and then came out of him.</u>*

    Mark 1:23 – 26 NLT (emphasis added)

I explained to her that the demon had retaliated because he didn't want to come out. When demons are cast out, they are tormented and, therefore, do everything they can not to come out; however, when the name of Jesus is used, they must obey.

He shouted at the top of his voice, "What do you want with me, Jesus, Son of the Most High God? <u>Swear to God that you won't torture me!</u>" For Jesus had said to him, "Come out of this man, you evil spirit!"

Mark 5:7 – 8 NIV (emphasis added)

"Daisy," she said, "I can honestly say that I love you, and I've never said that before."

"I love you too, my sistah!" I said as we rejoiced at what God had done for her.

Now, let me mention that prior to deliverance and after, I explained to Leah the importance of not going back into the homosexual environment until she was strong enough to withstand the temptation. I also encouraged her to no longer be in contact with the "friends" that she'd had a *relationship* with, because it would place her in the way of temptation (and challenge her in maintaining her deliverance). However, if she had any friends that she hadn't had a relationship with or wasn't in that lifestyle, then it was okay to be friends with them.

Leah said pretty much all of her friends were one or the other; either they'd been in a relationship or they were in that lifestyle. Therefore, I encouraged her not to take their calls if they called. And if she absolutely had to take the call, then just let them know that she was working on getting herself together and wouldn't be available for a while; thereby, allowing her time to maintain her deliverance and become strengthened in that area.

The next day Leah said, "Daisy, I am soooo exhausted! I feel like I have picked five cotton fields! Can you believe my hands are still numb?"

"Being exhausted is expected; you were involved in a spiritual war," I reminded her. "What's with your hand? Did it start hurting when you were at my house or before? And has the pain been non-stop?"

"Man, Daiz. This experience is much more than I thought. My hand started feeling numb at your house. It was back and forth. It would be tingling numb, settled down to swollen, and then flared up to go numb again. It was the first thing I felt this morning waking up."

"What do you mean 'more than you thought'?"

"I thought I was going to come to your house and praise GOD, listen to music, pray, and be delivered, but instead, I was engaged in a spiritual battle, digging deep in *hidden emotional corners,* and telling all my lil' business in such a significant way. My body is sore, my head is all messed up, and my hands keep tingling. I see why you kept asking if I'm ready! You are a real Woman of GOD! You have touched my life."

"Let me ask you this," I said. "When you visited the hidden emotional corners, was anything revealed that you weren't aware of?"

"A LOT of things were revealed, emotionally, that I wasn't aware of! My mindset, ugh (just thinking about it). I didn't realize these things were as bad as they were; that's the reason why I felt it was okay. The reasons why I was doing these things were NOT okay."

"What made you realize that it wasn't okay?"

"My emotional scars; I realize it wasn't okay because the Lord revealed it to me during deliverance. The same thing kept coming up over and over. I never speak about it. I locked that so far back into darkness – like it didn't exist. When I realize the magnitude of it all, I can barely stand up."

"I know. That's why I constantly tell you do not underestimate the power of the enemy. He has ways of coming in that you can't even begin to imagine (and before you know anything, you're under his influence). That also speaks to why you have to close the doors once the Lord has revealed these areas to you."

"I need to go into my secret place and pray. I am not capable of handling or digesting this all. This is tough. I have never HATED my lifestyle as much as I do TODAY! I am full of regret."

"That's deliverance manifesting itself; allowing you to see sin as God sees it. Is your hand still hurting/numb?" I asked.

"My hand is still numb."

"I hate to say this," I said, "but it's a demonic manifestation of your disobedience and rebellion unto the Lord."

"Daisy, whew! The Lord was serious with us! I cannot thank you enough for speaking into my life, being obedient, and for your work! My God, My God! You called out so many things until it's none other than GOD. Wait," she said, "just so I can understand what you are saying, my hurting is, okay, wait, explain it. Also, it's crazy you should say that because I kept hearing the Lord say, 'SUBMIT!'"

"When deliverance is happening, there are different ways that the demons come out (or manifest themselves), which reveals that they've come out. And sometimes they retaliate, which manifests in the body by way of pain, swelling, and/or distortion, which is now in your hand."

"Daisy, it was the weirdest thing," she said as she went on to describe the experience. "I felt like I couldn't breathe! I had to take deep, deep breaths just to get air, and when I did, I was on the ground asking you to help me get up. By the way, I truly apologize for lying to you, trying to deceive you and causing mistrust between us."

"I forgive you."

Her experience was understandable and expected because demons are associated with breathing (or breath); they normally leave through the nose or mouth.

However, a few days later, as I continued to touch base with her to make sure she was okay, the enemy had showed up and challenged her faith regarding her deliverance.

"How are you?" I asked.

"I'm sad inside," she responded.

"Why are you sad?"

"I really can't deal with the person I was. I hated what was revealed about me, internally I can't digest it."

"Leah, it's over. You're not that person anymore. You are a new person. Remember, walk by faith. Focus on the new you!"

"I receive that! I am fighting for my life."

"What do you mean?"

"This spiritual journey is a battle. Things trying to pull me back and I'm fighting to save my life. I HAVE TO change and it's not easy. Daisy, something isn't right…"

"Why do you say that?" I questioned.

"I don't know how to say this, but I feel like I'm struggling with my strongholds right now and I wasn't feeling that way prior to deliverance. Does it take time? I'm really struggling over here, spiritually. My light won't shine. I can't find joy."

I understood her struggle and immediately I explained to her what she was experiencing:

As a result of deliverance, the Spirit was now revealing what was *in her heart.* The hidden things were now being exposed. The things she 'hid' in the emotional corners of her mind, the emotions that had been lying dormant that she refused to acknowledge, were now confronting her and demanding that she comes face to face with them. One thing was clear: she was not over the relationship that she'd been involved in (like she thought she was). Therefore, there was a war going on between her flesh and her spirit. And of course, the victor in her life would depend on which she succumbed to; the Spirit or the flesh (the enemy). So I advised her to meditate on the scriptures I gave her that would help her renew her mind to the things of God and win the battle.

Consequently, she was being bombarded with thoughts, memories, imaginations, and desires of her old lifestyle – wanting it desperately; mentally, physically, and emotionally challenged – tempted by the touch, embrace, and sex, as she struggled to hold on. Tempted by the manifestation of the ungodly soul-tie that unquestionably had her thinking the relationship was love. Tempted by the undeniable truth, which she had gone to great lengths to try to deny all of these years, that she missed and still wanted to be in that relationship. Challenged and struggling to keep from just giving in and going back into that lifestyle. And there was no doubt that the battle was overwhelming. But it was a battle that she *had* to fight (there was no way around it) in order for her to get the victory in her life over that lifestyle.

For the world offers only a craving for physical pleasure, a craving for everything we see, and pride in our achievements and possessions. These are not from the Father, but are from this world.

1 John 2:16 NLT

What we have to understand about deliverance is that while the battle had been won in the spirit realm (during the deliverance process), it had to now be won in the natural; in the flesh. The Lord had delivered her and had given her the power to overcome her sinful nature, but it was going to be up to her to use the power that she had been given to maintain her deliverance and remain free from the demonic oppression.

So, the battle she was now fighting was internal. She was fighting against her flesh – her soul – her mind, will, emotions – physical cravings and pleasures. So, the fight that was now going on was about *the* standards, values, beliefs, and ungodly ways of her thinking what a relationship was. *She was being challenged in her way of thinking what a godly relationship was.* Therefore, she was being challenged to *change* her standards, values, beliefs, and ungodly ways of thinking – because they were not acceptable to God.

You see, her attitude (belief) towards these things was *deeply rooted* in her heart. So, unless she allowed the deliverance process to continue, so that God could do a work in her and change her heart, the enemy (the flesh, the ungodly standards, values, beliefs) would prevail. Her mind had to be renewed and her heart transformed. And because God had delivered her she was now being held accountable for maintaining her deliverance: self-control. There was no more giving the impression of being holy while still holding on to worldly attitudes in her heart.

So I responded, "Yes, it's a process and it'll take time for you to really come to terms with all that has taken place. It's going to take your faith to get you through this. It's also important to surround yourself with people to help you get through this – that's why I didn't want you to be by yourself even though I know you don't feel like being bothered. Keep praising Him, reading your bible, and the scriptures I gave you. Your light will shine again. Don't worry, nothing's wrong, just stay in the spirit.

Remember, I told you the enemy was going to try to convince you nothing happened. Well, that's what's happening – he's bombarding you with your past, so you'll think nothing has happened. That's why you're struggling now more than you were before the deliverance – but if you give in to these feelings, you'll be right back where you started from, keep praying. This is his way of keeping you in bondage, entangled with your past."

When the people return to their homeland, they will remove every trace of their vile images and detestable idols. And I will give them singleness of heart and put a new spirit within them. I will take away their stony, stubborn heart and give them a tender, responsive heart, so they will obey my decrees and regulations. Then they will truly be my people, and I will be their

God. But as for those who long for vile images and detestable idols, I will repay them fully for their sins. I, the Sovereign LORD, have spoken!"

Ezekiel 11:18 – 21 NLT

It was time for her to nail her passions and desires to the cross and crucify them, and be led by the Spirit. She had been set free and given the power over sin; therefore, she no longer had to give in to the flesh. She was now responsible for committing to killing the flesh *daily* as she walked this walk of Christianity. And to do so, she would have to submit to God's control *daily* to crucify her sinful desires. And use the power He had given her *daily* to get the victory in her life. She'd have to meditate on His Word *daily* to be strengthened to fight this fight of faith.

Those who belong to Christ Jesus have nailed the passions and desires of their sinful nature to his cross and crucified them there. Since we are living by the Spirit, let us follow the Spirit's leading in every part of our lives.

Galatians 5:24 – 25 NLT

"Man," she said. "I understand. I cannot wait to overcome this. I should not be afraid and I will look to the Lord at all times. I am trying to keep from 'looking to the left and looking to the right' for comfort. Thank you, Daiz! You are so helpful right now. I am 'tripping.' I think I am going to find out a little more about stuff before I do it. I thought I was ready."

"You are ready!" I insisted. "I wouldn't have allowed you to go through it if the Lord hadn't revealed to me that you were ready. It's a process. It's hard because the old Leah is dying. And of course death doesn't feel good. Keep your faith. You know this is the right thing for you – even though it doesn't feel good. We've gotten in enough trouble because we did things that *felt good*. This isn't about feelings; it's about faith. Do you believe?"

"I do believe. I have wavering faith. I need to work on that."

"I want you to picture Jesus on the cross. Can you see him?"

"Yes."

"That's where you are right now; your flesh is being crucified. Do you know why He had to die on the cross? So that our sins could be forgiven; so that He could pay the price for us. And so that His purpose on the earth could be fulfilled – the same holds true for you. This is your cross; you are dying, so that your purpose on the earth can be fulfilled."

"That is deep when I think about it, I understand."

"It is deep – glad you understand."

"At first, I felt He was far from me: All in the bible, an immoral woman is THE WORSE kind of woman. I was that woman and didn't realize it. When I read all those chapters about detestable sins, I felt separated from His covering, love, and grace. I felt myself dying (like you said); that pain is real. There is no escape – only His word to comfort me. I have to learn and follow His principles, His laws. I really don't feel well. I am hopeful though for what the day will bring."

"What do you mean you don't feel well?"

"Mentally, I'm not doing well. I am consumed with sadness, worry, and doubt."

"What are you worried about?"

"I kind of don't want to face these things. I'm wishing they would just go away."

"That's normal. The things you've worked so hard to keep hidden have now come to the light."

"I'm worried about my well-being. I want to be stable. I feel like I'm fighting and losing mind battles."

"The battle *is* in the mind. Meditate on the scriptures that I gave you and this will bring stability to your mind. Read the ones specifically for your thoughts."

Now, I have to say that I was a little concerned about her because she'd started saying things like, *'I have wavering faith,' 'I'm consumed with sadness, worry, and doubt.'* But it didn't take long for me to find out why.

She went on to share with me that she had spoken to Tiffany. She told Tiffany that she'd gone through the deliverance process, and that she really *wasn't pleased* with what the Lord had revealed to her about her lifestyle and the decisions that she'd made in her life. (However, she didn't tell Tiffany that she'd been delivered from homosexuality.) Anyway, she also told Tiffany that she was struggling with coming *face to face* with the person that she'd been; she was ashamed of who she was.

And Tiffany said, 'I thought all deliverance was instant and if that were the case, there is no reason you should be feeling bad about yourself.' And of course, it was *then* that Leah started struggling with her faith. Consequently, the enemy had used Tiffany to cause Leah to **doubt** the deliverance process.

"I don't know, Daiz. I really don't know if I'll be able to continue in the process, it's too difficult."

Immediately, the Lord revealed *that* was why Leah's faith was now "wavering." **Disguised as her friend,** the enemy had come in and planted the seed of doubt. And just like the parable of the *Seed of the Sower*, before faith was able to take root in Leah's heart, Tiffany had come and snatched it from Leah (and planted the *seed of doubt* instead).

"The enemy used Tiffany to cause you to doubt that the deliverance was profitable," I responded angrily. I was mad at that devil! And I went on to explain to her that it was a trick of the enemy – to keep her from completing the deliverance process by getting her to doubt that God had delivered her, and that it should've been instantly. And this way, she'd continue to be wrapped up and tied up with her past and not able to move forward in her life.

The serpent was the shrewdest of all the wild animals the LORD God had made. One day he asked the woman, "Did God <u>really</u> say you must not eat the fruit from any of the trees in the garden?"

Genesis 3:1 NLT (emphasis added)

And just as the enemy had planted a seed of doubt with Eve, he'd done the same thing with Leah only this time he said, 'I *<u>thought</u>* all deliverance was instant and *if* that were the case, there is no reason you should be feeling bad about yourself.' Clearly, Tiffany didn't *know* the scriptures. She *thought*, but she didn't *know* if it were true or not. And *if* (by chance) she was right, Leah shouldn't be feeling bad. But guess what? It *wasn't* true – she was *wrong*; all deliverance *is not* instant. However, Tiffany's words had already taken root, and caused Leah to doubt that she'd be able to continue the deliverance process. Consequently, I explained to Leah that because she was vulnerable (weak in her faith), she had to be very careful of whom she listened to, and again, I explained to her that Tiffany wasn't as mature in the Lord as she thought.

They came to Bethsaida, and some people brought a blind man and begged Jesus to touch him. He took the blind man by the hand and led him outside the village. When he had spit on the man's eyes and put his hands on him, Jesus asked, "Do you see anything?"

He looked up and said, "I see people; they look like trees walking around."

<u>Once more</u> Jesus put his hands on the man's eyes. <u>Then</u> his eyes were opened, his sight was restored, and he saw everything clearly. Jesus sent him home, saying, "Don't go into the village."

Mark 8:22 – 26 NIV (emphasis added)

When Jesus laid hands on the blind man, *he wasn't healed instantly!*

It was a process:

- ✓ *First, he took the blind man by the hand.*
- ✓ *Second, he led him outside the village.*
- ✓ *Third, he spit on the man's eyes.*
- ✓ *Fourth, he put his hands on him.*
- ✓ *Then, he asked the man, "Do you see anything?"*

The man participated; he had to do something:

- ✓ *First, he had to be led by the Lord (and not just physically); desired the Lord to heal him*
- ✓ *Second, he had to allow the Lord to do the work (He spit on him; laid his hands on him)*
- ✓ *Third, he looked up (he looked to Jesus)*
- ✓ *Fourth, he was open to the Lords instructions*
- ✓ *Then, he responded, "I see people; they look like trees walking around." (He told Jesus the state he was in.) And yet, he didn't doubt.*

Once more – ***for a second time*** – Jesus laid hands on the man's eyes.

Then healing manifested:

- ✓ *His eyes opened*
- ✓ *His sight was restored*
- ✓ *He saw "everything" clearly*

Then, guess what? Jesus said, "Don't go in the Village." Why? ***Because there would be people there who'd question his healing.*** People like Tiffany; who don't know the Lord, the Word of God, or deliverance.

And because when the Lord delivers you *out of a thing,* you don't go back *into that thing!* That's why I explained to Leah the importance of not going back into the homosexual environment; not until she had been strengthened, not until she was able to maintain her deliverance.

And yet, I continued to encourage Leah to hold on to her faith – to maintain her deliverance. But even so, not only did Tiffany ***not know*** what she was talking about; I was more *concerned* that Leah *believed* Tiffany (in spite of her experience during the deliverance process or in spite of me encouraging her).

And yet again, on a number of occasions following her deliverance, Leah shared with me that she was struggling to *"walk the walk of faith,"* and maintain her relationship with Christ. She stated that because she was unorganized and had great difficulty with time management, she wasn't able to be consistent in her ability to get up in the morning and pray, read her bible, or just spend time with the Lord; she felt overwhelmed. And consistently, I'd encourage her in these areas. And as I continued to pray for her, the Lord ministered to me:

In a dream…

I was in the elevator and was holding the door open so that Leah could get in. But she just stood there. I was encouraging her to get in the elevator, but she wouldn't. She continued to just stand there. She was shaking her head as if to say, "No," which indicated she wasn't going to get in the elevator with me.

The interpretation…

The elevator represented elevation, increase, or a situation getting better. And while it was my desire to see Leah increase, mature and complete, maintain her deliverance, she had decided, "No," that wasn't what she wanted. She wasn't going to go forward with the deliverance process.

As a result of what the Lord revealed to me in the dream, my heart completely broke into a million pieces. My thoughts began to race, *how could she come this far and not continue? She wanted it so badly, desperately. And the Lord had done for her just what she'd asked Him to do. How could she not continue?* "Please, Lord," I pleaded, "You have to do something! Don't let her just walk away – do something, Lord!" But I knew it was confirmed; He was revealing that she wasn't going to continue with the deliverance process, she was done – it was over.

During the time that followed, I noticed that on a number of occasions, Leah had started to compare herself to Tiffany. However, I'd continuously advise her to focus on establishing *her* relationship with Christ, and to take her eyes off of Tiffany. (Now I must say, Tiffany and Leah were polar opposites – from one extreme to the other: Tiffany was outspoken, Leah was quiet. Tiffany knew one or two scriptures, Leah didn't know any. Tiffany was strong-willed, prideful; Leah double-minded, timid.)

However, Leah said that it was easier for her to relate to *Tiffany* in order to grow in her relationship with Christ than it was to relate to *me* because I was the Pastor. (I was on a different level.) And as a result of her "relating more to Tiffany," she started saying that she felt like she needed to *know* more. However, I wasn't sure how she thought she would "know more" if she wasn't reading her bible, praying, or spending time with the Lord. But I asked her, "'Know more' like what?"

"Like, what does 'test the spirit and try the spirit by the spirit' mean?" she asked.

Test the spirit and try the spirit by the spirit was something that Tiffany said often, but she herself didn't understand. And as I thought about what was going on with her relationship with Tiffany, immediately, the *spirit of intimidation* was revealed. So I told her, "There is a *spirit of intimidation* present regarding your relationship with Tiffany. You're trying to measure up to Tiffany. I know you think she's mature in the spirit and that you want to get to know just as much as she knows, but you need to take your eyes off of what Tiffany is doing and focus on *your* relationship with Christ. Tiffany is not as mature as you think."

"But I feel like I should be doing more. I should be learning more."

"The only thing you should be doing now is praying, reading your bible, studying, and getting your relationship with Christ established. You're constantly telling me that you can't find the time to pray, read your bible, or spend time with Him, so how do you expect to learn more? Focus on those things and you'll get to know more. Anything other than that, you don't need to be focused on."

However, it was apparent that my words had fallen on deaf ears.

~ A CALL TO PRAY ~

The last praise and worship gathering at my house was to be different from the others. The Lord impressed upon my spirit that during this gathering, we were to focus on prayer and He immediately reminded me of Jeremiah, chapter twenty-nine, verse seven:

"Also, seek the peace and prosperity of the city to which I have carried you into exile. Pray to the LORD for it, because if it prospers, you too will prosper."

Jeremiah 29:7 NIV

Therefore, the atmosphere was prepared far in advance to welcome the Lord's presence into the place. And as usual, the Lord had come to rest, rule, and abide in the midst of His people. As the people entered the room, the Lord was there to welcome them; His anointing filled the room and He was our only focus.

We honored Him with praise from our lips. And immediately, He made His presence known, which was apparent as Leah wept before the Lord the entire time we were there; one hour. She had been through a lot; her spirit was crying out to the Lord. I couldn't help but be reminded of her deliverance process and how desperately she needed God. Because the anointing was so heavy upon her in that place, she was unable to pray; she could only weep before Him.

And His glory was demonstrated as His anointing rested upon her.

The prayer began with praying for the city as instructed and ended with seeking God's face for His plan for our ministry, The Embassy of Grace, and for the New Year. Mighty were the prayers as we declared and decreed victory in the lives of the people: Men, Women, and Children. Amazing things were revealed during the prayer, which became apparent as the Lord moved by His Spirit in that place.

The anointing was so heavy in that place that Tiffany also wept before the Lord as she prayed the prayer of salvation for the lost.

The Lord's presence was so prevalent that even I struggled with just wanting to be quiet in His presence. It was evident that we were in the presence of our Holy God.

And true to who He is – We left the place knowing that our prayers had been answered.

~ ARE YOU READY? ~

We waited with anticipation for the day to arrive.

It was clear that for Leah, this baptism was an outward expression of an inward confession; that she was declaring her old lifestyle to be dead and now she would start a new life resurrected with Christ. It was also clear that she understood that the baptism didn't cause her to be in right standing with God, that it didn't wash away her sin, nor did it make her holy or righteous – nothing but the blood of Jesus could do that. She understood that this was for her benefit and no one else's, not even God's.

She had come to die; to lay down her life that it may be buried. She decided to not only hold herself accountable to live a life that is pleasing and acceptable to God, but that she wanted others to hold her accountable as well. Consequently, the announcement went out that Leah was getting baptized. And without hesitation, the people of God came.

The Lord filled the room with His presence as we worshiped Him. It was His presence that revealed He was in agreement with her decision. Her time had come – for her death, burial, and resurrection (to be raised to newness of life in Christ). She would take her own life and willfully lay it down.

All she had to do was answer the question, "Are you ready?" and death would come.

We were therefore buried with him through baptism into death in order that, just as Christ was raised from the dead through the glory of the Father, we too may live a new life.

Romans 6:4 NIV

And with a loud, resounding, "Yes!" she responded. Immersed completely in the water and quickly raised out – the first baptism of The Embassy of Grace was accomplished.

In the same way, count yourselves dead to sin but alive to God in Christ Jesus.

Romans 6:11 NIV

~ CHAPTER 4 ~

HIS WORD SHALL COME TO PASS

Due to the holiday season, we didn't really come together for ministry. However, as a token of our appreciation, Pastor Randolph and I decided to have a "Church-Family" outing. It was planned a couple of weeks before Christmas to allow everyone to relax and just enjoy the day with each other. So we all (including Leah and Tiffany's kids) went skating, and of course we all had a good time; it was some much needed relaxation.

For our Christmas service, we did something a little different. Everyone was to bring a gift that would be presented to Christ that would allow us to focus on our spiritual growth. So the gift we brought had to be reflective of the area of spiritual growth that we wanted, which was dedicated to Christ. So during the days that we were preparing, we continued to encourage one another during our "Morning Glory." Morning Glory was a vehicle we used via email to send scriptures, encouraging words, motivational and inspirational support to one another. So of course, everyone's gift was to be a big surprise. And of course, everyone thought their gift was going to be the best gift. During this time, Leah mentioned to me that Tiffany was going to "fast and pray" in hopes that the Lord would reveal to her what He wanted her to present to Him.

I, in turn, said that it wasn't that serious and made a joke about it in the email. The next thing I knew, Tiffany sent an email back and pretty much *blasted* Leah for telling me that she was fasting: "Dag, Leah, you don't have to tell her everything!" Anyway, for the service, we presented our gift and stated why we were presenting that particular gift. For example, I had a gold Christmas ornament that was a church. So, I presented it as the temple of God, which was reflective of me dedicating my temple (my body) to the Lord; I would focus on developing it spiritually (and I wanted to lose weight), so I could be "fit" for the kingdom. Anyway, it was awesome; we had a good time. Afterwards, we sat around eating and fellowshipping.

For Christmas, Leah and her son, Alex, came over and had Christmas dinner with my family. After dinner, Tiffany and her son, Jack, also came over. By the time Tiffany had come, Leah and I were just sitting at the dining table, talking, and listening to the Christmas music; relaxing for the most part, as Pastor Randolph and our son watched football on TV. Anyway, the atmosphere was quiet and relaxed. So when Tiffany came, we all came together to play board games, Uno, ate some more, laughed, and just enjoyed the holiday.

The next day, Tiffany called me and shared her observation of what took place the night before. She went on to say, "When I came in your house, everybody was all quiet just sitting around, but I was all "crunk." I thought, *oh, my gosh! They're all of the same spirit – everybody's all mellow.* But then I came in with my loud self!"

"Girl, you're crazy," I said laughing.

"I'm serious, Ms. Daisy," she said. "I felt so out of place. I was embarrassed."

"There's no need for you to be embarrassed. Are you kidding? We were waiting for you to come so we could start playing games and get the party started."

"Nah, Ms. Daisy. I was the only one who was loud out of everybody there. Even your son is quiet," she said. "I'm starting to think that maybe I should change so that I'm not the only loud one."

"Tiffany. You know you don't have to change. You bring balance to the rest of us that are quiet. Girl, just be you."

"Now I see where Jack gets it from," she said. "I'm so serious, Ms. Daisy. I don't know. I think I was really affected by that. I think that did something to me."

"Tiffany, don't be silly. We all had a great time. Don't you even think that. You don't have to change. Be yourself." And shortly after, we ended the call.

Immediately, I was reminded of what the Lord had said a month prior, *'When you lay hands on her, it's going to cause her to either worship or leave. She will not be able to stay in the presence of Truth,'* but I didn't say anything. I knew it would only be a matter of time.

During the Christmas holiday, Leah and I had scheduled our vacation at the same time. And every day she'd come over to my house and we'd just hang out. Again, we'd play games, Uno, and eat the leftover Christmas dinner – just having fun and enjoying being away from work. One day she came over, and as we were talking, she said, "I need some clarity on who I'm supposed to be in contact with and who I'm not supposed to be in contact with."

Now, I have to admit, that by this time, which was now the third time she'd asked me this same question, I was a little irritated. And in my spirit I had become a little concerned. I just couldn't seem to understand why we had to keep going over this – something wasn't right (but I guess I was getting ready to find out why). As we were talking, she mentioned how she thought it wasn't fair that I thought she was a liar, especially since she'd been saved. She felt judged. So I asked what she was talking about.

"Dawne had a birthday party, and Shauna, Lisa, Evelyn, and I went. And I bought Dawne a gift because she bought me a gift for my birthday…"

"Wait a minute," I interrupted. "Dawne had a birthday party, and you went?" I asked for clarity.

"Yeah."

"You never mentioned to me that she had a party and that you went."

"Oh, I thought you knew."

"How was I supposed to know?"

"I don't know. I just thought you knew."

"Whether I knew about the party or not – you never mentioned to me that you went to the party. Why hadn't you ever mentioned to me that you went to her party?"

"Oh, I don't know. I just forgot about it."

"Leah. You *are* a liar," I said as a matter of fact. "You know that I know Dawne was 'interested' in you *that's* why you didn't tell me."

It was awfully funny how she oh, so conveniently, brings up the fact that she'd been to Dawne's party several months after the fact, which was how she operated. Then she'd oh, so conveniently be able to say, "Oh, I forgot." She "forgot" because Dawne also lived a homosexual lifestyle, and she was interested in having a relationship with Leah. So anything or anyone that had to do with the homosexual lifestyle, Leah "forgot" to tell me about it. And, because she was so use to lying and covering it up, it was easy for her to conveniently say, "Oh, I forgot" and it'll be all good. But I was done playing games with her.

"Nah, that's not why. I just forgot about it," she continued to say. And consequently, she felt like I was being unfair and judging her for lying to me. But by this time, I really had no interest in going over that again. Either she wanted to get her life right or she wanted to continue trying to "cover up," either way – play time was over.

"Okay," I said sarcastically because we weren't getting ready to have that conversation. I was done with it!

Anyway, the conversation turned to us discussing the upcoming New Year's Eve service that we were planning for the ministry. By this time, Tiffany said she wasn't sure if she would make it because her Aunt had invited her to come visit for the holiday; but she'd let me know. (However, immediately, I knew in my spirit that she wasn't coming and shared this information with Pastor Randolph.)

Then Leah mentioned that Tiffany had called her and shared with her pretty much the same thing she had shared with me (how she felt she didn't fit in because she was 'crunk' and everyone else was more laid back. And how we were all of the same spirit, but she wasn't). And of course,

Leah tried to encourage Tiffany by telling her that she didn't need to change to try to fit in – "just be yourself," she said. And Leah also shared that based on the conversation she had with Tiffany, she thought Tiffany was *really* affected by that. Consequently, I wanted to be able to spend some time with Tiffany, so we made plans to go and get our nails/feet done at the nail spa.

However, after a few days of not hearing from Tiffany, it was confirmed in my spirit that she wasn't going to attend the New Year's Eve service. However, I continued to stay in contact with her to see how this was all going to unfold. So, every couple of days or so, I asked if she had heard from her Aunt, and she would just indicate that she hadn't. After a couple of times that I'd asked, she continued to just say no. But not only had she mentioned that her Aunt hadn't called her, but she hadn't reached out to her Aunt either (which confirmed my impression that she wasn't coming). And yet, while I was able to see that the separation had already begun, I didn't say anything.

We planned for the service to take place on Saturday evening (before the New Year). By Thursday, I sent Tiffany a text message to ask again if she was going to make it. This time she responded, yes. So I shared with her that service was going to start at 10 p.m. and that praise and worship would be for thirty minutes. I also asked if she had any suggestions for the service because we were still finalizing everything. She said that she'd like to see something prophetic, so I asked her what was the "word" jokingly (meaning the prophetic word). She responded, "The Pastor should know the Word." In which I was taken aback at how serious she was.

Anyway, on Friday, Leah said she wanted to sing a song and write a poem to contribute to the service. I told her to share this information with Tiffany because Tiffany was the praise leader. After Leah talked with Tiffany, she shared with me the conversation that they had:

"Tiffany said, 'I hope they don't think I'm going to do nothing.' And I said, You're going to have to lead praise and worship. Then Tiffany became adamant about not doing *anything* and just really got all bent out of shape about it because she said, 'I'm not going to do nothing!'"

Then shortly after speaking with Leah, I received a call from Tiffany, "Do you expect me to do something?" she asked defiantly.

"I expect you to lead praise and worship," I responded as I was shocked by her attitude.

"I feel very uncomfortable about doing the praise and worship because I just decided that I was coming on Thursday, and I didn't know you would be expecting me to do praise and worship."

"Tiffany, you don't have to worry about it," I relented. I had had enough. And immediately, *'When you lay hands on her, it's going to cause her to either worship or leave'* rung out in my spirit. And I knew this conversation wasn't really about her 'leading praise and worship.'

"Well, I *am* worried because this is what I'm supposed to be doing, but you hadn't told me that you were expecting me to do it," she snapped.

My immediate thought was, *if this is what you're supposed to be doing, why do I have to tell you to do what you know you should be doing?* But I said, "If you are the praise leader and I told you that the service was starting at 10 p.m., praise and worship is for thirty minutes, then I shouldn't have to tell you that you would be expected to do the praise and worship."

'...worship or leave,' I kept hearing.

"Well, I didn't know that's what that meant. I thought you were just telling me that service was starting at 10. Well, what if I hadn't come?"

'...worship or leave.'

"If you hadn't come, then we would've done the praise and worship without you, but if you're there, then that's your responsi...don't worry about it, Tiffany. I'll take care of the praise and worship." And we ended the call.

'...leave.'

That was it. In my spirit, I knew the "word" of the Lord had come to pass.

Shortly afterwards, she sent me a text message stating she wouldn't be attending the service, which I had anticipated.

~ CHAPTER 5 ~

TRANSITION

As Pastor Randolph and I were praying concerning the New Year's Eve service, I asked the Lord, "What's the purpose of this service, this New Year?"

"Transition," He responded; indicating that it was time for us, as a ministry, to transition.

"Moses my servant is dead. Therefore, the time has come for you to lead these people, the Israelites, across the Jordan River into the land I am giving them. I promise you what I promised Moses: 'Wherever you set foot, you will be on land I have given you-"

Joshua 1:2 – 3 NLT

As I continued to inquire of the Lord, He showed me a vision:

In a vision:

I saw a foot taking a step on a stair step.

The interpretation...

Take one step at a time.

According to Webster's New World Dictionary, transition means passing from one condition, place, etc. to another. Therefore, it was time for us to transition, go from one condition or place to another. It was time for us to take the ministry outside of the house. And in order for us to do so, we had to walk by faith. What the Lord was calling us to do was going to take faith to do it.

So, I'd like to take this opportunity to encourage you; it's time for you to transition. It's time for you to move! It's time to leave the place that you're in and cross over. One step at a time!

The LORD told Joshua, "Today I will begin to make you a great leader in the eyes of all the Israelites. They will know that I am with you, just as I was with Moses. Give this command to the priests who carry the Ark of the Covenant: 'When you reach the banks of the Jordan River, take a few steps into the river and stop there.'"

Joshua 3:7 – 8 NLT

It's time to go into the Promised Land. It's time for us to possess the land that the Lord has already given us as an inheritance. And just as the Lord had instructed the priests who were carrying the Ark of the Covenant, 'When you reach the bank of the Jordan River, take a few steps into the river and stop there,' When you've gone as far as you can go, stop there, and let the Lord do what He's going to do; watch Him make a way for you. All you have to do is walk in obedience to what He has commanded you to do – His presence is with you.

Take that step of faith; one step at a time and see what the Lord will do.

It was the harvest season, and the Jordan was overflowing its banks. But as soon as the feet of the priests who were carrying the Ark touched the water at the river's edge, the water above that point began backing up a great distance away at a town called Adam, which is near Zarethan. And the water below that point flowed on to the Dead Sea until the riverbed was dry. Then all the people crossed over near the town of Jericho.

Joshua 3:15 – 16 NLT

Whatever situation you may be facing, the *Jordan River* is symbolic of that situation. And when you take that step of faith, the Lord is going to cause everything that has been holding you back; everything that has been keeping you from crossing over; and everything that has kept you from getting what He promised you to begin backing up! It's harvest season! It's time to go in!

The Lord is going to make a way for you; a way out of no way. He'll create a door where there isn't a door. Walk in obedience to His command and see what He'll do for you. He'll make the way for you. It doesn't matter what you're faced with. It doesn't matter the challenges, struggles, or who comes up against you. God is getting ready to make a way for you. He's preparing you for something greater; a greater level of anointing, power, and authority.

THE SECOND TIGER / THE SECOND TRIMESTER: Transition

I believe this is the season where God is getting ready to do great and mighty things – Get up and move! Be encouraged, the Lord is with you.

For the next couple of weeks, Tiffany hadn't come to bible study. Therefore, I'd check on her to see if she was okay. But she wouldn't respond. Finally, I sent her an email and asked, "Why aren't you coming to bible study? Is everything okay?"

"I didn't feel like it," she responded.

Needless to say, I was taken aback by her response. It was clear, by her response, that she was no longer connected to our ministry. "Tiffany, that's unacceptable. When you're in a position where people are counting on you, you don't just say, 'I didn't feel like it.'"

"Jack didn't feel well," she said to appease me.

"Okay. I hope that he feels better soon and I'll talk to you later," I responded.

Three weeks had past, and Tiffany hadn't come to bible study. I knew she wasn't coming back. But I called her – and continued to call. Unfortunately, my calls went unanswered. Then one morning, I sent her a text asking her to call me. She sent a text back and said she'd call me later because she was getting ready to go to bed. But I took advantage of the opportunity and I called her because she was avoiding me. When I called, she answered.

"Tiffany, what's going on?" I asked. Initially she was skating around the question and didn't want to come out and say what was what.

"Everything is okay. Nothing serious is going on, I mean, I'm okay, the kids are okay. It's nothing, really."

"*Something* is going on and for whatever reason you're not saying," I said. Even though I knew the Lord had removed her from the ministry, I wanted to hear why she thought she was leaving. "Are you planning to leave the ministry?" I asked.

There was silence.

"Well, yeah. But I didn't know how to tell you."

"Why are you planning to leave?"

"I want you to know that I enjoy the fellowship and what I'm learning in bible study. I just don't think I'm getting what I need. I have to find someone who can see my gift and help me develop it."

Ahhh, the "gift" again, I thought. "So why didn't you just say that instead of not showing up for weeks and avoiding my phone calls?"

"Because you are my friend and I didn't want to hurt you."

"Did you think that I wouldn't be hurt by you not saying anything and just stop coming?" I asked. However, *in spite of me knowing that the Lord had removed her from this ministry,* I wanted to take that opportunity to minister to her. And hopefully, one day, she'd mature and come to the realization that she was *focused* on the wrong thing. She was *so* focused on the 'gift' but not the '*gift giver*'. "When we started this ministry," I continued, "we asked you to be a part of the ministry to help us grow; and that takes time. Before you're able to walk in your *gift,* you have to learn to serve. You have yet to submit to what the Lord has asked you to do. You're not going to go to a church and just start *walking in your gift,*" I said. Then I was reminded that she left the church she was attending because her *gift* hadn't been *seen or developed;* even though the Pastor had a prophetic school of ministry. All I can say is when the Lord revealed her gift to Pastor Randolph and me, it wasn't a prophetess.

"I've been in ministry for years, and before I was able to develop my gifts, I had to first learn to submit and be obedient," I continued. "And you've got to spend time with the Lord. To be *"a prophet"* you stay in the presence of the Lord – and to *praise and worship Him* is *who you are* and *what you do as "a prophet."* For you to struggle as much as you've struggled with just worshiping the Lord, you're not going to *ever* develop in your gift."

Now, I have to say, this struggle was not about Tiffany *being the praise leader* and it wasn't about *her submitting to the leadership* that the Lord had place over her. It went deeper than that. This was really about "her relationship with Christ;" everything that we'd been going through was just a reflection of what was going on in her private time with the Lord – *what you do in secret He rewards openly.* She wasn't struggling to be the praise leader; she was struggling with submitting to the Lord. She was struggling with getting a *real* relationship with God that's what this was about.

Anyway, she just listened as I continued to talk.

"The first step in developing your gift is submitting to the Lord. And if I've asked you as your spiritual leader or the Lord has instructed you to be the praise leader, then you be the praise leader. This is not about your *gift*. This is about your relationship with Christ. Here is what I would like for you to do; think about it, let the Lord minister to you; I'd love for you to be a part of this ministry and allow us to help develop you. If you decide to stay, we'll be excited, but if you decide to go, that's okay too."

I didn't know *how* or *what* the Lord was going to do to move in this situation, but I knew He would. I wanted to make sure *I* was doing everything *I* was supposed to do as her spiritual leader. And even so, I knew He had the final say.

"Okay," she said, and we disconnected the call.

However, as soon as I hung up the phone, I *knew* that was it – He had removed her from the ministry – she wasn't coming back. But knowing that God was in control didn't stop my heart from breaking as the tears began to fall from my eyes. I could see that the enemy had a hold on her and there was nothing that I could do – but let her go.

How I wished she'd *known* and *understood* the scripture:

If you receive a prophet as one who speaks for God, you will be given the same reward as a prophet. And if you receive righteous people because of their righteousness, you will be given a reward like theirs.

Matthew 10:41 NLT

You see, what Tiffany didn't know was – I'm a Prophetess.

And as I stood in the garden area in which I prayed every day, crying, the Lord began to minister to me as if answering my heart's cry.

She has a perverse spirit and the spirit of pride, which is why she wouldn't submit. A perverse spirit is a spirit that deviates from what is right or good; it's stubbornly contrary; obstinately disobedient. And a spirit of pride, as many of you may already know, is a spirit that causes the person to have an unduly high opinion of themselves; it's a haughty spirit; a spirit of arrogance.

In other words, the perverse spirit is *adamant about going against what is willed.* So she was dead set on coming into this ministry, getting a position, which she thought was as a prophetess. *That* was her motive for joining this ministry. And because she was only focused on developing what she thought was her "gift" she refused to do anything other than that.

She was deceived.

But we belong to God, and those who know God listen to us. If they do not belong to God, they do not listen to us. That is how we know if someone has the <u>*Spirit of truth or the spirit of deception.*</u>

1 John 4:6 NLT (emphasis added)

And immediately, I was reminded of the second vision:

> **I was drinking from a cup. The cup was full, it had a hole in it, and the water was coming out.**
>
> **After the second attack, I'd be spiritually full and yet, the affliction would cause the anointing to be released.**

Then Jesus left them a second time and prayed, "My Father! If this cup cannot be taken away unless I drink it, your will be done."

Matthew 26:42 NLT

LEADERSHIP ESSENTIAL

~ PROPHETIC ANOINTING: PROPHET ~

When we think of the prophetic anointing, prophet, or prophecy, for the most part, I believe, we automatically think of prophetic utterance; *speaking a prophetic "word" for the future* that's divinely inspired by God. Prophetic utterance gives us understanding of God's secret plans; revelation, special knowledge, teachings, words of encouragement, and/or warnings. In which we are to prophesy with the measure of faith that God has given us.

A divinely inspired *"word"* from God can either be received by a dream, vision, impression in our spirit, or the audible voice of God. And its message could be interpreted by impressions of sight, hearing, touch, taste, and even smell. To receive a divinely inspired *"word"* is to have the supernatural ability to receive from the Lord; via any means as mentioned above. These prophetic utterances, revelation aren't only in the form of words but are also given in the form of symbols or symbolic actions. These prophetic utterances that are spoken on the Lord's behalf are to encourage, instruct, and help strengthen us as we *fight the good fight of faith.*

Timothy, my son, here are my instructions for you, based on the prophetic words spoken about you earlier. <u>May they help you fight well in the Lord's battles.</u>

1 Timothy 1:18 NLT (emphasis added)

Receiving or speaking God's "word" is Him sharing what's in His heart, on His mind, and the plans He has for us; His people, the children of God – supernaturally. However, more often than not, I think, when we think of prophecy in particular, we more than likely, think of *prediction* (telling future events). Now while prophecy does include prediction, that's not the most important function or the only function. The most important function, the only function or the only purpose of the prophetic anointing, prophet, and prophecy is to proclaim the Word of God and the testimony of Jesus Christ.

The revelation from Jesus Christ, which God gave him to show his servants what must soon take place. He made it known by sending his angel to his servant John, who testifies to everything he saw—that is, <u>the word of God and the testimony of Jesus Christ.</u>

Revelation 1:1 – 2 NIV (emphasis added)

So, according to the above scripture reference, prophecy is God's revelation of His plan *of* Jesus, which He gave to Jesus. The plan was then revealed (by an angel) to John, who testifies to everything he saw – the Word of God and the testimony of Jesus Christ, am I right?

Whew! Let me say that again, *who testifies to the Word of God and the testimony of Jesus Christ.* Amen? So simply put:

- ✓ Prophecy is God's revelation of His plan of Jesus.
- ✓ The prophet testifies to the word of God and the testimony of Jesus Christ.
- ✓ The prophetic anointing is the supernatural ability to reveal God's plan of Jesus.

So, again, prophecy is God's plan of Jesus revealed.

The purpose of the prophet is to testify to the Word of God and the testimony of Jesus Christ.

The prophetic anointing is the supernatural God-given ability to reveal God's plan of Jesus.

Then the vision was before me:

In a vision...

I saw God sitting on the throne.

The interpretation...

Immediately, I was enlightened as He revealed Himself, the Spirit of Prophecy, sitting on the throne bearing witness to who Jesus Christ is.

It is God Himself, the Spirit of Prophecy, sitting on the throne bearing witness to who Jesus Christ is. Prophecy is the *essence, nature, core, heart of His Spirit;* God Himself. *It is who He is. He* is the *One* who bears witness to who Jesus is. Therefore, if God Himself bears witness to who Jesus is, whenever we operate in the prophetic anointing, then we're operating in Him, *His Spirit;* the *Spirit of Prophecy.* It is His Spirit that enables us to function in the prophetic anointing. And consequently, if He *bears witness* to who Jesus is, and we're operating in His Spirit, then we're *bearing witness to who Jesus is – testifying to the Word of God and the testimony of Jesus Christ.*

Now, according to the above-mentioned scripture, Jesus revealed God's plan to His servant, John, in a vision, which allowed John to *see, hear,* and *speak* about events that took place while John was in the Spirit. Therefore, operating in the prophetic anointing enables us, the men and women of God, to *see, hear,* and *speak* about events or things that the Lord reveals to us while we're in the Spirit. These events, the things that are revealed, allow us to then testify to the Word of God and the testimony of Jesus Christ. Therefore, prophecy is what God reveals to us, visually or audibly, concerning His plan for Christ; of Christ.

Consequently, since prophecy is to testify to the Word of God and the testimony of Jesus Christ, then to understand the prophetic anointing and the prophet, we should look to Jesus:

After his baptism, as Jesus came up out of the water, the heavens were opened and he saw the Spirit of God descending like a dove and settling on him. And a voice from heaven said, "This is my dearly loved Son, who brings me great joy."

Matthew 3:16 – 17 NLT

Now, if we pay close attention to what took place ***after*** Jesus' baptism, as he came up out of the water, we'll see the,

- ✓ prophetic anointing
- ✓ prophet
- ✓ prophecy

First, and foremost, the scriptures tell us that after Jesus was baptized, the heavens were opened. The "heavens opened" or "open heavens" is a very familiar term in the prophetic realm. When there is a reference to an open heaven, it means that we have access to the spirit realm; the third heaven where God is. *Therefore, we have access to God.* We have access to the secret things of God; His revelation. And consequently, we're able to see, hear, and speak concerning what's revealed to us – the things that are taking place in heaven, in the spirit realm.

The scripture says that Jesus *saw* the *Spirit of God* descending like a dove and settling on Him. He saw God Himself come down from heaven in the form of a dove and anointed Him; anointing Him with a prophetic anointing and endowing Him with power; giving Him the supernatural ability to reveal God's plan. We see the Spirit of God, God Himself ordaining Jesus, if you will, preparing Him for His ministry; to carry out God's plan.

Now, I'd like to point out that Jesus wasn't the only one who saw the heavens opened; John the Baptist also saw the heavens opened. And therefore, he also saw the Spirit of God descending like a dove and settling on Jesus.

Then John testified, "I saw the Holy Spirit descending like a dove from heaven and resting upon him. I didn't know he was the one, but when God sent me to baptize with water, he told me, 'The one on whom you see the Spirit descend and rest is the one who will baptize with the Holy Spirit.' I saw this happen to Jesus, so I testify that he is the Chosen One of God."

John 1:32 – 34 NLT (emphasis added)

So John testifies that God spoke to him prophetically, and *told* him that 'The one on whom you *see* the Spirit descend and rest is *the One* who will baptize with the Holy Spirit.' So that means the prophetic anointing was also resting on John in order for him to, first of all, *hear* the voice of God and then *see* the Spirit resting on Jesus. As John stated, he didn't know that Jesus was the One. So basically, God *told* John how he would be able to identify who the Chosen One of God is. And as John stood baptizing Jesus, and the Spirit of God descended and rested on Jesus, John was able to testify to the *Word of God* and *of Jesus Christ*. John was operating in the prophetic anointing as well, so that he'd be able to testify or bear witness to what he heard God say to him and what he saw concerning Jesus, the Chosen One of God.

Now notice, God didn't tell John *who* the Spirit would rest on, but rather He told him *how* he would be able to identify Him; He told him **how** he would **know** who the Chosen One of God is: 'The one on whom you *see* the Spirit descend and rest is the One...' So clearly you have to have the prophetic anointing – the supernatural ability in order to be able to *see* into the spirit realm and be able to *discern* the things of the Spirit. Otherwise, John would've only seen a dove – not knowing that it was the Spirit of God.

I couldn't help but wonder after God spoke to John, how many people had John baptized before he baptized Jesus. Consequently, I realized that out of all the people John had baptized, he had to be attentive, watching, expecting, and open to the Spirit to *see* who the Spirit would descend on. And ultimately, allowing John to say, "I *saw* the Holy Spirit." John seeing the Holy Spirit descend and rest on Jesus was the prophetic sign that confirmed the Word that God had spoken. So when the heavens were opened, and John saw the Spirit, it gave John access to the *secret things of God*; God's revelation *concerning* Jesus Christ, so that John could testify to the Word of God and the testimony of Jesus Christ. And for the most part, I also believe, we all know that John had been chosen to be the forerunner for Jesus:

God sent a man, John the Baptist, to tell about the light so that everyone might believe because of his testimony. John himself was not the light; he was simply a witness to tell about the light. The one who is the true light, who gives light to everyone, was coming into the world.

John 1:6 – 9 NLT

In addition to John testifying that Jesus is the Chosen One, the scriptures state: a voice from heaven said, "This is my dearly loved Son, who brings me great joy," which is a reflection of God's prophetic voice; *God bearing witness to who Jesus is. His Spirit* also bore witness to who Jesus is as demonstrated by the dove resting on Jesus. And consequently, we see the Trinity revealed: *God the Father speaks,* "This is my dearly loved Son, who brings me great joy." *God the Son (Jesus) is baptized*, and *God the Holy Spirit (the dove) descends on Jesus.*

So, as reflected above, Jesus Christ Himself did not enter His ministry without first being "anointed with the Holy Spirit and endowed with power":

And you know that God anointed Jesus of Nazareth with the Holy Spirit and with power. Then Jesus went around doing good and healing all who were oppressed by the devil, for God was with him.

Acts 10:38 NLT

I'd like to point out that as we've seen the prophetic anointing of the Spirit of God, the Spirit of God is reflective of the *sevenfold Spirit of God.*

> And the Spirit of the LORD will rest on him—
> the Spirit of wisdom and understanding,
> the Spirit of counsel and might,
> the Spirit of knowledge and the fear of the LORD.

Isaiah 11:2 NLT

Therefore, we see a prophetic depiction of Jesus walking in the fullness of God as the *sevenfold Spirit of God.* In other words, when operating in the prophetic anointing, we operate in:

- ✓ The Spirit of the LORD
- ✓ The Spirit of Wisdom
- ✓ The Spirit of Understanding
- ✓ The Spirit of Counsel
- ✓ The Spirit of Might (power)
- ✓ The Spirit of Knowledge
- ✓ The Spirit of the Fear of the Lord

This scripture embodies what is known in the prophetic realm as the *sevenfold Spirit of God, the seven spirits of God,* and is another name for *the Holy Spirit.* The sevenfold Spirit of God represents the presence of the Holy Spirit and is a reflection of the sevenfold expression of His Spirit. Therefore, the prophetic anointing allows us to operate in the fullness of God; the *sevenfold Spirit of God* as His Spirit enables us.

Then you have a prophetic interpretation of Jesus' anointing and power:

> The Spirit of the Lord GOD is upon me;
> because the LORD hath anointed me
> to preach good tidings unto the meek;
> he hath sent me to bind up the brokenhearted,
> to proclaim liberty to the captives,
> and the opening of the prison to them that are bound;

Isaiah 61:1 KJV

Allow me to *first* point out the Spirit of the Lord GOD was upon Him because the LORD:

- ✓ Anointed Him (to preach the gospel), and
- ✓ Sent Him (to destroy the works of the enemy)

His anointing and power are to:

- ✓ Preach good tidings (the gospel) to the meek
- ✓ Bind up the brokenhearted
- ✓ Proclaim liberty to the captives
- ✓ Proclaim the opening of the prison to them that are bound

The purpose of the anointing as indicated above reflects the need for salvation, redemption, and deliverance from sin (bondage), death (spiritually and physically), and hell (eternal judgment), which are under the power of Satan. You see, it's the Holy Spirit who enables us to operate in the anointing with power in order to defeat Satan by preaching the gospel to the poor, healing the brokenhearted, proclaiming liberty to the captives, and setting free those who are bound. We, just like Jesus, need to be anointed and endowed with power to do the work of Him who has sent us.

The anointing is a manifestation of the Holy Spirit, the Spirit of God; His presence, His power. And when the anointing is imparted or rested upon an individual, it allows the person to experience the fullness of God; His supernatural presence, power, and authority. Just as it was with Jesus when the dove rested on Him – He received God's presence and was endowed, anointed with power to do the work; ministry. Initially, God's anointing rested upon an individual, as in the Old Testament (O.T.), to enable an individual to do the work, which means the anointing was only to allow the person to complete the assignment that he'd been given and then the anointing would be removed (or lifted). Thereby, when the Spirit *came upon* or *rested upon* someone in the O.T., it was temporary. You'll see in the O.T. a number of times that indicate the Spirit of the LORD *came upon* or *rested upon* someone, which enabled the person to do what God wanted accomplished in the earth.

For example, when the Lord took the same Spirit that was on Moses and gave it to the seventy elders:

So Moses went out and reported the L*ORD*'s words to the people. He gathered the seventy elders and stationed them around the Tabernacle. And the L*ORD* came down in the cloud and spoke to Moses. Then he gave the seventy elders the same Spirit that was upon Moses. And when the Spirit <u>rested upon them,</u> they prophesied. <u>But this never happened again.</u>

Numbers 11:24 – 26 NLT (emphasis added)

When Samson killed the Philistines with a donkey's jawbone:

As Samson arrived at Lehi, the Philistines came shouting in triumph. But the Spirit of the L*ORD* <u>came powerfully upon Samson,</u> and he snapped the ropes on his arms as if they were burnt strands of flax, and they fell from his wrists. Then he found the jawbone of a recently killed donkey. He picked it up and killed 1,000 Philistines with it.

Judges 15:13 – 15 NLT (emphasis added)

However, the prophet Joel prophesied that the Lord promised His Spirit would be poured out upon all people. And as a result, there would no longer be a need for His Spirit to *come upon* or *rest upon* someone to do the work, but rather His Spirit would *dwell within* the individual:

'In the last days,' God says,
  'I will pour out my Spirit upon all people.
Your sons and daughters will prophesy.
    Your young men will see visions,
    and your old men will dream dreams.
In those days I will pour out my Spirit
    even on my servants—men and women alike—
    and they will prophesy.

Joel 2:28 – 29 NLT

Now, prior to the Lord's Spirit being poured out upon all people, Jesus made it very clear that the apostles were not to go out to do ministry without first receiving His Spirit; the baptism of the Holy Spirit – the outpouring of His Spirit as follows:

Once when he was eating with them, he commanded them, "Do not leave Jerusalem until the Father sends you the gift he promised, as I told you before. John baptized with water, but in just a few days you will be baptized with the Holy Spirit."

Acts 1:4 – 5 NLT

On the day of Pentecost all the believers were meeting together in one place. Suddenly, there was a sound from heaven like the roaring of a mighty windstorm, and it filled the house where

they were sitting. Then, what looked like flames or tongues of fire appeared and settled on each of them. And everyone present was filled with the Holy Spirit and began speaking in other languages, as the Holy Spirit gave them this ability.

Acts 2:1 – 4 NLT

Peter's words pierced their hearts, and they said to him and to the other apostles, "Brothers, what should we do?"

Peter replied, <u>"Each of you must repent of your sins and turn to God, and be baptized in the name of Jesus Christ for the forgiveness of your sins. Then you will receive the gift of the Holy Spirit.</u> This promise is to you, and to your children, and even to the Gentiles—all who have been called by the Lord our God."

Acts 2:37 – 39 NLT (emphasis added)

So, what should you do? Repent of your sins, turn to God, and be baptized in the name of Jesus Christ (for the forgiveness of your sins), *then* you will receive the *gift* of the Holy Spirit.

Now before I go any further, I just want to talk a little about John's baptism. John's baptism was a baptism of *repentance.* In other words, John told the people to believe in the One who would come after him, Jesus. Therefore, John's baptism didn't cause a person to receive the *gift* of the Holy Spirit. It resulted in some *believing* but *not receiving* the gift of the Holy Spirit:

While Apollos was in Corinth, Paul traveled through the interior regions until he reached Ephesus, on the coast, where he found several <u>believers.</u> "Did you receive the Holy Spirit when you believed?" he asked them.

"No," they replied, <u>"we haven't even heard that there is a Holy Spirit."</u>

"Then what baptism did you experience?" he asked.

And they replied, <u>"The baptism of John."</u>

Paul said, "John's baptism called for repentance from sin. But <u>John himself told the people to believe in the one who would come later, meaning Jesus."</u>

As soon as they heard this, they were baptized in the name of the Lord Jesus. Then when Paul laid his hands on them, the Holy Spirit came on them, and they spoke in other tongues and prophesied. There were about twelve men in all.

Acts 19:1 – 7 NLT (emphasis added)

John prepared the way for the Lord. By being baptized in the name of Jesus Christ and by the laying on of hands, they received the *gift* of the Holy Spirit; resulting in an outward appearance of the manifestation of the Holy Spirit's presence just like on the day of Pentecost.

Now as a result of His Spirit being poured out upon all people, we, as believers, were given spiritual gifts to operate in, so that we could accomplish what the Lord wants us to accomplish:

- ✓ Preach good tidings (the gospel) to the meek
- ✓ Bind up the brokenhearted
- ✓ Proclaim liberty to the captives
- ✓ Proclaim the opening of the prison to them that are bound

Ultimately, what we're to accomplish is to testify to the Word of God and the testimony of Jesus Christ. Amen?

There are different kinds of spiritual gifts, but the same Spirit is the source of them all. There are different kinds of service, but we serve the same Lord. God works in different ways, but it is the same God who does the work in all of us.

A spiritual gift is given to each of us so we can help each other. To one person the Spirit gives the ability to give wise advice; to another the same Spirit gives a message of special knowledge. The same Spirit gives great faith to another, and to someone else the one Spirit gives the gift of healing. He gives one person the power to perform miracles, and another the ability to prophesy. He gives someone else the ability to discern whether a message is from the Spirit of God or from another spirit. Still another person is given the ability to speak in unknown languages, while another is given the ability to interpret what is being said. It is the one and only Spirit who distributes all these gifts. He alone decides which gift each person should have.

1 Corinthians 12:4 – 11 NLT (emphasis added)

So that we understand the purpose of the gifts that are given, they're given so that we can *help;* encourage, strengthen, each other – accomplish His will in the body of Christ. Every believer has been endowed with spiritual gifts. And it is the Spirit who decides which gift each person has. However, the spiritual gifts are not to be confused with the ***ministry gifts*** in Ephesians:

Now these are the gifts Christ gave to the church: the apostles, the prophets, the evangelists, and the pastors and teachers. Their responsibility is to equip God's people to do His work and build up the church, the body of Christ. This will continue until we all come to such unity in our faith and knowledge of God's Son that we will be mature in the Lord, measuring up to the full and complete standard of Christ.

Ephesians 4:11 – 13 NLT (emphasis added)

Notice that the *ministry gifts* were given **to the church** whereas spiritual gifts were given **to individuals.** Therefore, the apostles, prophets, evangelists, and the pastors and teachers are responsible for equipping God's people (the church) to do the work and build up the church – the body of Christ. (Of course, I have to point out the fact that when I refer to the ministry gifts I'm referring to men and women of God.) And while it was clear with the outpouring of His Spirit that we were endowed with spiritual gifts, I'd like to point out that there is a distinction of these gifts. While an individual may have the *ability* to prophesy, it doesn't make that individual a prophet. Again, the spiritual gift of prophecy is the ability to prophesy, to help, encourage, and strengthen each other (testify to the Word of God and the testimony of Jesus Christ) while the prophet equips (teaches, instructs, informs, prepares, trains) the people to do the work.

Are we all apostles? Are we all prophets? Are we all teachers? Do we all have the power to do miracles? Do we all have the gift of healing? Do we all have the ability to speak in unknown languages? Do we all have the ability to interpret unknown languages? Of course not!

1 Corinthians 12:29 – 30 NLT

So when it comes to prophecy, my focus is not on "speaking a divinely inspired word of God" because again, because an individual is able to prophesy doesn't mean they are a prophet. Now, in the book of First Corinthians, Paul exhorts us to desire to prophesy.

Let love be your highest goal! But you should also desire the special abilities the Spirit gives – especially the ability to prophesy.

1 Corinthians 14:1 NLT

I, as well, encourage all believers to desire to prophesy. However, I'd like to make mention that this encouragement is so that our focus is on using the gifts that would build up the church; not that prophecy supersedes any of the other spiritual gifts. Our focus should be on helping others not on the fact that we have the gift, which reminds me of the disciples when they "realized" they had the power to cast out demons:

When the seventy-two disciples returned, they joyfully reported to him, "Lord, even the demons obey us when we use your name!"… "Yes," he told them… "But don't rejoice because evil spirits obey you; rejoice because your names are registered in heaven."

Luke 10:17; 20 NLT

It's not about the gifts you have; it's about advancing the Kingdom of God. So to think for any reason that Paul was indicating that prophecy is the most important spiritual gift is incorrect. Therefore, anyone who desires the ability to prophesy for their own gain or selfish reasons doesn't understand the purpose of the gift, the Word of God or the testimony of Jesus. Now while we have gifts that *build us up* as believers, speaking in tongues for example, our ultimate focus should always be on *prophecy: testifying to the Word of God and the testimony of Jesus Christ.*

But one who prophesies strengthens others, encourages them, and comforts them. A person who speaks in tongues is strengthened personally, but one who speaks a word of prophecy strengthens the entire church.

1 Corinthians 14:3 – 4 NLT

PROPHET (SEER)

Prophecy, whether spoken by an individual with the *gift of prophecy* or spoken by the *prophet,* is the supernatural ability to speak on behalf of God (the heart, mind, and wisdom of God). And don't forget, it testifies to the Word of God and the testimony of Jesus Christ. Therefore, a prophet is considered the mouthpiece for God; the voice of God. Prophets couldn't prophesy unless God had given them the authority to do so; this was their purpose, as the Lord reveals His plans in visions and dreams:

And the LORD said to them, "Now listen to what I say:

"If there were prophets among you,
I, the LORD, would reveal myself in visions.
I would speak to them in dreams.

Numbers 12:6 NLT

Now the Bible is clear, God spoke directly and audibly with Moses. However, during the three centuries of rule by judges, His Word became rare. Therefore, by Eli's time, the prophets weren't speaking God's messages to Israel because the people refused to listen.

"The time is surely coming," says the Sovereign LORD,
"when I will send a famine on the land –
not a famine of bread or water
but of hearing the words of the LORD.
People will stagger from sea to sea
and wander from border to border
searching for the word of the LORD,
but they will not find it.
Beautiful girls and strong young men
will grow faint in that day,
thirsting for the LORD's word.

Amos 8:11 – 13 NLT

The people weren't interested in hearing the Word of God when the prophets spoke. And as a result, God said He'd send a famine on the land so that the people wouldn't be able to hear the words – even if they did hunger and thirst for the Lord, they wouldn't find it. And consequently, the word became rare. The prophets weren't speaking God's messages.

Now in those days <u>messages</u> from the LORD were very rare, and <u>visions</u> were quite uncommon.

1 Samuel 3:1b NLT (emphasis added)

Consequently, when the prophetic was rare, it was said that there was "no open vision."

(In those days if people wanted a message from God, they would say, "Let's go and ask the seer," for <u>prophets used to be called seers.)</u>

1 Samuel 9:9 NLT (emphasis added)

The *seer* is a particular type of prophet. A seer receives prophetic revelation through visions and dreams. (Visions and dreams are their primary means of communicating with God.) They have the God-given, supernatural ability to *see* into the spirit realm and receive prophetic messages from God, as well as foresee future events. The unique distinction of a seer is that the prophet *sees* things just as God Himself sees them. They're able to see past all of the external, all of what a person says, all of what a person does, and see right into the internal; the condition of the person's spirit. As a seer, the prophet receives visions, dreams, and revelations from God which enables them to convey spiritual messages to God's people.

I am a Seer.

The next morning the word of the LORD came to <u>the prophet Gad, who was David's seer.</u> This was the message: "Go and say to David, 'This is what the LORD says: I will give you three choices. Choose one of these punishments, and I will inflict it on you.'"

2 Samuel 24:11 – 12 NLT (emphasis added)

When it comes to prophetic revelation, for the most part, I believe, we're familiar with the prophet who *hears* the Word of God and then declares it. However, not as familiar is the seer who *sees* the Word of God and then declares it. The Word of God is *visual* for the prophet who's a seer. Therefore, the prophetic anointing that a seer has is like when someone says, *"Do you <u>see</u> what I'm saying."* The Lord speaks and the prophet *sees* what He's saying.

Visual? Yes. Seers are prophets who see visions and dreams in a consistent and regular manner. So rather than receiving *words* that are spoken in the spirit, seers receive *visions and dreams* that are received either while sleeping or awake. The dreams are just as anyone would dream while sleeping. The differences, however, are the dreams that are revealed to a seer are from God and are prophetic. They're spiritual in nature and are messages from God. The visions, for the most, are like flashes of images, pictures, and impressions. Again, the differences in the visions a prophet may see are they're spiritual in nature and are messages from God. Consequently, once the Lord reveals the vision or dream to the prophet, the prophet *describes* what they saw. And that which is being described is the actual message that the Lord is conveying to His people. Now note, while the messages that are revealed are primarily for the people, visions and dreams are also a means by which the Lord communicates to the prophet concerning his own spirituality.

The visions and dreams that are communicated to the prophet is God providing words of encouragement, detailed instructions, warnings, corrections, and/or teachings (just to give you an idea of their purposes). Often times, the visions and dreams are symbolic, which God then provides the revelation (interpretation and understanding). And of course, the visions and dreams provide access to the heavenly, future events, angelic visitation, and demonic activity.

All of which I've received and encountered.

Now, because a seer's prophetic anointing is to primarily *see* doesn't mean that they don't *hear* the "word" of the Lord because they do. A seer's prophetic anointing just means that the *primary* way that the Lord communicates is through visions and dreams. And the same holds true for the prophet who *hears* the Word of God. He has the ability to *see* visions and dreams as well; however, that's not the *primary* way that God communicates with him. Consequently, all prophets can see, but all prophets are not seers.

One morning when I was having devotion, I was sitting in the Lord's presence and suddenly I heard the woman of God call my name, "Daisy." I sat there, quietly, in anticipation of what the Lord was getting ready to reveal. Then I heard her call my name a second time, "Daisy." Again, I continued to sit, quietly. And again, she called me a third time, "Daisy." Immediately, I was reminded of Samuel in First Samuel, chapter three, verses two through ten.

And just as Eli had realized that it was the Lord calling Samuel, I too, realized it was the Lord calling me. And I, like Samuel, answered, "Speak, your servant is listening."

"PROPHETIC ANOINTING, PROPHET; GET UNDERSTANDING," He said.

While on earth, Jesus was the full manifestation of the five-fold ministry: Apostle, Prophet, Evangelist, Pastor and Teacher given to the church. The *office of the prophet* is a manifestation of Jesus, the Prophet. And like Jesus, prophets are chosen, anointed, set apart and sent to do the work of the Lord. The *office* of the prophet is endowed with a prophetic mantle, anointing, power, and functions with an authority that far exceeds that of the *gift of prophecy.*

While the prophet is called to be the mouthpiece of God, they do more than just prophesy. Prophets are the eyes and ears of the church; the heart of God. Prophets are mediators between God and His people through intercessory prayer. Therefore, like Jesus, we see a prophetic depiction of the office of the prophet. In other words, the prophetic mantle, anointing, power, authority, and functions of the prophet's office allow the prophet to operate in the fullness of God; the *sevenfold Spirit of God*:

> And the Spirit of the LORD will rest on him—
> the Spirit of wisdom and understanding,
> the Spirit of counsel and might,
> the Spirit of knowledge and the fear of the LORD.

> *Isaiah 11:2 NLT*

✓ The Spirit of the LORD
   o The supernatural manifested presence of the LORD; God Himself. His nature, personality, qualities, character, and temperament.
✓ The Spirit of Wisdom
   o The supernatural ability to correctly apply and spiritually utilize the revelatory information God gives us.

- ✓ The Spirit of Understanding
  - o The supernatural ability to understand spiritual mysteries and spiritual truths with clarity and simplicity.
- ✓ The Spirit of Counsel
  - o The supernatural ability to stand or wait upon the Lord, in His presence, to get guidance and direction.
- ✓ The Spirit of Might
  - o The supernatural power, strength, and ability to carry out the Lord's plans; to do His will.
- ✓ The Spirit of Knowledge
  - o The supernatural ability to receive information by revelation from God.
- ✓ The Spirit of the Fear of the Lord
  - o The supernatural reverent ability to recognize He is God. To know Him; acknowledge and understand His holiness. To walk in obedience to Him.

The office of the prophet gives the prophet the authority to: build up the church - encourage, exhort, edify, comfort, exhort, strengthen and confirm. They provide guidance, instruction, train, and develop the people of God; they raise-up other prophets. They preach the word of God that leads to true repentance, salvation and obedience unto Christ. They bring revival, restoration, inspiration and/or correction to the church. They do deliverance; leading the people out of bondage and captivity to set them free. They are prayer warriors. They ordain, confirm, and activate those called into leadership through the laying on of hands (prophetic presbytery). They protect the people; they blow the trumpet in Zion to warn, rebuke, and correct the people of God to avoid looming judgment.

The prophet weeps in secret for the people of God.

Today I appoint you to stand up
   against nations and kingdoms.
Some you must uproot and tear down,
   destroy and overthrow.
Others you must build up
   and plant."

Jeremiah 1:10 NLT

God reveals Himself to the prophets in visions and speaks to them in dreams; making known the will and mind of God. They are the servants of God; the apple of His eye.

...Touch not mine anointed, and do my prophets no harm.

1 Chronicles 16:22 KJV

Now, as if I hadn't gotten the message, I attended a prophetic conference one evening. And the next day, during my morning devotion, the Lord began to minister to me. And before I knew anything, *the* absolute strangest thing happened that I'd ever seen:

In a vision…

I saw what appeared to be an eye; and just as suddenly as it had appeared, it disappeared. Then another eye appeared and disappeared; then another, and another, and another, and another, and another – one by one. And I noticed that each eye was different – it wasn't the same eye.

The interpretation...

The Lord began to speak into my spirit the seven eyes of God.

Then I saw a Lamb that looked as if it had been slaughtered, but it was now standing between the throne and the four living beings and among the twenty-four elders. He had seven horns and <u>seven eyes, which represent the sevenfold Spirit of God that is sent out into every part of the earth.</u>

Revelation 5:6 NLT (emphasis added)

Consequently, I felt compelled to go back to the conference over the next couple of days. Then, as if the visions weren't enough, the last night of the conference the woman of God (who was a prophetess of course) ministered prophetically to the people in the congregation. And of course – she called me out.

"You're a prophetess," she said. "You're a seer," to be more specific.

I shook my head to confirm she was right. And she continued to minister as the Lord allowed.

As Samuel grew up, the LORD was with him, and everything Samuel said proved to be reliable. And all Israel, from Dan in the north to Beersheba in the south, <u>knew that Samuel was confirmed as a prophet of the LORD.</u>

1 Samuel 3:19 – 20 NLT (emphasis added)

Now, in the above scripture reference it indicates Samuel was confirmed as a prophet of the LORD; then, First Chronicles, chapter twenty-nine, verse twenty-nine states: All the events of King David's reign, from beginning to end, are written in The Record of ***Samuel the Seer…***
And it's stated in the scripture reference below:

"I am the seer!" Samuel replied.

1 Samuel 9:19a NLT

So, Samuel was a prophet *and* a seer as was Gad:

The next morning the word of the LORD came to the prophet Gad, who was David's seer.

2 Samuel 24:11 NLT

The prophetic revelation, information, or message from God is received in a number of different ways: visions, dreams, impressions, audible voice of God, trances, and experiences in the third heaven. Once the revelation is revealed, it must be interpreted in order to understand the message that God is conveying. Now, what I'd like to point out is, even with accurate revelation, even if you've described the vision or dream accurately, it's possible to misinterpret the message. You may ask, "How is that possible if the message is from God?" It's possible because, first of all, we're human and we make mistakes. Secondly, the message could be misinterpreted if we rely on interpretation from visions or dreams that we've had in the past, as well as if we don't understand the symbolism of the revelation.

"What symbolism?" you ask.

When a vision or dream is revealed, God uses "symbols" to convey His message. So while a person may be able to, at least, describe what they saw or heard in a vision or dream, the understanding or the prophetic interpretation of the message is hidden. The message is hidden because it is a *spiritual message* that the human mind can't understand or interpret unless the individual has the special, God-given ability to interpret the vision or dream as was the case with Daniel.

God gave these four young men an unusual aptitude for understanding every aspect of literature and wisdom. <u>And God gave Daniel the special ability to interpret the meanings of visions and dreams.</u>

Daniel 1:17 NLT (emphasis added)

So just because a person has a vision or dream which may, in fact, be prophetic in nature, doesn't necessarily mean the person is able to interpret it. So, why would God give a prophetic vision or dream to someone who doesn't have the ability to interpret it?

It is *God in heaven who reveals secrets;* secrets that are revealed in dreams (as was the case with King Nebuchadnezzar in the book of Daniel, for example) and in visions (to Daniel, who was given the ability to interpret the dream). And not only to show what would happen in the future, but because God wants us to understand what He's communicating to us; what He's saying (especially if the person is an unbeliever like King Nebuchadnezzar).

But not with my servant Moses.
Of all my house, he is the one I trust.
I speak to him face to face,
clearly, and not in riddles!
He sees the LORD as he is.

Numbers 12:7 – 8a NLT

When the vision or dream is interpreted, the unbeliever gets to know God in a way that they've never known Him before. And ultimately, they'd want to get to know Him more. Prophetic visions and dreams show who God is and what He's like. Therefore, when visions and dreams are interpreted, they're revelations of God; Him revealing Himself, His word, and the testimony of Jesus Christ. And just like He determines which spiritual gift each person gets, He also determines who He gives the special, God-given ability to interpret visions and dreams.

In the book of Numbers, God told Aaron and Miriam that when He speaks prophetically, He, get this, *reveals Himself* in visions and *speaks* in dreams:

…"If there were prophets among you,
I, the LORD, would reveal myself in visions.
I would speak to them in dreams.

Numbers 12:6 NLT

Now as stated above in Numbers, chapter twelve, and verse seven, He didn't speak to Moses in riddles, which is how He speaks to us today – in riddles – parables, if you will; the same way He spoke to His disciples. The symbols, riddles, parables are to get us to exercise our spiritual resourcefulness in responding to what He has revealed to us. It causes us to try to discover its meaning. Ultimately, it causes us to seek after Him to get the interpretation and understanding, which then prompts *us* to get to know Him in a way that we've never known Him before. And it results in us wanting to get to know Him more.

And, not only do you need prophetic interpretation to get understanding of the symbolic message, but often times, God will only reveal a message in part. For example, there are some visions and dreams that are revealed, however, it'll be years before He reveals the interpretation and understanding because the vision or dream is for a set time. So needless to say, it's crucial that we have understanding before we try to convey the revelation or message of a vision or dream to someone. Then, there are some visions and dreams that are revealed in part; God doesn't give us the interpretation and understanding until what was revealed in the vision or dream actually happens.

You see, there are times when the revelation or interpretation of the vision or dream isn't revealed *until* it is acted on by faith. For example, I'm reminded of a dream I had, but I *didn't* know the interpretation of the dream. And yet, I felt lead in my spirit to reach out to the individual who the dream was about. *After* I shared the dream with the person, the prophetic interpretation was *then* revealed. This is how it was revealed:

When I talked to Alex, I asked him, "May I share with you a dream that the Lord revealed to me?"

"Of course!" He said as he laughed. "The Spirit already revealed to me that you had a "word" to share with me."

Then I shared the dream with him:

In a dream...

"I saw you crying in the spirit. You came to me and said, 'I was looking for you.' (You wanted to let me know that you were leaving the company.)

Now what I received in my spirit was the company was letting you go."

"Can you bear witness to what was revealed in the dream?" I asked.

"Well," he responded. "I actually resigned from my position. They're not replacing me and who knows what would have happened. I was able to get a job that I desired and applied for two times before, but was turned down; the third time I got it."

When Alex said he had applied for the job two other times, but hadn't gotten it, immediately, the Lord gave me the *interpretation and understanding* of what the dream meant. So I prophesied to Alex; I said to him what I heard the Lord say to me:

The interpretation...

"Alex, 'the company letting you go' means you were being "released" from the company in the spirit (by God), which speaks to your third attempt and finally getting the job. The Lord wants you to know that this move was orchestrated by Him. He's getting ready to do a mighty work in you concerning ministry.

You crying in the spirit is a reflection of the work He's getting ready to do; separation. You are going to have to let go of some things in your life (things and people) as God does the work. He also wants you to submit your will to His will because He knows what's best for you.

This will be a season of humility for you; a season of you humbling yourself under the mighty hand of God. He has His eye on you, He cares for you, and you are on His heart. He's getting ready to bless you in a way that you have never seen before," says the Spirit of Grace.

"Amen. Praise the Lord," he responded. "This is confirmation on so many intimate levels! (It's involving ministry and my personal walk with the Lord.) The closer I walk with God, the more He allows me to see the different levels of humility. My God! My Lord! I have been praying on this for some time, and when I left the company, it was truly a spiritual separation; and God's hands were involved in every step. Thank you for your obedience and for delivering the 'word.' I'm extremely grateful to the Lord for you," he said.

"Amen," I responded. "To God be the glory."

Now I'd like to give you a little more clarity on how not having the interpretation or understanding could happen:

In the book of Acts, the tenth chapter states: in Caesarea there lived a Roman army officer named Cornelius, who was a captain of the Italian Regiment. He was a devout, God-fearing man, as was everyone in his household. He gave generously to the poor and prayed regularly to God. One afternoon about three o'clock, he had a vision in which he saw an angel of God coming toward him. "Cornelius!" the angel said.

Cornelius stared at him in terror. "What is it, sir?" he asked the angel.

And the angel replied, "Your prayers and gifts to the poor have been received by God as an offering! Now send some men to Joppa, and summon a man named Simon Peter. He is staying with Simon, a tanner who lives near the seashore."

As soon as the angel was gone, Cornelius called two of his household servants and a devout soldier, one of his personal attendants. He told them what had happened and sent them off to Joppa.

The next day as Cornelius's messengers were nearing the town, Peter went up on the flat roof to pray. It was about noon, and he was hungry. But while a meal was being prepared, *he fell into a trance.* He saw the sky open, and something like a large sheet was let down by its four corners. In the sheet were all sorts of animals, reptiles, and birds. Then a voice said to him, "Get up, Peter; kill and eat them."

"No, Lord," Peter declared. "I have never eaten anything that our Jewish laws have declared impure and unclean."

But the voice spoke again: "Do not call something unclean if God has made it clean." The same vision was repeated three times. Then the sheet was suddenly pulled up to heaven.

Peter was very perplexed. What could the vision mean? Just then the men sent by Cornelius found Simon's house. Standing outside the gate, they asked if a man named Simon Peter was staying there.

Okay, if I may interrupt, there's something I'd like to point out: first of all, if you notice, the men were *"looking for Peter"* just as Alex was *"looking for me"* in my dream. Secondly, during the time the men were looking for Peter, Peter had a vision. In addition to the vision, the Lord spoke to Peter. And after Peter heard the voice and saw the vision three times, the passage of scriptures state *Peter was very perplexed and asked what the vision meant.*

Well, the same held true for me. Although Alex was looking for me, and the Lord had revealed to me in a dream that he was looking for me, I still didn't know what the dream meant.

Now let's continue. Meanwhile, as Peter was puzzling over the vision, the Holy Spirit said to him, "Three men have come looking for you. Get up, go downstairs, and go with them without hesitation. Don't worry, for I have sent them." (I, on the other hand, was lead to go and share the dream with Alex.)

So Peter went down and said, "I'm the man you are looking for. *Why have you come?*"

They said, "We were sent by Cornelius, a Roman officer. He is a devout and God-fearing man, well respected by all the Jews. A holy angel instructed him to summon you to his house so that he can hear your message." So Peter invited the men to stay for the night. The next day he went with them, accompanied by some of the brothers from Joppa.

Let's stop here again. Okay, the men told Peter the angel of the Lord had Cornelius send for Peter because Peter had *a message* to share with Cornelius. So it was with Alex, the Lord had revealed to Alex that I had *a message* or a *"word"* for him. When I talked to him, he said, 'The Spirit had already revealed to me that you had a *"word"* to share with me.' That's why the Lord revealed to me in the dream that Alex was looking for me even though, I, like Peter, didn't know what the message was. And yet, I knew in my spirit that the Lord wanted me to go to Alex.

Peter told them, "You know it is against our laws for a Jewish man to enter a Gentile home like this or to associate with you. But God has shown me that I should no longer think of anyone as impure or unclean.

Wait! I have to stop you right here. If you noticed, the *interpretation* of the vision that the Lord gave to Peter has now been revealed. Initially, when the Lord revealed the vision to Peter, he declared, "No, Lord, I have never eaten anything that our Jewish laws have declared impure and unclean." However, if you'll notice, now that he's talking with Cornelius, he said *God has shown me that I should no longer think of **anyone** as impure or unclean.* So Peter now has the interpretation and the understanding that the vision of the *animals, reptiles, and birds* wasn't about the *meat that you eat,* but rather it was about the *Gentiles, a people, who were considered "unclean."*

Now let's continue. "So I came without objection as soon as I was sent for. Now tell me why you sent for me."

Now, get this, while Peter at least understands that the vision wasn't about meat, but rather was about *a people,* he still doesn't know *why* he's there as he says to Cornelius, *"Now tell me why you sent for me."* So Cornelius shared with Peter what he experienced when the holy angel appeared to him and instructed him to send for Peter. Then in verse thirty-three Cornelius says,

"Now we are all here, waiting before God *to hear the message the Lord has given you.*" Then guess what? It's not until *then* that Peter gets the full understanding and interpretation of the message:

Then Peter replied, "I see very clearly that God shows no favoritism. In every nation he accepts those who fear him and do what is right. This is the message of Good News for the people of Israel—that there is peace with God through Jesus Christ, who is Lord of all.

So, how do I know he received the interpretation and understanding? Because Peter said, "I *see very clearly,"* as he refers to the vision. And says, *"God shows no favoritism,"* as he refers to the voice of the Lord. Again, as I mentioned previously, sometimes God doesn't give us the interpretation and understanding until what was revealed in the vision, in this case, actually happens or manifests.

When God reveals things to us, whether by visions, dreams, impressions, trances, the audible voice of God, or experiences in the third heaven, it's known as "revelation." So in essence, visions and dreams from God are revelation; they're the secret things of God – revealed. There are different levels of prophetic anointing and revelation that a prophet operates in, which are equivalent to or parallel to the different dimensions or levels in the spirit realm. And the more God reveals to the prophet, the greater the level of satanic attacks he endures by demonic forces.

I will reluctantly tell about visions and revelations from the Lord. I was caught up to the third heaven fourteen years ago. Whether I was in my body or out of my body, I don't know—only God knows. Yes, only God knows whether I was in my body or outside my body. But I do know that I was caught up to paradise and heard things so astounding that they cannot be expressed in words, things no human is allowed to tell.

2 Corinthians 12:1b – 4 NLT

So to keep me from becoming proud, I was given a thorn in my flesh, a messenger from Satan to torment me and keep me from becoming proud.

2 Corinthians 12:7b NLT

Therefore, the prophet who operates in a high level of prophetic anointing and revelation is also exposed to a high level of *prolonged testing and intense spiritual warfare.*

NEW LEVELS – NEW DEVILS

And with that being said, we have to also be aware that all visions and dreams are not from God. That's why we have to have the spirit of discernment or at the very least inquire of the Lord whenever we have a vision or dream. Now I have to say, I always thought *if someone passed away who was a Christian, then the dream* **had to** *be from God.* For example:

Shortly after one of my loved ones passed, I saw her in a dream.

It wasn't until I had *that* particular dream (which surprisingly disturbed my spirit) that I knew otherwise; all dreams of Christians are not from God.

Therefore, I started to seek the Lord concerning the matter. And the Lord began to minister to me. I was reminded of Saul and Samuel in First Samuel, chapter twenty-eight, verses five through nineteen. Saul was seeking Samuel (who had died) to get instructions from the Lord. *The spirit of Samuel appeared.* However, it wasn't the spirit of Samuel it was what is known as a *"familiar spirit."* A familiar spirit is a demon.

"Then the rich man said, 'Please, Father Abraham, at least send him to my father's home. For I have five brothers, and I want him to warn them so they don't end up in this place of torment.'

"But Abraham said, 'Moses and the prophets have warned them. Your brothers can read what they wrote.'

"The rich man replied, 'No, Father Abraham! But if someone is sent to them from the dead, then they will repent of their sins and turn to God.'

"But Abraham said, <u>'If they won't listen to Moses and the prophets, they won't be persuaded even if someone rises from the dead.'"</u>

Luke 16:27 – 31 NLT (emphasis added)

The **Word of God** tells us that no one who has passed away would come back to visit; there would be **no messages and no warnings** (as the psychics and fortune-tellers proclaim). These are **familiar spirits, demons** that the enemy uses to divert or deflect us from God. Therefore, we don't have to *worry* if the person is "okay" or *wonder* if they had trouble "crossing over." Nor do we have to try to figure out if they're "trying to tell us something." (So when the psychic and fortune-tellers have messages for you from your love ones who have passed – be mindful that these "love ones" are familiar spirits; they are demons!)

The **Word of God** is absolute about the death of the righteous: to be absent from the body is to be present with the Lord!

Yes, we are fully confident, and we would rather be away from these earthly bodies, for then we will be at home with the Lord.

1 Corinthians 5:8 NLT

We do not want you to be uninformed about those who sleep in death, <u>so that you do not grieve like the rest of mankind,</u> who have no hope.

1 Thessalonians 4:13 NIV (emphasis added)

'I am the God of Abraham, the God of Isaac, and the God of Jacob.' <u>So he is the God of the living, not the dead."</u>

Matthew 22:32 NLT (emphasis added)

PART

V

THE
THIRD
TIGER

THE THIRD TRIMESTER

~ CHAPTER 1 ~

YOU KNOW YOU BE LYING

After I talked to Tiffany and it was confirmed that she wouldn't be coming back, I shared the information with Pastor Randolph. And the following week we shared it at bible study. Unable to do anything about the Lord removing her from the ministry, it was still sad to see her go.

A few days later, Leah said, "I'd like to talk to you."

"Sure, about what?"

"I'm concerned that y'all didn't treat Tiffany the same way y'all treated Maria when she left the ministry."

Now considering I hadn't told Leah about the conversation that Tiffany and I had, I assumed she was *concerned* based on what Tiffany may have told her. Still, I asked, "How did we treat Maria and how was it different than the way we treated Tiffany?"

"I don't know. I can't explain it, but it was different."

"Let me see," I said to recount both situations, "when Maria left, she told us she was leaving then we announced to everyone that she wouldn't be returning to the ministry. And when Tiffany left, (after several weeks of not showing up, and not returning my calls), we also announced that she wouldn't be returning to the ministry. So there wasn't a difference in the way we treated them. Especially considering in both situations I encouraged them to stay." Immediately I thought, *She's got a lot of nerves! She, out of all people, who has gotten the absolute most from this ministry – was concerned about how 'she felt' we had treated Tiffany differently, somehow!*

She said, "I'm concerned about what's going to happen in the ministry now that Tiffany is gone. I'm wondering if you're going to ask me to step up and do what you asked Tiffany to do."

"No. I won't be asking you to step up to do what I asked Tiffany to do," I said. *As a matter of fact,* I thought, *I won't be asking you to do anything.*

Then, she went on to say, "I want to write the overview for bible study to share with the people who weren't able to make it. But I don't want you to pressure me to get it done by a certain time and date because you know I have trouble balancing my time and obligations."

"Thanks for wanting to do the overview, but if you can't have it done when I ask you to do it, then I don't want you to do it."

"I also want to talk about the time you hurt my feelings…"

"When did I hurt your feelings?" I interrupted curiously.

Now, Leah had a habit of being late (no matter what she did or who she did it with, she was *always* late). And this particular day she got off work at 6 p.m., which gave her plenty of time to get to the bible study that started at 7:30; especially after she specifically changed her schedule so that she could make it to bible study on time. Leah stated *she had been talking to the girls at work and the time just got away from her.* Therefore, I asked them (her and Tiffany) to try to make sure they came in a timely manner (considering they had to get their kids situated).

So, as a result of how I handled the situation, her feelings were hurt. She felt like she had to *explain* to me why she was late, which she didn't have to do. I never asked her why she was late. She just mentioned she was talking and the time got away from her. However, I apologized because I didn't know that I had hurt her feelings. Anyway, it became clear after that incident, she didn't want water/ice/juice, snacks – nothing – from me, which was evident by her bringing her own; however, I continued to be hospitable, and she continued to decline.

A few days later, Leah was all excited because she had something to tell me and could hardly wait. Anxiously, she prefaced the conversation, "Ever since I told Tiffany about my deliverance and how I had been lying to you, whenever I talk to her on the phone, she always say to me, 'You know you be lying,' at some point in our conversation. It doesn't matter what the conversation is about, she somehow seems to find a way to fit it into almost *every* conversation that we have. It really bothers me that she would continuously say that." Then she paused and looked at me.

Because she paused, I thought she wanted me to say how I thought she should respond to Tiffany calling her a liar. But I had to pause myself because I was surprised – wait! She didn't seem to have a problem with telling *me*, *'You're judging me by thinking I'm a liar.'* And yet, *every* conversation she has with Tiffany, Tiffany blatantly calls her a liar and yet she says nothing. And even more surprising, she didn't feel *judged. Was I missing something?* I wondered. But as soon as I opened my mouth to say what I thought…

Hesitantly, she continued, "So," she said slowly, "I just told her what I had been delivered from."

"You told her?" I asked surprised (because she said she wasn't going to tell anyone).

"Yeah, I told her."

"Wait!" I said. "Let me get this straight. You just came out and said, 'I was delivered from homosexuality'?"

"Well, not exactly. We were talking and she said, 'You know you be lying.' And I just got sick and tired of hearing her say that, so I just told her so she'd understand why I had been lying to you."

"Oh, so you only told her to get her to stop calling you a liar?" I said because that demon (the *spirit of manipulation*) had used Tiffany to manipulate Leah!

"Yeah, I guess. I was just sick of hearing it. So I thought if she knew why I had been lying she'd stop saying it."

"So it wasn't because you were excited that you had been delivered and just wanted to share with someone what Jesus did for you, but rather because she kept tormenting you and calling you a liar?" I said shedding light on what happened.

"Well, I guess; if that's how you put it."

"So let me ask you this, if she hadn't kept calling you a liar, would you have told her?"

"No, because I didn't want her to know. I just figured that since she's no longer a part of the ministry, that if she knew, then I don't have to worry about her mistreating me, being afraid to hug me, or just treating me differently. So since I don't have to see her anymore – I didn't care; I just told her…"

"And because you wanted her to stop calling you a liar." I interjected, but not without being confronted by my heart as it broke at the thought of the torment she's had to contend with as a result of this lifestyle. I fought back the tears as she expressed the pain of not wanting to be discriminated against; rejected.

"Yeah, and so she'd stop calling me a liar," she said. "Oh, man! I was all excited that I told someone. I thought that was a good thing."

"That was a good thing. But you *really* didn't want to tell her. You only told her in order to get her to stop calling you a liar. You had the wrong motives, so God doesn't get the glory."

Leah was absolutely right! By telling Tiffany, it *would* get her to stop calling her a liar. But only after Tiffany had manipulated her into telling her what she wanted to know – why Leah had been lying to me. That's exactly how the *spirit of manipulation* works. By Tiffany continuously saying to Leah, "You know you be lying," it put Tiffany in a position to control Leah's reaction; her response. If it bothered Leah for Tiffany to say that, then Leah would *do something* to get her to stop saying it. Either she'd tell Tiffany that it bothered her and asked her to stop or she'd tell her what she wanted to hear, which was the case.

Now I have to say, Tiffany wasn't the only one using manipulation. Leah was doing some manipulating of her own. In an attempt to "cover up" the *lying spirit,* the attention was diverted to the *homosexual spirit*, which resulted in her telling Tiffany about her deliverance. The only way she'd be *bothered* by Tiffany continuously saying, 'You know you be lying,' is if the spirit was there, otherwise, she wouldn't care. Not only that, but she was also trying to avoid the shame, embarrassment, and discrimination that she had *yet* to overcome by thinking she'd never see Tiffany again – so she told her.

"What did she say when you told her?" I asked.

"She said, 'I knew it! I was right! I had discerned in the spirit that you were gay! I could tell by your mannerisms!'"

"How did you feel about her saying you were *gay*?" I asked because immediately I was reminded of a conversation that Leah and I had about her realizing and admitting that she was gay, which was a part of the deliverance process. However, this girl refused – I mean *absolutely* refused – to say she was gay. So it was interesting, to say the least, to hear how she responded to Tiffany calling her *gay*.

"I guess I'm okay with it. I don't have to see her anymore, so it doesn't bother me," she responded. "Then Tiffany said, 'I'm excited for you. You don't have to be afraid to go back around the people in that lifestyle because it would give you an opportunity to let your light sh...'"

"The enemy is using Tiffany." I interrupted. "He has sent her to confuse you about maintaining your deliverance. I've already shared with you the importance of you not going back into that environment because you're not ready. And the fact that you *struggled* to even tell Tiffany about your deliverance is an indication that you're not ready; there are still some areas that you need to deal with and overcome before you can go back into that environment."

So yet again, immature, lacked understanding, and in error of the scriptures, Tiffany had advised Leah incorrectly; *'You don't have to be afraid to go back around the people in that lifestyle because it would give you an opportunity to let your light shine,'* and it angered me that the enemy was using Tiffany. Unfortunately, Leah didn't have a *light to shine* because she was still struggling with her deliverance.

My heart broke under the weight of her words that continued to ring out in my spirit, *'I don't have to worry about her mistreating me, being afraid to hug me, or just treating me differently.'* Her words spoke volumes to the realization of the pain she had to endure by being discriminated against, mistreated by others who don't either understand the homosexual lifestyle or are intolerant of it. Being concerned about being discriminated against was something that she had never said before. Consequently, it was clear that she wasn't ready to go back into that environment until she was stronger.

~ CHAPTER 2 ~

CONTRACTIONS

One night after bible study, Leah and I were talking and she brought up the conversation about me agreeing with our friend, Lisa, about her being late all the time: One of our friends, Shanta, was graduating with her bachelor's degree. So Leah, Lisa, and I agreed we'd all go to the graduation together. And as we were working out the details of when and where we'd meet, Lisa said that she liked being on time. (Clearly, this was intended for Leah, who was known for being late all the time.) So I, in turn, agreed with Lisa and started laughing.

"Wasn't that funny?" I said to Leah. "Everyone in the department knows you're always late for everything."

"I didn't appreciate that. And I'd appreciate it if you didn't do that."

"Are you kidding me? I thought it was funny. You need to get your act together!"

"I'm always late; I've always been that way all of my life, and I'm not going to change because that's how I am," she said. "Your methods of trying to get me to '*get it together*' aren't effective and they don't help me."

Initially, I was taken aback by how serious she was. Then, I was reminded of the "methods" that she was referring to. She came to me and asked me to help her *"get it together"* when her supervisor kept pressuring her about being late *all the time*. So I advised her to do some of the things that she did in the morning the night before to free up time in the morning. Then she'd say why that wouldn't work. Then I suggested waking up earlier; leaving the house earlier – she'd say why that wouldn't work. Then I suggested taking a different route to work – she'd say why that wouldn't work. Okay, so nothing I suggested worked, but not because she had tried it. So, after several unsuccessful attempts to assist her with being on time, I was being confronted with "my methods aren't effective and don't work for her."

So I responded, "If I recall correctly, *you* asked *me* to help you *get it together.* I'm the same person that tried to give you suggestions on how to *get it together,* but for one reason or another you always seemed to find an excuse why you couldn't follow through." And we continued to go back and forth about her being late, she'll never change, that's how she is, so on and so on. As I stood there arguing with her I thought, *I can't believe I'm having a conversation with someone who doesn't want to change. Someone who's defending why she's always late and will always be late – opposed to being open to changing.* And ultimately, as she had so eloquently stated, "Don't try to change me." The conversation had become extremely exhausting and so draining – then I realized, I was in warfare.

The conversation had taken such a rapid turn from her asking me to help her to my methods weren't effective and didn't help her, which released the attacks disguised in the form of contractions. Extremely exhausted and unable to bear the weight of the attacks (the contractions), I wanted to push. *If I rebuke this devil, it'll be over!* I thought. And just as I had gotten to the point that I could no longer endure the warfare and would rebuke her, the Lord said, "Hold your peace."

Ready and filled with expectation of this birthing, the Lord revealed that I wasn't in position to push. He also revealed that if I pushed, I'd do damage to myself and to the baby; damage to my purpose and ministry. So it took everything that I had within me to keep from pushing – to keep from rebuking that demon! I was tired and I wanted this to be over.

The tears welled up in my eyes because I was exhausted and didn't think I would be able to carry this thing (ministry/baby). I desperately wanted nothing more than to be obedient to the Lord and *hold my peace.* Ultimately, I knew the pain of the contractions (attacks) would become more intense and more frequent in order for me to deliver what the Lord was birthing in me. Consequently, the thought of the warfare that had been launched against me was overwhelming and caused me to, once again, determine *the next time she comes at me like that, I'm going to rebuke her!*

And just as suddenly, the Lord rebuked *me*, "Hold your peace!"

By this time, I was very much aware of the third tiger's assignment – kill this ministry; stop it from going forth.

And consequently, the Lord ministered to me and revealed that Leah wasn't connected to the ministry. For the most part, she was just going through the motion. So I continuously asked if she was having personal prayer time (outside of the praying we were doing at lunch) and she said, "Yeah, when I can find the time."

"Are you reading the bible, studying, praying, and spending time with the Lord?"

"Yeah, for the most part," she said. And of course I continued to challenge her in these areas since the Lord had already revealed that she wasn't connected. Therefore, I already knew that she wasn't reading her bible, studying, praying, or spending time with the Lord.

"I am the true grapevine, and my Father is the gardener. He cuts off every branch of mine that doesn't produce fruit, and he prunes the branches that do bear fruit so they will produce even more. You have already been pruned and purified by the message I have given you.

Remain in me, and I will remain in you. For a branch cannot produce fruit if it is severed from the vine, and you cannot be fruitful unless you remain in me.

"Yes, I am the vine; you are the branches. Those who remain in me, and I in them, will produce much fruit. For apart from me you can do nothing. Anyone who does not remain in me is thrown away like a useless branch and withers. Such branches are gathered into a pile to be burned. But if you remain in me and my words remain in you, you may ask for anything you want, and it will be granted! When you produce much fruit, you are my true disciples. This brings great glory to my Father.

John 15:1 – 8 NLT

One day after Leah and I finished praying she said, "I don't think I should have to pray if I don't feel like praying." Now, let me say this, by that time, Leah and I had had this same conversation on a number of occasions. And each time, I tried to explain to her the importance of not only me praying, but her praying as well. Her praying was helping her with her relationship with Christ. However, *this time* when she said it, I had had enough. I was tired of going back and forth with her about this same subject.

"If you don't want to pray, you don't have to pray." Therefore, it was impressed upon my heart not to ask her to pray anymore. So thereafter, she came to prayer every day and just sat there while I prayed. Not only did she not want to pray, but her participation in bible study, as well as praise and worship were limited. It had become a struggle to get her involved.

As I thought about the Lord revealing to me that Leah wasn't connected, I became concerned as I was reminded of how it appeared that Leah had been hanging onto Tiffany's every word. And as if the Lord had answered my concern, He revealed *Tiffany had taken the seed from Leah before it was able to take root in her heart.*

The Parable of the Sower

"A farmer went out to plant his seed. As he scattered it across his field, some seed fell on a footpath, where it was stepped on, and the birds ate it. Other seed fell among rocks. It began to grow, but the plant soon wilted and died for lack of moisture. Other seed fell among thorns that grew up with it and choked out the tender plants. Still other seed fell on fertile soil. This seed grew and produced a crop that was a hundred times as much as had been planted!" When he had said this, he called out, "Anyone with ears to hear should listen and understand."

Jesus Explains the parable:

His disciples asked him what this parable meant. He replied, "You are permitted to understand the secrets of the Kingdom of God. But I use parables to teach the others so that the Scriptures might be fulfilled:

'When they look, they won't really see.
*   When they hear, they won't understand.'*

"This is the meaning of the parable: The seed is God's word. The seeds that fell on the footpath represent those who hear the message, only to have the devil come and take it away from their hearts and prevent them from believing and being saved. The seeds on the rocky soil represent those who hear the message and receive it with joy. But since they don't have deep roots, they believe for a while, then they fall away when they face temptation. The seeds that fell among the thorns represent those who hear the message, but all too quickly the message is crowded out by the cares and riches and pleasures of this life. And so they never grow into maturity. And the seeds that fell on the good soil represent honest, good-hearted people who hear God's word, cling to it, and patiently produce a huge harvest.

Luke 8:5 – 15 NLT

As a result of what the Lord had revealed, my heart went out to Leah. As I thought about Leah's relationship with Christ, it was clear that the enemy had used Tiffany to come against Leah to steal the Word of God from Leah before it was able to take root in her heart. Every time I would tell her something, Tiffany would say something different, which planted seeds of doubt:

- ✓ *I said deliverance is a process*
    - ○ *Tiffany said that deliverance is instant.*
- ✓ *I said she needs to maintain her deliverance before going back into the homosexual environment*
    - ○ *Tiffany said don't be afraid to go back around the people in that lifestyle – let your light shine.*

You were running the race so well. Who has held you back from following the truth? It certainly isn't God, for he is the one who called you to freedom. This false teaching is like a little yeast that spreads through the whole batch of dough! I am trusting the Lord to keep you from believing false teachings. God will judge that person, whoever he is, who has been confusing you.

Galatians 5:7 – 10 NLT

Any yet, I continuously tried to encourage Leah to keep the faith.

But I fear that somehow your pure and undivided devotion to Christ will be corrupted, just as Eve was deceived by the cunning ways of the serpent. You happily put up with whatever anyone tells you, even if they preach a different Jesus than the one we preach, or a different kind of Spirit than the one you received, or a different kind of gospel than the one you believed.

2 Corinthians 11:3 – 4 NLT

Clearly, the things that Tiffany had been sharing with Leah didn't line up with the Word of God. Therefore, these false teachings resulted in Leah's faith (and her walk with Christ) being threatened. There were a number of times Leah said that she felt overwhelmed with just trying to keep up with her personal prayer, reading the bible, or even just spending quality time with the Lord. And unfortunately, while she thought it was important to keep up with Tiffany (because it was easier for her to relate to Tiffany opposed to me because I was the Pastor), she lost sight of her relationship with Christ.

And while there wasn't any doubt that the enemy had been using Tiffany to keep Leah from believing (and receiving), it was also clear that the confusion that Tiffany was creating in Leah's life was apparently accomplishing the goal that she was assigned to accomplish. This explained why Leah would ask me two and three different times the same things that I'd advised her on before (because Tiffany was advising her otherwise), which caused her to become confused.

As the Lord continued to minister to me, it just broke my heart. Just like Eve lost focus and listened to the enemy, Leah had lost focus and was distracted by Tiffany's demonic activity that she obviously mistook for godly activity. By this time, Tiffany hadn't been a part of our ministry for a few months and she hadn't been connected to another ministry either. So basically she was back at home – backslidden. And there was no doubt in my mind that Tiffany, under the influence of demonic activity, was influencing Leah in a way that *sounded good and seemed to make sense,* at least to Leah. Unfortunately, because Leah was so focused on Tiffany (and clearly confused), Tiffany was able to lead her astray.

Who was Leah *really* serving…which tree was she *really* allowed to eat from???

~ CHAPTER 3 ~

THE ENEMY IS IN THE GARDEN

The Bible talks about the Garden of Gethsemane, which is where Jesus was, once again, confronted by Satan himself. The Garden of Gethsemane was the place where Jesus experienced the greatest intensity of spiritual warfare before being betrayed and then going to the cross to complete His God-given purpose. In the garden, He agonized over drinking from the cup of affliction; grief-stricken, sorrowful unto the point of death, and tormented. He wrestled with eating the bread of adversity; weighed down, burdened, and challenged physically, spiritually, mentally, and emotionally as Satan tried to stop Him from accomplishing God's will. This garden, which was an olive orchard, with its oil press, proved to be a place of pressing.

Then Jesus went with them to the olive grove called Gethsemane, and he said, "Sit here while I go over there to pray."

Matthew 26:36 NLT

Allow me to share with you the significance of the olive and the oil press, which makes the Garden of Gethsemane such a powerful place:

- ✓ The olive represents *the vessel* – the person God uses to accomplish His will.
- ✓ The olive press or oil press represents *the process* – which God uses to produce the oil from the olive.
- ✓ The oil from the olive represents *the anointing* – God's presence, power, and purpose.

So the process of the olive and the oil press is a representation of the Lord producing the anointing in an individual's life.

- ✓ Therefore, we must understand first and foremost, all of the olives or vessels that are pressed – are handpicked – chosen by God.
- ✓ After the olives have been picked or the vessel has been chosen, they're washed; they go through a process of separation – separating the leaves and stems from the olives or separating the vessel from the people who aren't a part of what God is doing in their life.
- ✓ Then the olives (including their pits, I might add – *everything*) are crushed into a paste; the *flesh* is crushed, just as the vessel (including mind, body, soul, and spirit, I might add – *everything*) is crushed into the will of God; the *flesh* of the vessel is crushed unto death.

That was the case with Jesus as He prayed in agony in the Garden of Gethsemane:

"My soul is crushed with grief to the point of death."

And there was no way of stopping this assignment from happening, nor was there any other way that this could be accomplished. Therefore, He became vulnerable, weak, and defenseless – exposed to the physical, emotional, and mental pain and agony of dying on the cross; His *flesh* being put to death – crushed.

  ✓ He struggled.

"My Father! If it is possible, let this cup of suffering be taken away from me. Yet I want your will to be done, not mine."

And during this process, the oil that is trapped in the paste is then put in the press,

  ✓ ...and squeezed.

"My Father! If this cup cannot be taken away unless I drink it, your will be done."

  ✓ ...and squeezed.

"My Father! If this cup cannot be taken away unless I drink it, your will be done."

  ✓ During the pressing, the olive oil *naturally* separates; just as the anointing *naturally* comes forth.

While Jesus was here on earth, he offered prayers and pleading, with a loud cry and tears, to the one who could rescue him from death. And God heard his prayers because of his deep reverence for God. Even though Jesus was God's Son, he learned obedience from the things he suffered.

Hebrews 5:7 – 8 NLT

One day Leah and I were in the garden getting ready to pray. And she looked me dead in my face and said, "You look tired." This same person that said time and time again, 'I shouldn't have to pray if I don't want to pray,' sat there as if she was taunting me because I had grown tired.

"I am," I responded. And immediately the vision was before me:

In a vision...

Immediately as I looked in Leah's face, it had been contorted into that of Satan; taking pleasure in the fact that I was getting worn down.

The interpretation...

I was face to face with Satan.

I was looking into a face that was decomposed, decayed – the face of death.

THE ENEMY WAS IN THE GARDEN.

"Look, my betrayer is here!"

Matthew 26:46b NLT

So Jesus told him, "What you are about to do, do quickly."

John 13:27b NIV

~ WHAT HAS THE LORD SAID TO YOU? ~

I continued to be concerned about Leah and her relationship with Christ. So, one day after prayer, Leah and I were talking and I said, "Leah, it's important for you to heed what I'm saying to you in order for you to grow. I've been placed in your life to help you grow spiritually. As the Lord shares things with me concerning you, I'll share those things with…"

"The Lord isn't going to tell you something that He hasn't already told me," she said abruptly.

Immediately, I was taken aback because that was something that Tiffany often said. And still, I tried to explain to her what Tiffany said wasn't true. Then, I challenged her. "That sounds like Tiffany; did she tell you that?"

She sat there looking lost and uncertain; unsure of what she had said, why she had said it, or what to say next. "Yes," she replied. "I don't believe that the Lord will tell you something that isn't in my spirit."

So I asked her, "What has the Lord said to you?"

She just sat there.

"What has the Lord said to you?" I challenged her again. "Since you believe that He isn't going to say something to me that He hasn't already said to you, what has He said to you?"

"I don't know."

"I know you don't know because you don't even know the voice of the Lord! So how are you going to sit here and tell *me* that 'He's not going to say something to me unless He also tells you'?" And yet again, I tried explaining to her that when the Lord spoke concerning the people, he spoke to the leaders, not to the people – that's why you have leaders and pastors in the church. And considering the relationship that she had established with Tiffany, I said again, "You need to be careful of who you're listening to – especially if it's not your spiritual leader."

She just sat there.

When it came time to leave the prayer area, I could hardly move. I struggled to get up because the weight of the warfare that I was enduring was heavy. It was so devastating to see her (and Tiffany) being used by the enemy.

In the garden...

~ YOU DON'T KNOW IF I'VE BEEN DELIVERED ~

Although the Lord had revealed that Leah wasn't going to continue the deliverance process, I was still concerned about her well-being. So one day after prayer, I asked how she was doing with meditating on the scriptures that I had given her to help her maintain her deliverance.

"That's the best thing you could've done for me; giving me those scriptures because they work (especially the one for my thoughts). I had a thought, I used the scripture, and it worked!" she said almost as if she was surprised that it worked. But we were both excited.

Then, from out of nowhere, she said, "You don't even know if I've been delivered because you haven't even spent any time with me. You haven't even asked me about what's going on with me, so you have no idea if I've been delivered."

Taken aback, I couldn't even begin to tell you how shocked I was. Only to come to the realization that the demonic forces were present but I responded, "I know you've been delivered and I know it's a process; it takes time. And not only that, but you haven't even applied the principles that I've given you to help maintain your deliverance. When have you even meditated on the scriptures that I gave to you?"

"I read the *one* scripture about my thoughts, which surprisingly worked. So I can say that was the best thing that you could've taught me because it worked. However, I don't think you are really concerned about me and me being delivered because you always make me feel judged."

Her words, once again, gave way to the demonic attack and released warfare. And immediately the demonic forces rushed in to oppress me as the agony of the pressure rung out in my spirit. *OMG!* I thought, *here we go again.* And just as suddenly, the heaviness caused me to struggle as I responded. "Leah," I said exhausted. "I can't believe you would even fix your mouth to say something like that when I'm the very person that has gone to bat for you. I'm the one that wanted to see you get delivered. And in case you forgot, I'm the one that the Lord used to bring forth your deliverance. If I were judging you, I wouldn't have gone through all that I've gone through with you to see you set free."

"I don't think that's the case."

"Well, that is the case with me!" I said in a raised and uncompromising voice. I had had enough of her foolishness. "If I were judging you, then…"

"Hold your peace," the Lord interrupted, and I just stood there on the verge of tears. I was so tired of the demonic oppression. I had had enough! I was getting ready to let her have it!

"You always think that I'm a liar," she continued. "If you weren't judging me then you wouldn't think that."

"Our friendship has been built on lies; that's the foundation that *you* built our friendship on. And because you've consistently lied to me over and over throughout our friendship, what makes you think that all of a sudden I'm not going to think that you wouldn't lie to me anymore? What have you done to change that behavior? Nothing! So why shouldn't I think that you would lie to me again?"

"But you are judging me."

"I'm not judging you. I've *never* said anything to you to judge you. I have spiritual discernment – so I'm able to discern when you're lying or telling the truth."

"If you continuously think somebody is lying to you, when I'm not, then you're judging me. And that's not right."

"When have I judged you? Give me an example of when I've judged you."

"Whenever I'm telling you something, you automatically think I'm lying."

"Give me an example of when I'm judging you."

"I don't have an example. But I know you're judging me."

"Your sins are telling your mouth what to say.
   Your words are based on clever deception.
Your own mouth condemns you, not I.
   Your own lips testify against you."

Job 15:5 – 6 NLT

I was done! As far as I was concerned, this conversation was over.

"That's her insecurity. And she's projecting them onto you," the Lord said.

Projection is a psychological defense mechanism that allows an individual to take their own insecurities and project them onto other people, me, in this case. However, Leah didn't know that she was doing it; it's subconscious. This was her mind's way of defending her ability to deal with the undesirable emotions that she wasn't capable of handling as a result of the deliverance process. And instead of admitting or dealing with the undesirable emotions – she had projected them onto me. Basically, I acted as a mirror for her. When she saw me, she would see her insecurities, which made her *think* they were coming from me; when in fact, they were coming from *within* her. *That's* why she kept saying *I* was judging her.

You see, *she* was judging *herself* as a result of the lifestyle she'd lived for years and the lies that she'd told to "cover up" that lifestyle. And psychologically, she was unable to accept this negative feeling because it had become repulsive to her, which speaks to why she had a hard time dealing with the person she **was** prior to deliverance. And it also explained why Tiffany was able to constantly say to her, 'You know you be lying,' *but she never felt judged.*

Then I said, "I am not judging you. That's your own insecurities that you're projecting onto me."

"I didn't expect you to take responsibility for what you're doing."

"You're absolutely right. I'm not going to take responsibility for something *you're* doing – and *thinking* I'm doing."

"Not only that," she continued. "You can't make me like you! I'm my own person! Don't try to make me like you."

"How am I trying to make you like me?" I asked as I let out a sigh because the warfare was wearing me out.

"Because I know the principles that you live by and I know that some things that you say are based on the way you live, not because it's what the bible says. And just because you live that way doesn't mean that I'm going to live that way. And, you called me unholy."

"I didn't call you unholy; I said your situation was ungodly."

Leah had a friend, Dwayne, who'd been romantically interested in her for years. However, as a result of her not returning the same romantic interest, he became involved with someone else, and then they got engaged. However, on several occasions, when Dwayne would be "away on business," he would stay at Leah's house, in which they'd end up sleeping in the same bed – "fooling around" with each other.

"Well, I know that's the way that *you* live and that's not in the bible; therefore, you can't make me do things because that's the way *you* would do things."

"Leah, you don't think that you laying up with a man who's engaged to someone else is wrong?"

"No, I don't. And it doesn't matter what you say because I know you're just trying to make me like you, which I'm not going to let you do because I'm my own person, and I do what I want to do."

"If you're trying to live a holy life, what is it about you laying up with a man who's engaged to another woman that makes you think that's okay to do?" I asked.

"It's okay because we have an understanding. He knows nothing is going to happen between us because I already made that clear; we would not be having sex."

"So that explains why he went out the other night and bought condoms – *because he understands that you wouldn't be having sex* – is that right?"

"That's right! And I'll continue to do it because I don't see anything wrong with it."

"Okay," I relented. "If you don't see anything wrong with it – that's on you."

And basically, she went on to say that if I shared anything else with her, I would have to show it to her in the bible. Otherwise, she knew it would be me just trying to tell her how to live; me trying to turn her into me.

So prepare your minds for action and exercise self-control. Put all your hope in the gracious salvation that will come to you when Jesus Christ is revealed to the world. So you must live as God's obedient children. Don't slip back into your old ways of living to satisfy your own desires. You didn't know any better then. But now you must be holy in everything you do, just as God who chose you is holy. For the Scriptures say, "You must be holy because I am holy."

1 Peter 1:13 – 16 NLT

In the garden...

~ YOU LET ME DOWN ~

Again, right after prayer, Leah and I were headed back to work when she stopped me, and said she had something that she *had* to tell me; something she wanted to get off her chest. Now I have to say that by this time, not only had I had enough, but enough was enough! I knew the enemy was about to show up, which he'd often done after prayer; therefore, I determined that I was going to just *hold my peace* as the Lord had instructed me.

"I remember when I first started trying to live my life right," she said, "and you encouraged me to spend more time with my spiritual sisters. But then when Tiffany left the ministry, you let me down because I took it hard and you didn't help me through it," she said.

She took it hard? I thought. Immediately, I was overwhelmed by the demonic forces that continued to come against me. The heaviness of standing there in the midst of warfare was agonizing; I was barely able to stand. And the weight of having to hold my peace and not just rebuke this demon was starting to become painful. Then I thought, *what, if anything, did she want me to do about Tiffany leaving the ministry? How was I in control of who stayed and who left?* But I stood there and said nothing. As a matter of fact, I had already determined that this was not going to be a discussion. I was done trying to explain (or defend) myself; not only to her, but to the demons who were influencing her to attack me.

Therefore, I acted as if she wasn't even talking to me; the conversation hadn't even taken place. And just as soon as she had finished talking, one of our co-workers walked up and just started talking to us – interrupting what was supposed to be a conversation. And I just walked away.

I can't begin to tell you how angry I was at the thought of her suggesting that I should've done more than what I'd done to "help her" through *whatever* difficult time she experienced. Leah and Tiffany had only known each other for all of a couple of months. So, I'm not really sure of what *"difficult time"* she experienced.

But what angered me even more was her saying, 'you let me down,' because again, that's something she got from Tiffany. That's right. One day Tiffany called and told me that Viola had attempted to commit suicide. And consequently *Tiffany* said, "Her Pastor let her down."

I told Tiffany, "You can't say, 'Her Pastor let her down,' because you don't know what was going on between her and her Pastor. You don't even know if she had a relationship with her Pastor."

"You're right," she acknowledged.

And now, Leah was saying that exact same thing to me, *"You let me down,"* which no doubt, she'd gotten from Tiffany (because she told me Tiffany had told her about Viola as well).

In the garden...

~ YOU DIDN'T PREPARE ME FOR THE RIGHT BATTLE ~

Yet again, you guessed it, after prayer, from out of nowhere, Leah said, "You failed me."

"What do you mean, 'I failed you'?" I asked puzzled.

"You weren't there to support me while I was going through. When I was being attacked by Henry, I didn't even know that I was being attacked until Ms. Sonja said I was being attacked. She was the one that brought it to my attention that I was in spiritual warfare. She was the one that told me that ever since I'd been reading my daily scriptures for spiritual warfare, the enemy was now attacking me."

Not only was I being attacked yet again, but the attacks were so frequent that it was really extremely difficult (and getting more and more difficult) for me to *hold my peace.* In my mind, I still just wanted to rebuke that devil and be done! But I knew that wasn't going to allow me to be victorious. So again, I stood there while she accused and attacked me.

Then I responded, "In spite of me encouraging you not to give in to Henry's attacks, you're telling me that I didn't support you? And in spite of me telling you that the enemy was using him to attack you because of your deliverance, you weren't aware that you were being attacked? I encouraged you *every – day, all – day,* not to give in to his attacks."

"You didn't support me!" she said. "And not only that, but you encouraged me to turn my back on my friends from that lifestyle."

"No," I said as a matter of fact, "I encouraged you to get *yourself* together *first, then* go back when you were strong enough."

"Nah, you encouraged me to turn my back on them. I know what you said! That doesn't make sense! I should've been showing the love of Jesus to these people; letting my light shine."

Okay, "Tiffany," I thought. The *"let your light shine"* issue, again. In spite of me telling her that she wasn't prepared to go back into that environment, she was telling me basically, because *Tiffany said* she should've been *"letting her light shine,"* then she should've been letting her light shine. *I was infuriated with that devil!* "Leah, how are you going to let your light shine and you don't even *have* a light; you're still *struggling* with your deliverance. How are you going to go and 'let your light shine'?" I said as a matter of fact. It was very challenging, difficult to say the least, for me to stand there and see how the enemy had continuously used Tiffany to deceive, manipulate Leah, time and time again, by misleading her. And it reminded me of Eve:

And the LORD **God said unto the woman, "What is this that thou hast done?" And the woman said, "The serpent beguiled me, and I did eat."**

Genesis 3:13 KJV

The enemy was only able to beguile (trick, mislead, or deceive) Eve because she wanted what he had tempted her with; she saw that the tree was beautiful and its fruit looked delicious, and she wanted the wisdom *she thought* it would give her – she wanted to be like God, knowing good and evil.

And it was no different with Leah; she wanted what she *thought* Tiffany had – knowledge. She saw what she *perceived* as Tiffany being mature in the spirit, but she had no idea that Tiffany was operating in a spirit of divination. They both had been deceived and was being used by Satan.

Her words interrupted my thought as she continued, "Well, you didn't prepare me for the right battle. You should've prepared me to handle it all," she continued.

"Leah, you couldn't handle it all. How are you going to get delivered one day and just go back into that environment the next, talking about 'Jesus this or Jesus that'? They don't want to hear that."

"There you go again judging people! You don't know if they want to hear that or not!"

Now, I have to say, at that point, I was like King David:

I said, "I will watch my ways and keep my tongue from sin; I will put a muzzle on my mouth as long as the wicked are in my presence." But when I was silent and still, not even saying anything good, my anguish increased. My heart grew hot within me, and as I meditated, the fire burned; then I spoke with my tongue:"

Psalm 39:1 – 3 NIV

"Let me tell you something! If I don't know anything else, I know deliverance! I've been doing deliverance for a very long time, and I *know* what you are capable…"

"Hold your peace," the Lord said. I was done!

"You didn't prepare me for the right battle because *that's* my struggle."

So, there you have it. This wasn't about her going back into that environment to "let her light shine." She was struggling with her deliverance and wanted to go back into that environment to satisfy her flesh; she wanted to have sex. I just stood there as her words tugged at my heart as a cry for help. *But I couldn't help her.*

"You prepared me for the wrong battle because now that's my struggle. I'm struggling with wanting to go back into that environment, but I turned my back on them. And with that lifestyle, once you turn your back on them, there is no going back," she said.

As I stood there, my heart was overwhelmed. And to see her struggling, broke my heart into a million pieces as her cry for help pierced my ears. I wanted desperately to see her healed, delivered, and set free. My mind raced to try to figure out how we'd gotten to this place; it was clear she was struggling with her deliverance. "Once you're strong enough," I said with conviction, "the Lord will send you back."

"There is no going back! You don't get it!" she screamed.

"That's the world's way; that's not how the Lord operates," I said to try to reason with her.

"You don't understand. That's what I'm dealing with right now!"

I stood there.

No one understood better than I. My tears beheld my heart's pain.

I was reminded of the children of Israel and their plight with deliverance as well:

It so happened that after Pharaoh released the people, God didn't lead them by the road through the land of the Philistines, which was the shortest route, for God thought, "If the people encounter war, they'll change their minds and go back to Egypt."

Exodus 13:17 (The Message Bible)

While it was clear that the Lord had delivered the children of Israel from Egypt, it was also clear that they weren't prepared *mentally* to encounter war or any challenges; otherwise, like the Lord thought, *they'd change their minds and want to go back to Egypt.* So to avoid facing any challenges or having to go to war with the Philistines (even though this would've been the faster route), the Lord took them the longer route. Otherwise, the Philistines would've killed them. Therefore, while the Lord had taken them the longer route, He knew they would get there – without any challenges.

Well, the same held true for Leah. In the bible, *Egypt* represents the world. And although she had been delivered from Egypt (homosexuality; a worldly lifestyle), she wasn't *mentally* prepared to go back into that environment, otherwise, if she would've encountered any challenges, temptations; someone to entice her, *she would've changed her mind and gone back into that lifestyle.* Obviously, Tiffany didn't know *that* when she told her to let her light shine. So to keep her from facing any challenges, any temptations, the Lord took her the longer route. Otherwise, she'd face a situation that she wasn't prepared to fight; and there would be no way she would win – she'd surely be defeated. And while He had taken her the longer route, He knew she would get there – without any challenges or temptations – ***had she decided to continue the deliverance process.***

But somehow she thought, by being influenced by Tiffany of course, that because she hadn't "let her light shine" that *I hadn't prepared her for the "right" battle* or that I hadn't prepared her to handle it all.

The issue wasn't that *I* hadn't *prepared* her for the *right* battle; the issue was that she wasn't *fighting* the *right* battle. She was trying to fight the battle that *Tiffany* had encouraged her to fight; "let your light shine" instead of *preparing mentally* with prayer, bible study, spending time with the Lord, and meditating on the scriptures that I had given her as her *weapons* to *fight* with. And now she was facing a challenge that surely *there was no way that she was going to win.*

Her defeat was imminent.

What she failed to realize, and I tried to teach her, was that the battle was in her mind. And if she wasn't prepared mentally, she'd change her mind and go back into that lifestyle, which is exactly what she was struggling with – wanting to go back into that environment. And now she was left to fight the battle on her own.

I wanted desperately to help her, but there was nothing I could do. This was *her* battle to fight. It was her decision not to continue with the deliverance process. And as I shared with her after the deliverance session, there was a ***war*** going on between her flesh and her spirit (and the victor in her life would depend on which she succumbed to), the Spirit or the enemy (the flesh). She was now being controlled by demonic forces, which was evident by her struggle to want to go back into that environment and by the many attacks that I'd endured at her hands. And it was heartrending that the enemy was able to deceive her into thinking that *I hadn't prepared her for the right battle.*

Unfortunately, because she turned her back on God after He delivered her from the hand of the enemy, unlike the children of Israel, she was about to encounter the *Philistines;* war – the enemy – and her defeat was certain.

My heart was grieved.

Day and night your hand of discipline was heavy on me. My strength evaporated like water in the summer heat.

Psalms 32:4 NLT

In the garden...

~ A LOSING BATTLE ~

One day after I had prayed, Leah and I were talking when it became apparent that she was disturbed about something. Immediately, I knew something wasn't right. And when I asked her about it, she said that she couldn't talk to me about it at work, which confirmed my suspicion. So that night when I got home, I called her to see what was going on. (Calling her wasn't something that I normally did because we were together all day at work; we'd text if something came up after work.) Anyway, when she answered the phone, immediately, I could hear the distress in her voice as she struggled to tell me what was going on. So I encouraged her until she was able to tell me.

"I sacrificed my celibacy," she managed.

Immediately, I was reminded of the dream the Lord had revealed to me months earlier:

In a dream...

I saw Leah on the toilet defecating. Then I noticed that she had a handful of feces and she was putting it in her purse (as if she was trying to save it).

Then she started eating it.

As I stood there watching, I said to myself, I'm not going to just stand here and watch her do this.

Then I tried to stop her from eating it.

Then I woke up.

The interpretation...

The Lord revealed that the dream was a reflection of Leah's decision to get involved with Sanford (a supervisor that we worked with).

Being involved with Sanford was the same as her defecating and then eating it.

Basically, she'd be eating the waste that she'd spent years getting rid of by being celibate.

And now she was trying to hold on to it, which indicated she wanted it.

As a dog returns to its vomit, so a fool repeats his foolishness.

Proverbs 26:11 NLT

Immediately, great disappointment came over me as my heart was deeply saddened by her deafening revelation. It felt like someone had pinned me down, as the weight of her words was so heavy, and I wasn't able to move. I sat there, frozen in my spirit. While at the same time, I tried desperately to keep her from knowing the great disappointment that had overtaken me. I was extremely distressed by the fact that after many attempts, Satan had finally succeeded; she hadn't heeded the warning that God had given her, even though I shared the dream with her months ago. I explained to her that God said, "You getting involved with Sanford is like you making a bowel movement and then eating it." But she wanted it.

My spirit was profoundly grieved.

The enemy had dealt me yet another devastating blow; the wind had been knocked out of me. And in an attempt to get myself together, it was very difficult to gather my words to respond. So the only thing I was able to say was, "What did you say?" as if the first time she said it wasn't devastating enough.

My spirit cried out for God *Oh, God!* She had lost the battle that she'd been fighting for a very long time; years. And immediately, the tears rushed to the surface waiting to be released, but I fought to keep them back. I was hurt and devastated as if *I* had fallen into sin. I wanted nothing more than to hang up the phone and just be in the Lord's presence. The enemy had not only attacked her, but it was an attack against me as well because I was her spiritual leader; I was the one praying and interceding for her and encouraging her not to give in. And because I had been covering her it caused me to be subject to the enemy's attacks, for helping her.

"Was it in the area that you were delivered in?" I asked even though the Lord had just revealed to me who it was with. But I had no idea what to say; it was very difficult gathering my words.

"No. I thought the other way would be better."

"They're one and the same; sin is sin," I said as I sat there lost for words. There was no need for her to try to explain because the Lord had already revealed in the dream what was really in her heart; she wanted it. And her intense struggle with wanting to go back into the homosexual environment was just the boiling point, Satan turning up the heat. But that didn't stop the pain of me knowing that she had *lost the battle.* And without permission, the tears rolled down my face as my heart broke at her defeat.

The thought of what she'd sacrificed, after all that she'd been through, *for a man that cared absolutely nothing about her made me sick to my stomach.* The tears continued to just roll down my face. I did everything I could to keep her from knowing how devastated I was at the fact that the enemy had gotten the victory over her. She had been defeated; defeated *after* the Lord had delivered her and had given her the victory.

"What happened, My Love?" I managed.

As I sat listening to her explain, the tears continued to roll down my face. I was very careful to allow her to say what she felt she had to say in an attempt to get it off her chest and acknowledge what she had done. No one knew better than I how challenging this temptation had been for her, and after *all* that she'd been through, she had fallen.

Sacrifice – but no reward.

And I wanted desperately to hang up the phone and just cry out to God for her. I anxiously hoped this was just a cruel joke, so she could see if I *really* cared about her well-being; she was going to say that she was only testing me to see how I'd react, but that wasn't the case. My heart was overwhelmed with sorrow to know that *now* she would have to face the consequences of her actions. In spite of the many times I had warned her about the importance of maintaining her deliverance:

When an evil spirit leaves a person, it goes into the desert, seeking rest but finding none. Then it says, 'I will return to the person I came from.' So it returns and finds its former home empty, swept, and in order. <u>Then the spirit finds seven other spirits more evil than itself, and they all enter the person and live there. And so that person is worse off than before.</u>"

Matthew 12:43 – 45b NLT (emphasis added)

She had gotten delivered, but had failed to fill her life with the things of God; His word, and His Holy Spirit, which left room for the demons to come back. And not only had they come back, but seven times worse than before she had gotten delivered.

"Well, Daiz," she said as she continued to struggle to face what she had done. "I have been falling out of fellowship with the Lord for a while now." (*A while* turned out to be shortly after she was baptized and shortly after Tiffany had left the ministry). "I don't want you to think that you have to help me through this because this was my mistake, and I'll just have to get through it."

"The reason I'm here is to help you carry your burdens," I said.

"I'll be all right. I know that I'll have to pay the price for my sin; I made the mistake, so I'll suffer the consequences. I don't want you to think that you need to help me through this."

Immediately, I was disturbed in my spirit as I wondered *what kind of response was that?* I had become concerned because of what she was saying. While it was clear that she had struggled to tell me what happened, *there wasn't any remorse.* I thought, *who says, 'I've sinned, but you don't have to help me – I'll get through it'? Who says that?* Anyway, I sat there as my spirit had now become concerned for a different reason. I continued to listen. I decided that I didn't want to hear the details because the Lord had already revealed *why* it happened. And surely, she didn't have to say who she'd been intimate with because the Lord had revealed that as well.

"My Love, I'm sorry this has happened," I said. "But what's important at this point is that you repent…"

"It just happened," she interrupted obviously feeling the need to explain.

And through the tears that continued to stream down my face, which caused me to keep putting my phone on mute so she couldn't hear me, I said, "This didn't just happen. You allowed it to happen. You knew when the call came, it was going to happen."

Aside from what she was saying and what the Lord had revealed in the dream, *we were under attack.* But we were going to get through this, so again, I asked her if she had repented.

"I haven't because I'm trying to wrap my mind around what has happened and how it happened."

"The first step of you getting back in right standing with God is that you have to repent. And until you repent, you'll be separated from Him – because our sin separates us from God."

"Well, before I repent, I want to make sure that my heart is in the right place. I don't want to just be repenting and not mean it. I want to make sure I mean it. And until I'm able to wrap my mind around what happened, I don't think that my repentance would be sincere."

As if a grenade had gone off in my spirit, her response was just as devastating as her admission of *falling into sin.* Clearly, the enemy had a strong hold of control on her and he was still present. He wasn't going to let her go. *She wasn't sorry for what she'd done.* Yes, I know she said she wanted to wrap her head around what had happened so that she could make sure when she repented it would be sincere; however, that was a trick of the enemy. Her trying to "wrap her head around what happened" was to keep her from repenting. She was deceived.

Anytime someone sins, immediately, the *spirit of conviction* comes and you're either convicted or you're not. The spiritual state that you're in would be the deciding factor of which you'd respond to. And because she *wasn't* convicted or remorseful I knew her spiritual state was worse off than *she* had realized. In spite of her spiritual state, I assured her that we'd get through this together.

After we disconnected the call, and because I had become so burdened, immediately, I fell to my knees and cried out for the Lord to help her! I was so devastated; the spiritual warfare, all of the attacks, and now this devastating blow. And as I laid prostrate before the Lord, the only thing I could do was cry. I wasn't even able to pray – for her or myself – I was so devastated. Tired and drained spiritually and emotionally, I just went to bed knowing everything would be okay in the morning. However, I was sadly mistaken. My spirit was still grieved and immediately the tears that had been held back the night before surfaced when I thought about what happened.

I contemplated not going to work because I couldn't seem to get myself together; I couldn't stop crying. But I knew I had to press on. So I went to work and tried desperately to focus and just get on with my day, but I was unsuccessful. So I called one of the young ladies that was a part of the prayer group to come and pray for me. When she came over, the flood of tears burst forth as I tried to explain to her that I needed prayer. My spirit was overwhelmed, grieved, and greatly distressed. Immediately, she prayed for me and I just let the tears flow. By the time she finished praying, the burden had been somewhat lifted (at least to the point where I could go back to work and make it through the day).

The next day, Leah didn't come to work. However, I called her to check on her and to try to get her to see the importance of her repenting. I also explained to her how concerned I was about her spiritual state, which was reflected in her "falling out of fellowship with the Lord for a while" and her not repenting.

"I'm okay. I'm just tired," she answered.

"I'm sure you are. You're in a spiritual war." And again, I tried explaining the importance of her repenting. "Even if you came to prayer, bible study, and/or praise and worship, the Lord wouldn't respond to you until you've repented. Are you sorry for what you've done?"

"I don't know."

Oh, my God, Lord, please help me get through to her, I thought. "What do you mean, 'you don't know,' either you are or you aren't."

"I told you, I'm trying to wrap my head around what happened so that I can understand and be able to move forward from there."

"Leah. There is no 'wrapping your head around what happened.' You know what happened, and either you're sorry that you allowed it to happen or you're not."

"I don't know. I haven't made a decision yet about what I'm going to do."

"You 'haven't made a decision yet about what you're going to do'? Either you want to repent and get back in right standing with the Lord or you don't. What decision is there to make?" And immediately, I was prompted in my spirit that she doesn't *want* to live for the Lord. So I asked her, "Do you *want* to live for the Lord?"

"I don't know."

"You don't know? What do you mean?"

"Well. I want to live for the Lord, but I don't know if I want to repent because I liked it; it felt good. I'm just being honest – I liked it. And I think I want to continue in what I'm doing."

Oh, God, help me get through to her, I prayed. "Of course your flesh liked it. But you know that you can't live this way and serve God. You can't live for God and continue to live in sin. Either you're going to live for God or you're going to stay in the mess that you're in."

"How is it that there are people in the church who live this way?"

"I don't know one Pastor who stands in the pulpit and allows this type of behavior. People who actively participate in sin (and don't repent) are separated from God, whether they attend church or not. But if this is how you want to live, then you go right ahead – that's your choice."

"I just haven't made a decision."

"Well, you need to make a decision. Because whether you know it or not, the longer you take to decide – you've made a decision. *No decision is a decision.*"

"I don't know, Daiz."

"Okay. Then you decide."

If she thought that she was going to be able to continue to live in sin; sexual sin – fornication *and* live for God, she was sadly mistaken. Her sin separated her from God and until she repented, she'd remain separated. Now, obviously, we know there are people *in* the church who are involved in sexual sin; fornication, adultery, or otherwise. However, anyone who is actively involved in sexual sin (or any other sin), go to church, and *think* you're worshiping a Holy God, and *think* that's okay; they're deceived. God will not be mocked.

Be not deceived; God is not mocked: for whatever a man soweth, that shall he also reap.

Galatians 6:7 KJV

Obviously, we've become confused and have lost sight of the purpose of the church. Don't be fooled by those who try to excuse their sin, for the anger of God will fall on all who disobey Him. The church, God's holy presence, is there to expose your sin – not to "cover it up."

Be sure your sin will find you out.

That evening when Leah came to bible study, she was low-spirited, depressing, and it grieved my spirit to just be around her. The manifestation of the sin was revealed in her face; her facial appearance had become darkened, gloomy, heavy – deadly. And as if the demons were taunting me, it was very difficult for me to look at her in that state. I had no authority to rebuke the demons; she had given them legal right to be there by having sex. Therefore, after bible study, we prayed for her and asked the Lord to stay the hand of the enemy so that she could repent and live for the Lord. However, after several days of unsuccessful attempts to get her to repent, like the apostle Paul said – I handed her over to Satan so that her sinful nature would be destroyed; in an attempt to get her to come back to God.

I can hardly believe the report about the sexual immorality going on among you – something that even pagans don't do. I am told that a man in your church is living in sin with his stepmother. You are so proud of yourselves, but you should be mourning in sorrow and shame. And you should remove this man from your fellowship.

Even though I am not with you in person, I am with you in Spirit. And as though I were there, I have already passed judgment on this man in the name of the Lord Jesus. You must call a meeting of the church. I will be present with you in spirit, and so will the power of our Lord Jesus. <u>Then you must throw this man out and hand him over to Satan so that his sinful nature will be destroyed and he himself will be saved on the day the Lord returns.</u> Your boasting about this is terrible.

1 Corinthians 5:1 – 6a NLT (emphasis added)

As a result of her not repenting, I informed her that the prayer time during lunch was cancelled. And consequently, I had limited interaction with her during bible study and praise and worship. There was no texting or communicating during or after work. But I continued to pray for her and pleaded with the Lord that He'd deliver her.

When I wrote to you before, I told you not to associate with people who indulge in sexual sin. But I wasn't talking about unbelievers who indulge in sexual sin, or are greedy, or cheat people, or worship idols. You would have to leave this world to avoid people like that. <u>I meant that you are not to associate with anyone who claims to be a believer yet indulges in sexual sin,</u> or is greedy, or worships idols, or is abusive, or is a drunkard, or cheats people. Don't even eat with such people.

1 Corinthians 5:9 – 11 NLT (emphasis added)

It isn't my responsibility to judge outsiders, <u>but it certainly is your responsibility to judge those inside the church who are sinning.</u> God will judge those on the outside, but as the Scriptures say, "You must remove the evil person from among you."

1 Corinthians 5:12 – 13 NLT (emphasis added)

I couldn't help but think about what was going on. I'm not sure if there were *really* any words to describe how devastated I was. My heart was heavy and my spirit grieved. I was overwhelmed. But I knew it had to be done. Then the Lord began to minister to me that Leah was walking in *spiritual pride.* To have sinned against God and yet say, 'I liked it,' 'I think I want to continue to live this way,' is prideful. Just as the above scripture states: *you are so proud of yourself, but you should be mourning in sorrow and shame.*

Her behavior had to be disciplined; otherwise, left unchecked would divide the ministry. It couldn't be ignored – deliberately sinned, felt no remorse, and wouldn't repent – couldn't be tolerated. There was no 'wrapping her head around what happened.' Either she'd repent or she wouldn't.

I (Pastor Randolph and I) have a responsibility to other believers.

SO I TURNED HER OVER TO SATAN.

"Why don't people say to God, 'I have sinned, but I will sin no more'?

Job 34:31 NLT

~ YOU WEREN'T THERE WHEN I NEEDED YOU ~

As a result of Leah not repenting, our relationship was strained for several weeks. Then one day, she came to me and asked if she could talk to me. Needless to say, I wasn't going to tolerate her thinking that it was okay to continue sinning and not repent. Initially, I was hesitant because I figured the conversation would be pretty much the same as they'd been in the past. However, she expressed how it was *important* for her to speak with me. Therefore, I wondered if she had repented and wanted to share the news with me.

When she started the conversation, I could not believe it, she brought up the same many conversations that we had already discussed time and time again in the past. Unfortunately for her, I told her that we'd already discussed those topics and they weren't up for discussion anymore; I was done! Only this time she said, "I just want to let you know that the reason I didn't tithe was because I thought you were trying to manipulate me."

"Let me tell you something," I said, "we, this ministry, doesn't want for anything. There is *nothing* that you can give to this ministry that would cause us to *need* your tithe. Your tithe is so that *you* can get blessed – not *us*," I said as a matter of fact.

"Well, that's how you made me feel. I felt like you were trying to manipulate me."

"Are you serious?" I said sarcastically. We were *not* going to have that discussion. I was washing my hands of her. But before I walked away I said, "Leah, let me apologize to you for anything that I've done to you. I'm sorry for *whatever* it is." I hadn't realized it but I had gotten kind of heated, and my voice was raised, but I continued. "I don't know what you want from me. What *do you* want from me? Every time I talk to you, it's something that *I* could've done, should've done, made you do, made you feel! What do you want from me?" Talking to her was sooo exhausting; the warfare was grueling.

"Well, I want to apologize to you too, for looking at you as *my mother*; for expecting unconditional love from you. Because it seems that right when I needed you the most, you weren't there for me."

Immediately, the power of her words caused the pain of my contractions to surface. As a result of the difficulty of turning her over to Satan, to try to win her back to the Lord, I had been laboring in prayer for her. '*When I needed you the most, you weren't there for me,*' rung out in my spirit. It took everything that I had within me to keep from just completely breaking down and crying right then and there, as her words struck like a hammer and broke my heart into a million pieces. "Whether you know it or not," I said as my voice cracked and I struggled to keep it together, "I'm here for you more than you'll *ever* know." And as I stood there, her words *'for looking at you as my mother, for expecting unconditional love from you,'* pierced my spirit and pulled on my heart strings, which caused it to shatter. I knew the pain that she was in because the enemy had control over her. I grabbed her and hugged her as I fought back the tears to keep from crying.

However, that wasn't the case when I got in the presence of the Lord. I laid before Him and cried out for her; asking Him to have mercy on her. And the realization of her now being in Satan's hands was *too painful* for me to bear. And it was that much more heart breaking to know that *I* had *handed* her over to him. But I was done!

I continued to labor in prayer for her.

A few days later, Pastor Randolph and I were talking when my phone beeped to signal I had a text message. I looked at the phone. The message was from Leah:

"Daisy, I need you. I am seeking deliverance and I need your help."

And sure enough, that which I had dreaded the most had happened – she was in Satan's hands; she had to suffer the consequences of her actions. And true to the very words that *she* spoke, *she would have to fight this fight on her own; without my help.*

Unable to respond to the text, my legs began to give way, weakened by the thought of the torment she was enduring. I held onto the counter to keep myself from falling as I cried out to the Lord, "Nooo, Lord." Surely, I couldn't take anything else. The weight of the attacks had become too much, which was evident as the tears began to fall from my eyes. I cried out to the Lord, "Pleeease, release me from this assignment! I've had enough! Please, Lord, let this cup pass from me! I can't do this! And just as if *I* were being tormented, the pain was excruciating.

Why wouldn't she just repent? My heart cried.

The Lord was silent.

In the garden...

~ MY NEEDS AREN'T BEING MET ~

In spite of all that we were going through, apparently, it wasn't enough.

One day Leah said, "Do you think Pastor can teach on something else, I don't feel like my needs are being met…."

Immediately, I could hear Tiffany saying this very same thing when she left the ministry. And I was reminded of an email that Tiffany had sent during the Morning Glory. The email was asking (indirectly) why would you stay somewhere if your needs aren't being met. And it was almost as if she was encouraging the person to leave. Consequently, I responded to the email several times asking her what she meant by the email, but she never did respond. Now, it made sense.

Leah continued, "I need to be taught life application stuff that will help me with everyday life."

"Life application, like what?" I asked, hoping my frustration hadn't come through in the tone of my voice.

"You know, like how to handle a man that's interested in me; things like that." So apparently, *all* of the conversations that *we* had in the past regarding this were no longer relevant.

"I understand. But I would encourage you to focus on your relationship with Christ. Pastor doesn't just decide what he wants to teach in bible study. He teaches based on what the Lord tells him to teach, which speaks to you learning the foundation of your faith; not only who you believe in, but why."

"I understand that, but sometimes I just find it difficult for me to handle the challenges that I face in life and I know I need some help in these areas."

"I know. But he teaches based on what the Lord tells him to…"

"I know the Lord dictates what you teach," she interrupted. "I'm just wondering if you can teach me this to help me, and then we can go back to the teaching."

Immediately, I discerned her need for "life application" was really a plea to *help her* get through the torment she was experiencing. But Pastor, life application, or I couldn't help her. Jesus was the only one who could help her at that point. And there was no one who understood more than I that she wanted "life application" and didn't want to hear about "Jesus." I also understood she wanted to deal with a *physical* need. But what she didn't know was that the answer to her *physical* need was *spiritual*.

This battle was **not** about stuff that would help her with everyday life. This battle was **not** about how to handle a man that's interested in her. This battle **was** about her relationship with Christ.

So I said, "I understand. But if you're paying attention in bible study, the teachings provide you with ***life application.*** Have you applied what you've been learning? It may not necessarily be what you want to hear, but it's what you need."

"Okay. I just thought I'd ask."

"I know."

Life application – you don't have sex if you're not married.

Life application – you repent when you have sex if you're not married.

By the time I made it home, she sent a text stating she had thought about what I said and realized that I was right.

~ SPIRITUAL DEPRESSION ~

My spirit had become so burdened, so heavy, that it was difficult for me to even get in the Lord's presence. It was a struggle everyday – all day – because of the warfare. "I cannot take any more, Lord. Please, help me!" I cried out. And there was nothing I could do to stop my spirit from seemingly, spiraling out of control, in a downward spiral. It was tearing me apart – my spirit was so grieved.

And the Lord was silent.

Then I was reminded of King David:

As the deer longs for streams of water, so I long for you, O God. I thirst for God, the living God. When can I go and stand before him?

"O God my rock," I cry, "Why have you forgotten me? Why must I wander around in grief, oppressed by my enemies?"

Why am I discouraged? Why is my heart so sad? I will put my hope in God! I will praise him again – my Savior and my God!

Psalm 42:1 – 2; 9; 11 NLT

I had become spiritually depressed. Overwhelmed by the hand of the enemy because of all the attacks; I was hard pressed on every side, crushed, perplexed, and in despair as I struggled to keep my eyes on God.

Day and night, the bread of tears and the cup of affliction were my portions.

I was deeply discouraged by the anguish of the warfare; like a raging sea, the agony and suffering swept over me.

I continued to press my way into His presence.

In the garden...

~ YOU'RE NOT READY ~

The next day at work Leah asked if I had received her text and wanted to know if I was ignoring her because she needed my help.

"Why do you need my help?" I asked.

"Because I'm struggling in certain areas and I know I need deliverance."

"What makes you think you need deliverance?"

"I can't shake the thoughts of what I've done. They just keep coming up and there's nothing I can do to stop them. I'm overwhelmed with the thoughts."

Of course I knew she was being tormented by the very demons that she had allowed back into her life. *These same demons that she took pleasure in and said, she liked, were now tormenting her.* But there was nothing I could do to help her. So I asked her, "What are you doing to help yourself?"

"I'm praying and reading my bible."

Of course you are, I thought. "Does this mean you've repented?"

"Why do you keep asking me that?!" she snapped as it was clear she was irritated.

"Because your sin has separated you from the Lord; therefore, until you repent, you shouldn't expect the Lord to do *anything* for you."

"Yes. I repented."

Of course she had, now that she was being tormented. And now she just wanted to be delivered, but that's not how deliverance works. Unfortunately, she was going to have to **suffer** the consequences of her actions. And until *she made the decision* that she wanted to live for Christ, she'd continue to suffer.

"What made you repent?" I asked curiously.

"I talked to Tiffany," she said, "because I wanted to know some things. And then I asked her if it were true that if someone sins, would they be separated from God. And she basically said yes."

Oh, you talked to Tiffany, I thought, *the witch who has control over you; the person who operates in a spirit of divination. Because 'she' said you'd be separated from God you repented. But I'm the one you come to for deliverance. What? Tiffany couldn't do deliverance and help you?*

Unfortunately, as I sat there, the Lord revealed that she still wasn't remorseful. She may have repented with her mouth but certainly not with her heart. And until she was *sorry* for what she had done, she would continue to **suffer,** she would continue to be tormented by the demons that she took pleasure in and had allowed back into her life.

"You're not ready for deliverance," I said. "You'll have to continue to pray and the Lord will bring forth deliverance *when you're ready.*"

"Okay. I understand."

And we walked away.

In the garden...

~ THE SPIRIT OF DIVISION CALLED OUT ~

We used what we called the "Morning Glory" as a vehicle to send encouraging words and scriptures (via email) to one another. (Tiffany was no longer a part of the ministry, but continued to be encouraged by the daily emails.) So, the next morning, after speaking with Leah, during our Morning Glory, it appeared that Tiffany's email was speaking directly to Leah's issue. Consequently, I figured Tiffany knew about Leah's struggle. But I didn't want Tiffany using the Morning Glory to discuss it. Not only that, but it led me to believe that Leah had been discussing with Tiffany some of the things that Leah and I had talked about. So I went over to Leah and asked her about it.

"Have you been discussing with Tiffany the things that you and I have been talking about?"

"Tiffany knows more about my struggle than you do," she said as a matter of fact. "But to answer your question, I don't talk to Tiffany about you; and I don't talk to you about Tiffany." Immediately, I was taken aback. She was sharp and frank.

"Okay," I said, but not without being reminded that she's a liar. (Clearly, the email Tiffany sent reflected things that Leah and I had discussed). Not only that, but I was also concerned that she was still getting advice from Tiffany, who, at that point, still hadn't been in church for several months (since leaving our ministry).

So, as she was trained to do, she was back at home because her "gift" wasn't recognized. Therefore, she had no covering and was in a backslidden state. And with that in mind, I said, "Leah, you have to be careful who you're listening to, especially if they're not your spiritual leader."

"Okay," she said.

I walked away.

Shortly after talking to Leah, I went to pray during my lunch.

"There's a *spirit of division* present," the Lord said. So I started warring against the spirit of division; binding and loosing, declaring and decreeing, until the Lord had given me the victory.

And surely, victory had come.

As soon as I got back to my office, I received an email from Tiffany:

Hi, Everyone:

First, I want to say that I repent if I have offended anyone for any reason or have caused anyone to question anything that doesn't line up with God. I'm sorry.

My reason for this email is because I don't want it to be a situation where anyone is looking at me as an influence or to cause confusion. It is not in my heart to bring division. Mr. Randolph and Daisy, I want you guys to know that I respect you as Pastors and I also consider you as friends. I also want to bring to the light that Leah and I are also friends. I will NEVER tell Leah anything that will cause her to be confused. Leah has to make choices and seek God for herself. I would be a fool to come in between what God is telling her and what her leaders are telling her. Yes, there are things I may not agree with but that doesn't mean that I am in the wrong, Leah is in the wrong, or either of you because we don't agree. My experience and her experiences are totally different because we are on different levels with God. I have shared with her things and situations based on my experiences, and I am not in no form comparing them to hers. Yes, Leah has talked to me about certain things that she is experiencing, but I always encourage her and tell her the truth; to self-examine first. Please understand and discern the spirit I am operating out of. I mean no harm. I hope this email helps and clears some things up.

Let me first of all say, "The Lord never ceases to amaze me." When I received this email from Tiffany, I almost fell out of my seat! I could not believe (and unbeknownst to Tiffany) *that demon* had been exposed! ***The spirit of division had been called out and revealed itself!*** It was not by happenstance that she wrote that email – that devil had been called out! And of course, she *was* sent to cause division, which is what she'd been doing all along. Although she wasn't able to discern that the enemy had been using her, we, Pastor Randolph and I, were very much aware of it. Just as the Lord had revealed, the enemy had been using Tiffany to steal the word from Leah before it was able to take root in her heart, so that she couldn't believe. This hindered her faith and caused her to be deceived – *and created division within the ministry.*

And now I make one more appeal, my dear brothers and sisters. Watch out for people who cause divisions and upset people's faith by teaching things contrary to what you have been taught. Stay away from them. Such people are not serving Christ our Lord; they are serving their own personal interests. By smooth talk and glowing words they deceive innocent people.

Romans 16:17 – 18 NLT

It just broke my heart to see how the enemy had used Tiffany to cause division within the ministry. And it was also heartbreaking to see how Leah had been controlled and manipulated by that devil. And in spite of all of my many efforts to try to get Leah to see that Tiffany was in error, I was unsuccessful; *watch out for people who cause divisions and upset people's faith by teaching things contrary to what you have been taught.* Tiffany was just another strategy the enemy used to deceive Leah (just as he had done Eve in the Garden of Eden except he used *Tiffany* instead of *fruit*).

Consequently, it was evident that Tiffany was influencing Leah, which resulted in division among us. Influenced or somehow impressed that Tiffany called herself a prophetess and prophesied. But, what Leah didn't know was that Tiffany was operating under the influence of satanic powers. She herself didn't have a relationship with Christ; she wasn't connected to the Spirit. Therefore, Tiffany had become just like the yeast that spreads throughout the whole batch of dough and causes the whole batch to become corrupt. That demonic spirit transfers from one person to another and before you know it, the entire church is divided.

I am telling you this so no one will deceive you with well-crafted arguments.

Colossians 2:4 NLT

Now, there was no doubt in my mind that Leah was easily influenced because of their personalities, Tiffany's *perceived* maturity, and Leah's desire to have one foot in the church and the other in the world. Therefore, she was never really able to get access to the spiritual weapons that she needed to defeat the enemy: studying the word, prayer, reading the bible, and spending time with the Lord, which was the only way that she'd be able to combat being deceived by Tiffany's false teachings. And clearly, as the email stated: *Yes, there are things I may not agree with…* and *I have shared with her things and situations based on my experiences…* these conversations were disguised as well-crafted arguments that helped to sway the demonic influence that was in operation.

If people are causing divisions among you, give a first and second warning. After that, have nothing more to do with them. For people like that have turned away from the truth, and their own sins condemn them.

Titus 3:10 – 11 NLT

Again, as the email revealed, Leah and Tiffany *had been* discussing me **and** the ministry. Anyway, now that the Lord had exposed *them,* the demonic activity, I was amazed and maybe even in shock at the fact that Tiffany mentioned in her email – *I hope this email helps and clears some things up.* It absolutely did! It confirmed everything that I already knew.

However, after receiving the email, I asked Leah if she had seen the email that Tiffany had sent, but of course, she played crazy and said, "No." So I printed the email and gave it to her to read as she stood in my office. You see, the issue I had with Leah that was revealed in the email was Tiffany stated, *I don't want it to be a situation where anyone is looking at me as an influence or to cause confusion.* Based on that statement alone, I knew Leah had told Tiffany what I said. "Did you tell Tiffany what I said?" I asked.

"Said about what?" she responded. Immediately, I knew she was playing crazy because she was caught in her lie. Needless to say, she didn't have to admit it because the email had already confirmed that she *had.*

"Did you tell Tiffany that I said, 'You have to be careful who you're listening to; especially if they're not your spiritual leader?"

Initially, she tried to divert the conversation by trying to draw my attention to something else that Tiffany said in the email. But I confronted her again. "You ran and told Tiffany what I said, which is why Tiffany wrote this email! *You* are the one that has been stirring up this mess. I specifically asked you if you had discussed with Tiffany what you and I had been talking about, and you sat there and **lied to my face** saying, *'I don't talk to you about Tiffany, and I don't talk to Tiffany about you.'*"

"That's not true."

"What's not true?"

"I didn't *run* and tell Tiffany." I could see that lying demon squirming, because she was being exposed; caught in her lie. It took everything that I had in me not to strangle this girl because she was playing word games.

"Just because you didn't *run* and tell her doesn't mean you didn't tell her! Whether you ran or you walked, you told Tiffany what I said."

"What you said about what?" she said as she pretended to be confused about the conversation.

"Leah!" I said with exhaustion. "Did you tell Tiffany that I said 'you have to be careful who you're listening to, especially if it's not your spiritual leader'?"

"Yeah, I said that, but I didn't say the other part."

"What other part?"

"I told her that you said, 'I have to be careful of who I'm listening to.'"

"But you didn't say that I said, 'especially if it's not your spiritual leader'?"

"No. I didn't say that."

And immediately I knew when she said that, she meant it in a malicious way, which is why Tiffany wrote: *I will NEVER tell Leah anything that will cause her to be confused...I would be a fool to come in between what God is telling her and what her leaders are telling her.*

"But Daisy, if you look at the email, what is she talking about when she said, *"Yes, there are things I may not agree with but that doesn't mean that I am in the wrong, Leah is in the wrong, or either of you because we don't agree."*

Of course I recognized the *spirit of manipulation.* She was trying to change the subject in order to get the spot light off of her; lying and maliciously gossiping.

"This isn't about Tiffany. It's about you maliciously twisting what I said. I have no idea what she's talking about in the email and I don't care. Whatever it is, she had plenty of time to come and talk to me about it. I don't have time to try and figure out what you and Tiffany are sitting up discussing about me."

However, I have to say, I was reminded of Miriam and Aaron when they didn't *"agree"* with Moses:

While they were at Hazeroth, Miriam and Aaron criticized Moses because he had married a Cushite woman. They said, "Has the LORD spoken only through Moses? Hasn't he spoken through us, too? But the LORD heard them. (Now Moses was very humble – more humble than any other person on earth.) So immediately the LORD called to Moses, Aaron, and Miriam and said, "Go out to the Tabernacle, all three of you!" So the three of them went to the Tabernacle. "Aaron and Miriam!" he called, and they stepped forward. And the LORD said to them, "Now listen to what I say:

"If there were prophets among you,
    I, the LORD, would reveal myself in visions.
    I would speak to them in dreams.
But not with my servant Moses.
    Of all my house, he is the one I trust.
I speak to him face to face,
    clearly, and not in riddles!
    He sees the LORD as he is.
So why were you not afraid
    to criticize my servant Moses?"

The LORD was very angry with them, and he departed.

Numbers 12: 1 – 9 NLT (emphasis added)

Like Miriam and Aaron, the email revealed Tiffany had a *critical spirit*. You see, instead of Tiffany being able to face the real issue, her pride, rebellion, and deception, she resorted to criticizing me and the ministry. And who did she complain to? Leah. By her complaining to Leah, it allowed her to plant seeds of mistrust, doubt, and confusion in Leah. And once these seeds were planted, the spirits transferred, which attached themselves to Leah because she was open to receive the criticism – she believed it.

So these *"things* that she may not be in agreement with" weren't *really* about me or the ministry, they were really about her pride, rebellion, and deception. Because she couldn't have things her way, someone to recognize her gift as a prophetess, she resorted to criticism. And just like Miriam and Aaron, she too, thought, *hasn't he [the Lord] spoken through me, too?* Thereby, she was able to control Leah with her *well-crafted arguments*. By this time, Leah was very much deceived into thinking Tiffany was a prophetess, but I'm sure Tiffany did some persuading of her own to prove that the Lord spoke through her as well, and may have been prophesying to Leah by way of satanic powers.

"But Daisy, this isn't about you. Tiffany has her own issues with you that she didn't think that she could talk to you about," Leah said.

"Of course this is about me!" I assured her. "This is *my ministry* and *anything* that goes on in this ministry is about me! Let me tell you something! This isn't a game, this isn't high school, and it isn't a social club, this is *my ministry!* And I'm not going to tolerate this foolishness!" Needless to say, I was furious. But on the other hand, I was also relieved that the Lord had allowed all of this to come to the light. That way, neither of them would be able to deny what they had been doing in this ministry. It was clear that they had been sent to kill and destroy this ministry to keep it from advancing. But God said, "Not so!"

When I got home, I tried quieting my spirit before the Lord to see what the Lord was saying. As I sat before the Lord, everything played over and over in my mind. Then I was reminded of King David:

I said to myself, "I will watch what I do and not sin in what I say. I will hold my tongue when the ungodly are around me." But as I stood there in silence – not even speaking of good things – the turmoil within me grew worse. <u>*The more I thought about it, the hotter I got, igniting a fire of words:*</u>

Psalm 39:1 – 3 NLT (emphasis added)

I was furious with them. *One thing was certain – they are going to hear from me tomorrow,* I thought. *When I respond to that email, they are going to get to know me in a way that they have never known me before.* I was so mad!

"Hold your peace," the Lord said.

My heart was saddened.

But, of course, there must be divisions among you so that you who have God's approval will be recognized!

1 Corinthians 11:19 NLT

Consequently, the next day, I knew I had to at least accept Tiffany's apology because she had asked. So I simply responded:

My Love,

Your apology is accepted.

But the LORD stands beside me like a great warrior.

Before him my persecutors will stumble.

They cannot defeat me.

They will fail and be thoroughly humiliated.

Their dishonor will never be forgotten.

Jeremiah 20:11 NLT

~ BRAXTON HICKS ~

The hurt and the pain that I experienced had only been a rehearsal of the pain that was to come. Pain disguised as contractions. The contractions proved to be more about the preparation than it was about the pain. Birthing ministry, at that point, was like having Braxton Hicks. Those of you who've ever experienced being pregnant and going into labor may be familiar with Braxton Hicks.

Braxton Hicks are false labor pains.

The contraction is flexing the muscles that prepare you for the *true* labor pains. And as a result of the Braxton Hicks, it was just an opportunity for the Lord to flex His muscles to *prepare* me for true labor – *birthing ministry.* Consequently, He was showing me just how much I *could* take.

As He prepared me for the moment of true labor, the pain would then push me out of the womb and command me to accomplish my purpose and fulfill my destiny.

The pain would come and go; giving me just enough time to practice my breathing: Inhale; take it all in. Exhale; let it all out. Inhale; take it all in. Exhale; let it all out.

As the birthing process drew to its end, the contractions became more frequent, intense, and painful.

However, the pain alone was not enough to birth the ministry.

I had to push!

In the garden...

~ REPAIR THE BREACH ~

A couple of weeks had past and Leah had started missing days at work, as well as coming in then leaving early on other days, so I hadn't been seeing her much. One day I had taken off work and when I returned, one of my co-workers, Darnell, said, "You need to check on your girl because she came to work yesterday and she looked like crap!" I was reluctant to call her because I had to be careful not to get in the way of what the Lord was doing. But I called her.

"I'm calling to check on you. What's going on?" I asked.

"I'm in so much pain that I'm on the verge of going to the emergency room; it's too much for me to take," she said in a forced whisper.

Immediately, I became concerned. "What's wrong?" She explained the symptoms that she was experiencing but ultimately indicated she was going to be okay. "Okay. Well, I'll continue to check on you to see how you're doing," I said, which I did. The next day, she showed up for work and as usual, I checked on her, and was very attentive to her. And of course, for lunch, I prayed – specifically for Leah.

So he said he would destroy them – had not Moses, his chosen one, stood in the breach before him to keep his wrath from destroying them.

Psalm 106:23 NIV

My heart was continuously heavy concerning her; therefore, I started praying for her and asked the Lord to have mercy on her and to forgive her for her sins. I started declaring and decreeing her healing and restoration to wholeness. While I was praying, I heard my cell phone ring, but I ignored it. And as the tears rolled down my face, I did everything that I could to keep myself together because my heart was so heavy. So I continued to cry out to the Lord on her behalf.

As a result of turning her over to Satan, I knew there were a number of ways that the enemy would attack her as a result of her "suffering the consequences of her actions" – including sickness in her body, as he'd done with Job.

As I was praying, the Lord said, "Repair the breach."

But Moses tried to pacify the LORD his God. "O LORD!" he said. "Why are you so angry with your own people whom you brought from the land of Egypt with such great power and such a strong hand? Why let the Egyptians say, 'Their God rescued them with the evil intention of slaughtering them in the mountain and wiping them from the face of the earth'? Turn away from your fierce anger. Change your mind about this terrible disaster you have threatened against your people!"

Exodus 32:11 – 12 NIV

I pleaded with the Lord that He would have mercy on Leah and forgive her for her sins. I prayed that he would command the enemy to loose her and let her go! "Heal her, O Lord," I cried. I started to bind sickness and disease in her body and loosed healing, wholeness, and restoration. I continued declaring and decreeing on her behalf. I prayed that He'd release her from the hand of the enemy. I prayed and cried. I cried and prayed. I wanted desperately for the Lord to deliver her. "Prove Yourself to her!" I pleaded. "Let her see You in a way that she's never seen You before." I prayed until I couldn't pray anymore.

When I finished praying, I left the area. I walked around until I was able to get myself together to go back to work. As soon as I got back to my office, Sandra came running over and said, "I tried to call you. Leah needs to go to the emergency room, she's not doing well."

It took everything within me not to just completely break down. But without hesitation, I jumped up to go find her. My heart broke at the thought of what she was experiencing and I struggled to fight back the tears. *Lord, answer my prayer!* I pleaded in my spirit.

"She's out in her car," Sandra said.

So I went to go see about her.

"I tried calling you, but you didn't answer."

"I heard the phone, but didn't want to be disturbed while I was praying," I managed.

"When I walked by the prayer area I saw you there, but then when I came back to get you, you weren't there. And I didn't know what to do."

By the time we got to the car, Leah was getting out. And immediately, I could see that she had been crying as the attack on her body proved to be devastating. And she went on to say that she had called the hospital but there wasn't anything they could do to help her.

"Meet me in the bathroom," I demanded. "I'm going to get my oil, and I'm going to lay hands on you."

"I don't think that's going to help," she said.

"We're going to let the Lord be the judge of that! I'll meet you in the bathroom; I'm going to get my oil."

Dear brothers and sisters, if another believer is overcome by some sin, you who are godly should gently and humbly help that person back onto the right path. And be careful not to fall into the same temptation yourself. Share each other's burdens, and in this way obey the law of Christ.

Galatians 6:1 – 2 NLT

When we went into the bathroom, I laid hands on her and anointed her body with oil. I prayed over her and declared and decreed her healing. And later when I checked on her, she said that she felt one hundred percent better, as we laughed at Sandra saying she didn't know what to do!

And over the next few days I continued to be prayerful regarding her healing. And when she got the report back from the doctor, it confirmed that the Lord had moved in a mighty way. The report reflected that all of her vital signs had been reduced by half of that when she entered the hospital initially. And we thanked the Lord for her healing, as we rejoiced.

"In that day I will restore the fallen house of David. I will repair its damaged walls. From the ruins I will rebuild it and restore its former glory."

Amos 9:11 NLT

Consequently, she returned to prayer, and I was excited to see her; it did my heart good that she'd come. I grabbed her by the hand, wrapped it into mine, and we just started to walk (hand in hand) and prayed; just declaring the goodness of God. Then she started to share with me what she had experienced.

"You don't have to tell me what happened," I assured her.

"But I want to. I want you to know that after everything that I've been through, I've decided that I want to live for Jesus!" And we both rejoiced that she had made that decision; I was overjoyed! "I have to tell you," she continued, "when all of this started happening, I found myself in the deepest, darkest, black hole that I'd ever been in, in all of my life, and there was no way out. I thought I was going to die. I had come as close to death as I could get without dying. I knew I needed someone to help me because there was no way that I could make it on my own. So I went to look for help and before I knew anything, everything just spiraled out of control and I found myself in the midst of this whirlwind. But of course, I can't thank the Lord enough for you, and all that you've been to me and have done for me. And I knew there was no way I could've come through this if you hadn't come and helped me. And I know that I never want to experience that again."

I was so glad to hear that after all that she'd been through, the Lord was merciful and had stayed the hand of the enemy. And my spirit rejoiced at her declaration that she would *live for Jesus.* "But Daiz," she said. "I don't know why I had to go through all of that. I know I made a mistake by having sex, but I didn't think it was going to take all of that!"

"Well, I'm glad it took all of that because now you see the consequences of your actions, and you've now declared that you want to live for Jesus!"

"You're right about that! I thought I was going to die!"

"First and foremost, you had to make a decision of who you were going to serve," I explained. "Either you were going to repent and serve God or you would live in sin and serve Satan. And even though you'd been in the midst of bible study, prayer, and praise and worship, you weren't connected. And each day that you weren't connected, you were dying spiritually until eventually you *fail into sin.* When you chose not to repent, you were serving Satan. Therefore, the Lord allowed Satan to have his way with you – until you decided that you wanted to serve the Lord…"

"But I thought I did," she interrupted.

"You did with your mouth, but not with your heart. You were just going through the motion. And ultimately, because of your disobedience, you had to suffer the consequences of your actions. And even though the Lord revealed to me that you had "fallen out of fellowship" shortly after you were baptized and Tiffany left the ministry, *you* never said anything to me about "falling out of fellowship" in spite of me continuously asking you about your relationship with Christ. It was clear that you didn't want my help even though I continuously extended it to you. Therefore, the enemy was able to defeat you in the battle."

"Daiz, it just happened."

"No, it didn't. You allowed it to happen."

"I mean, I hadn't planned for it to hap…"

"Yes, you did," I interrupted.

"Let me tell you what happened."

"You don't have to tell me what happened or who it happened with because I already know."

"I want to tell you," she insisted. "I got a new telephone and I wanted to make sure the numbers were programmed correctly, so I accidentally hit his num…"

"It wasn't by accident."

"It was. I wasn't trying to see him. I was just trying to make sure my numbers were programmed correctly. And when I realized I had called him, I quickly hung up. Then he called me back."

"Leah. You knew when the call came in what was getting ready to happen. So don't try to tell me that it just happened. When the Lord revealed the dream to me months ago, it was revealed *then* that that's what you wanted."

"But I've been able to fight off this temptation for years prior to coming to know Christ. I just don't understand how I wasn't able to fight it off this time."

Allow me to explain. You see, just as with the children of Israel, the Lord's anger burned against them as a result of Him delivering them from Egypt, and yet they didn't trust him – but rather sinned against Him. Well, the same held true for Leah. The Lord had delivered her, and yet, she didn't trust Him, which ultimately caused her to sin against Him by having sex. In due course, when it came down to it, in spite of all that Leah and I had been through, her not heeding my instructions, not trusting me – it wasn't *really* about me – it was the Lord that she didn't trust. Who am I? It was Jesus that she was going against, rebelling against, not me. I was just the vessel He used – by His Spirit. It was useless for her to try to fight against His will.

"This wasn't something that you've been doing on your own," I said, "The Lord has had mercy on you all these years and has *kept* you. But because you became arrogant and filled with pride that *you* were doing this He had to show you that you weren't in control – He is. How many times have I said to you, 'don't underestimate the power of the enemy,' and you'd say, 'I got this! I've been doing this for a long time.'? You've been playing with fire, but it's been the Lord's grace and mercy that has kept you from getting burned." I said.

Jesus replied, "You hypocrites! Isaiah was right when he prophesied about you, for he wrote,
'These people honor me with their lips,
But their hearts are far from me."

And then he added, "It is what comes from inside that defiles you. For from within, out of a person's heart, come evil thoughts, sexual immorality, theft, murder, adultery, greed, wickedness, deceit, lustful desires, envy, slander, pride, and foolishness. All these vile things come from within; they are what defile you."

Mark 7:6; 20 – 23 NLT

In the dream, the Lord was also revealing the condition of her heart. *That's* what was in her heart. And as you can see, deliverance doesn't come to those whose heart is not towards God. Her "relationship" with God wasn't motivated by her wanting to be intimate with God, but rather it was motivated by her desire to "appear" to be holy, "appear" to be living a lifestyle of holiness. **But God is not mocked, that which she sowed to the flesh, she also reaped.** Her focus at some point had changed from *God* to *people (Tiffany);* where she appeared to pray, she appeared to praise and worship Him, and she appeared to study the Word while her heart was far from God.

~ SHOW ME YOUR GLORY ~

The following week, after all that we'd been through, I was expecting the Lord to show up in a great and mighty way in bible study to bring us all some relief. So prior to bible study, I started to set the atmosphere with praise, worship, prayer, and declaring the glory of the Lord. So when the praise and worship started, the Holy Spirit came in right away. We praised and worshiped Him as Leah took the liberty of singing a song to Him. And it didn't take long before I started crying as the Lord began to lift the weight of the battle that I'd been fighting. And before I knew anything, I was lying prostrate before the Lord as I allowed Him to have His way; repentance rung out in my spirit. I *was* sorry for anything that I had unknowingly done to hurt Leah. I was also godly sorrowful for the times I wanted to give up and not fight for her because the burden had become too much for me to bear.

As I continued to cry out before the Lord, I could hear other people were crying as well. I knew without a shadow of a doubt the Lord had moved mightily. As I was trying to get myself together, I looked up and saw Leah was also crying. She had taken a seated position on the floor as she hung over the couch, weeping. The spirit of repentance was in that place.

We just remained in the Lord's presence because the anointing was so heavy; we were unable to have bible study. For the entire time, the Lord just ministered to us in such a powerful way. He left us all in awe of His glory as His Holy Spirit came through the place like a whirlwind and knocked us all down on our faces in reverence and repentance.

As we continued to allow the Lord to have His way, I had somewhat gotten myself together and just sat in the Lord's presence. I watched Leah as my heart went out to her. To see her in a position of worship unto the Lord, just did my heart good. She had finally submitted. She wept as her tears were evidence that she was *sorry* for what she had done. And I thanked the Lord that He had moved in a such a mighty way in her life, especially after *all* that she'd been through.

She continued to weep before Him.

An hour after bible study would have normally been over, she was still crying before the Lord.

In a vision...

I had a baby in a carrying case strapped across my chest.

The interpretation…

I was carrying Leah.

He will feed his flock like a shepherd. He will carry the lambs in his arms, holding them close to his heart. He will gently lead the mother sheep with their young.

Isaiah 40:11 NLT

In the garden...

~ YOU SHOULDN'T PRAY ABOUT REBELLION ~

The next day at work, Leah came over and grabbed me, hugged me, and kissed me on the forehead. "I'm sorry for any hurt that I have caused you," she said. There was no doubt that the Lord had done a mighty work concerning her; concerning us.

"I'm sorry as well," I admitted as I hugged her back.

Finally! The Lord had turned this thing around. She had *finally* gotten on board, so now we could move forward with the ministry. And the glory of the Lord brought some relief – all was well as we continued to give Him the glory for what He had done.

A couple of weeks after the Lord's glory was revealed, while praying during lunch, I was prompted in my spirit to pray concerning rebellion. In fact, I had been *arrested* in my spirit to do so for several days. So, for several days, I prayed continuously regarding rebellion; binding and loosing, casting out and casting down the spirit of rebellion, declaring and decreeing obedience.

Then one day after prayer, Leah said, "Daisy, you shouldn't pray about rebellion because every time you pray about rebellion you make me think you're talking about me."

"Well, if you're convicted, then I *am* talking about you."

"But you shouldn't pray about rebellion. Instead of praying about rebellion, you should try to encourage me."

Oh, my God! What the devil! I thought. *No this devil ain't back up in here trying to tell me what I should pray!* "Leah, I pray what the Holy Spirit tells me to pray; I'm not just picking something out of the sky. So if you feel convicted when I pray about rebellion, you should repent and do something about it to change."

In the meantime, we had a meeting to go to, which cut the conversation short. However, when we got in the meeting, I tried to continue the conversation because if this was something she was dealing with, I wanted to assist her. "Okay," I said as we settled into the meeting, "so you feel convicted when I pray concerning rebellion..."

"I didn't say that," she said. *Oh, Lord, are you kidding me!* I thought as I looked at her in amazement. But I didn't push the issue because I realized it was the enemy trying to dictate to me what I should and shouldn't pray. So I left it alone.

In the garden...

~ SQUARE ONE ~

It had been about three weeks since we'd come together for bible study because Leah had been sick; attacked in her body. Therefore, Pastor Randolph thought it was a good time for her to recuperate and not have to worry about coming to bible study. So it was good to be back together on one accord praising the Lord. Now, this particular Wednesday, as I was worshiping, Leah came in and as always she prepared her son's dinner then came into the living room. She sat on the couch, opened her bible, and appeared to read. However, I continued to set the atmosphere by worshiping the Lord.

When bible study started, Pastor Randolph joined us. We started to worship the Lord and shortly into the worship, just as I had expected, the Lord came right in and suddenly I began to weep before Him.

His presence was overwhelming, I could hardly take it. His glory was simply too much for me; therefore, I continued to weep. Then the Lord started to minister to me.

"Square one," He said.

And immediately, I was overwhelmed with disappointment and wanted desperately to just give up – I had had enough! And surely, at this point, there really was no way that I could go through any of this, again! The attacks had proven to be far too difficult for me (even after I thought I had given it all that I had to give). I was exhausted! I felt as if someone had grabbed me by my ankles and just slammed my body up against a brick wall. Surely, like the apostle Paul, *I was poured out like a drink offering;* I was empty!

Consequently, I cried out for the Lord to *please have mercy* on me and help me. I was breaking under the weight of the attacks and I knew there was no way that I could go any further than I had already gone. My whole heart had been poured out. I mean, with everything that was within me – I wanted desperately to just lay hold of that devil and rebuke him! I could not *hold my peace* anymore. I could not be silent any longer. Even though I had no words to say – I just could not hold it together any longer. I needed the Lord to do whatever He was going to do because I was done!

My spirit was broken. Spiritually, physically, mentally, and emotionally – I was about to break! I had stood for as long as I could stand. The crushing blows that I'd endured time and time again at the hand of the enemy had proved to be far more devastating than anyone could imagine.

Inside, I had been torn apart and was finding it very difficult to hold it all together. I struggled to "repair the breach" as my own defenses had been torn down and destroyed.

And yet, my strongest defense was to *hold my peace.*

As I continued to weep before the Lord, He revealed that Leah's heart still wasn't in agreement with the ministry. We were in fact, still at *square one. After alllll that we'd been through*, I thought. I was devastated.

Then He revealed, He was about to expose her.

They have done nothing to repair the breaks in the walls around the nation. They have not helped it to stand firm in battle on the day of the LORD.

Ezekiel 13:5 NLT

He was about to expose her and reveal what was *really* in her heart. The neglected condition of her *temple* would reveal how far she had strayed from God.

Bless those who persecute you. Don't curse them; pray that God will bless them.

Romans 12:14 NLT

In the garden...

~ THIS IS YOUR MINISTRY ~

One day, Leah came to me and was telling me about a text message that Henry had shared with her. The text message was about marriage equality that went something like: *If you don't agree that marriage equality is okay and you eat shrimp, wear jeans, then you need to shut up.*

I laughed because immediately I could see that Henry was, of course, trying to defend his lifestyle of homosexuality and marriage equality. Basically, he was using the text message to say that people who think marriage equality is a sin and they eat shrimp or wear jeans they were also sinning – because the bible states you shouldn't eat shrimp or wear jeans. And therefore, no one could judge him because they were also sinning.

Unfortunately, Henry's understanding of these scriptures was in error.

"Of all the marine animals, you may eat whatever has both fins and scales. You may not, however, eat marine animals that do not have both fins and scales. They are ceremonially unclean for you.

Deuteronomy 14:9 – 10 NLT

"A woman must not put on men's clothing, and a man must not wear women's clothing. Anyone who does this is detestable in the sight of the LORD your God."

Deuteronomy 22:5 NLT

So right away, I said to Leah, "The scriptures that Henry's using are not used in their proper context and it's clear that Henry really has no idea what these scriptures mean. I explained the scriptures to her:

The food restrictions were to indicate unclean and unhealthy habits and were used to remind the Israelites that they were a chosen people, set apart for God. And the second verse simply states that men and women should not try to reverse their sexual roles. The man shouldn't dress as though he's a woman and the woman shouldn't dress as though she's a man. The scripture isn't talking about fashion.

Shortly after talking to Leah, Henry came over and commented about the text message. However, I shared with him that the scriptures didn't mean what he thought they meant, and shared the meaning with him.

"Don't you think that because society has changed that the laws in the Old Testament don't apply?" He asked.

"No, I don't think that. The laws in the Old Testament still apply. When Jesus came, He fulfilled the laws; He did not make the laws obsolete.

"Do not think that I have come to abolish the Law or the Prophets; I have not come to abolish them but to fulfill them."

Matthew 5:17 NIV

"Now, prior to Christ coming, when we sinned, we were punishable by the law under the Old Testament; however, we're now covered by His grace when we sin. But make no mistake," I said for clarity, "because we're under grace doesn't give us the right to sin. We're still accountable for our sin."

What shall we say, then? Shall we go on sinning so that grace may increase? By no means! We are those who have died to sin; how can we live in it any longer? Or don't you know that all of us who were baptized into Christ Jesus were baptized into his death?

Romans 6:1 – 3 NIV

"And just because someone supports marriage equality, that doesn't change the Word of God: Homosexuality is still a detestable sin and those who participate in it will be punished," I continued.

"I was born this way," he said.

"If that were the case, then it's a result of a generational curse that's in your blood line; in your family history," I said.

"Now may the Lord's strength be displayed, just as you have declared: 'The LORD is slow to anger, abounding in love and forgiving sin and rebellion. <u>Yet he does not leave the guilty unpunished; he punishes the children for the sin of the parents to the third and fourth generation.</u>' In accordance with your great love, forgive the sin of these people, just as you have pardoned them from the time they left Egypt until now."

Numbers 14:17 – 19 NIV (emphasis added)

"So, how is it that out of all of my brothers and sisters, I'm the only one that turned out this way?" he asked.

"You 'turned out that way' because you acted on it. You gave in to the temptation and now the enemy has a stronghold on you." Unfortunately, our conversation was interrupted and we weren't able to finish. Therefore, I told Henry I was going to send him some scriptures that would help him understand this lifestyle of homosexuality:

"Do not practice homosexuality, having sex with another man as with a woman. It is a detestable sin."

Leviticus 18:22 NLT

Yes, they knew God, but they wouldn't worship him as God or even give him thanks. And they began to think up foolish ideas of what God was like. As a result, their minds became dark and confused.

So God abandoned them to do whatever <u>shameful</u> things their hearts desired. As a result, <u>they did vile and degrading things with each other's bodies.</u>

That is why God abandoned them to their shameful desires. Even <u>the women turned against the natural way to have sex and instead indulged in sex with each other. And the men, instead of having normal sexual relations with women, burned with lust for each other.</u> Men did shameful things with other men, and as a result of this sin, they suffered within themselves the penalty they deserved. Since they thought it foolish to acknowledge God, he abandoned them to their foolish thinking and let them do things that should never be done.

Romans 1:21; 24; 26 – 28 NLT (emphasis added)

Now, I'd like to respond to his initial concern about *marriage equality* and the *Old Testament laws* no longer being applicable. So, since he thinks that the Old Testament is outdated, let's look at the *New Testament* to see what the Lord has to say:

"Haven't you read the Scriptures?" Jesus replied. "They record that from the beginning 'God made them male and female.' And he said, 'This explains why a man leaves his father and mother and is joined to his wife, and the two are united into one.' Since they are no longer two but one, let no one split apart what God has joined together."

Matthew 19:4 – 6 NLT

I believe the scriptures are self-explanatory regarding *"marriage equality."* **God made them male and female.** This explains why a man leaves his father and mother and is joined to his wife. Now I have to say that what I think is interesting is the fact that in most homosexual relationships that I've encountered (and I do have friends who live in this lifestyle), there is always one person who plays the male dominant role while the other individual plays the more submissive role – that of the woman. So even though they are the same sex (whether two men or two women), they know one is to be the husband and the other is to be the wife – *imitating* the roles of marriage that God established *"in the beginning"* as the scriptures state.

Now this is not to say that all same sex relationships are like that, but that is the case with the relationships that I've witnessed. And I'd also like to speak to the fact that Henry stated that he was born that way. Now, I have to say that I cannot discuss this topic without making mention that if he (or anyone else) says they were "born that way," they would be saying that homosexuality is not a *spiritual* issue, but rather a *biological* issue. And for God to create an individual "that way" and then call it sin, He would not be a *just* God. To create someone and then curse them, He would not be a righteous God.

The Bible, the above-mentioned scriptures, clearly state that "the two are united into one." What "two"? Male and female. Thereby, giving a clear indication that **anyone** *other than male and female* are not united into one – they remain separate – two individuals.

Now, for the most part, I believe the majority of the people understand the scripture is referring to *one* as *consummating the marriage – having sexual intercourse.* It is the consummating of the marriage that causes the two to become one. However, we must understand that principle **only** applies to the "two" – "male and female." So, while there is sexual intercourse in the same sex relationships, the marriage isn't consummated because they are not male and female. (Nor is the marriage *consecrated; holy, set apart* because they are not male and female.) You see, the blessings that God established as a result of marriage are built on spiritual principles. Therefore, anyone that tries to imitate these principles in order to receive the blessings, but do not have a **marriage ordained by God** doesn't receive the blessings. They aren't entitled to the blessings because there isn't a *marriage*. Instead, anyone who tries to imitate these godly principles outside of the covenant relationship with God is acting in sin.

Therefore, it is only what God joins together – male and female – that no man shall split apart.

So, what more can *I* say? If Henry thought the Old Testament doesn't apply then *what say he* about the New Testament?

Shortly after sending Henry the scripture references, he in turn, sent me the same scriptures that we discussed earlier. So, after going back and forth with him for a little while, I realized that he wasn't really interested in hearing the *truth;* he was only trying to defend his position and get me to see his point of view and agree with him, which was not going to happen. Therefore, I told him when he was ready to hear the *truth,* then, let me know. And that was the end of the conversation.

As a result of Leah going through deliverance regarding her homosexual lifestyle, I shared with her the scripture references as well. I told her to meditate on them (get to know them intimately), so when someone came to her regarding the homosexual lifestyle or marriage equality, she'd have scriptures to reference (instead of telling the person to come see me). "After all," I said, "This is your ministry."

"Okay," she said enthusiastically.

A short time later Leah came to me and said, "Well, if you ask me, I think you closed the door. And I think that if he was ready to change, he wouldn't come to you. You can be a little harsh; sometimes you say things but you don't say them with love."

I had no idea what had just happened. *Where did this come from,* I wondered. She was standing right there with me when Henry and I had this conversation. *Did she not hear me speak the truth?* "First of all," I said, "you have to understand that I am not going to go back and forth with an individual that isn't ready to hear the truth, but instead is trying to defend their position. Sometimes you have to walk away, brush the dust off your feet, and keep it moving – especially if the person is not open to what you're saying. You'll learn *that* as you mature."

"I don't think he was trying to change. He just had questions. So I think you closed the door."

"I answered his questions; however, he wasn't interested in what I was saying. He was only interested in defending his position, which is why every time I shared something with him, he kept using those same scriptures."

"Well, if it were me," she reiterated, "I would never close the door on someone who's trying to get understanding or asking me questions about the bible or living right. That's just me. If they ask me the question, no matter how long it takes for me to explain it, I'll keep explaining it until they understand."

"I understand you'd want the person to get the understanding, but as you mature, you'll learn that if people are not receptive to what you're saying, if they're not receptive to the Word of God, you have to leave it alone. Sometimes one person plants the seed, another waters it, and God gives the increase."

...Each of us did the work the Lord gave us. I planted the seed in your hearts, and Apollos watered it, but it was God who made it grow. It's not important who does the planting, or who does the watering. What's important is that God makes the seed grow.

1 Corinthians 3:5d – 7 NLT

"That's just me. I wouldn't close the door if someone has questions about the bible," she continued.

Unfortunately, it was clear that Leah wasn't receptive to what I was saying either. Therefore, I knew, in spite of all that she'd been through, the enemy was still present (and was trying to convince me that I had *closed the door* on someone who was interested in hearing the truth). Therefore, as I prayed concerning this matter, the Lord prompted me to *teach* Leah how to identify the activity of the enemy. So the next day, prior to prayer, I advised her to bring a pen and paper so she would be able to take notes.

In the garden...

~ YOU ARE ABOUT TO BE EXPOSED ~

It was my desire to use the prayer time to teach her as I was prompted to do. However, there was a young lady that joined us for prayer; therefore, we prayed. Then, after praying, the young lady left, which gave me the opportunity to minister to Leah.

"I wanted to use this time as a teaching opportunity that's why I asked you to bring your pen and paper, so I want you to listen," I said.

"Okay."

"I want to use the incident with Henry to show you how to identify the enemy, his tricks, tactics, and schemes." She seemed excited, so I continued. "First, I want to point out, as we know, Henry was trying to use the scriptures to defend marriage equality. Because we already know what the Bible says about homosexual relationships and marriage equality; that was a clear indication that demonic activity was present, the enemy was present. Marriage equality goes against what the Bible constitutes as a marriage. So, anytime you're engaged in a conversation that is contrary to what the Bible teaches, right away, you are able to identify demonic presence," I said.

"Now, the fact that Henry indicated that the Old Testament is no longer applicable because times have changed is a *trick* of the enemy. It's a strategy that the enemy uses to make individuals not only *think* that times have changed, but it also encourages them to *participate* in that behavior. And consequently, they won't think anything is wrong with that lifestyle if the Old Testament no longer applies. This type of lifestyle results in the individual not only living in bondage to sin, but their minds, conscience will be dull to the things of God. Ultimately, they won't be aware that they're living in sin; they'll think that lifestyle is acceptable. The ultimate trick of the enemy is to make homosexuality acceptable to society, so if everybody's doing it, then it must be okay. This scheme is to blind the minds of individuals, so again, they aren't aware that they're living in sin, therefore, they would remain in bondage."

She just sat there.

"As we know, Henry is open about his homosexual lifestyle, so for him to use those scriptures and to say that he was "born that way," was an attempt to support and defend his decision to continue to live in that life…"

"I don't think he was trying to defend his decision," she interrupted. "I think he was just saying what he felt." The tone in her voice (and what she was saying) was a clear indication that she was not in agreement with what I said as she spoke in a matter of fact way and probably couldn't care less about what I was saying.

"May I finish?" I asked; however, she continued talking over me.

"I think I should have a right to say what I feel." She had become very defensive, very agitated.

"Leah, I want you to be able to see the demonic activity that took place, which you're missing. I want you to be able to identify the enemy's presence and his tricks."

"Whatever!" she said defensively.

"Anyway," I continued, "what happened with Henry was a trick of the enemy. We know that the enemy makes the person *think* that their decision to live that lifestyle is the right decision; that way, they'd remain in bondage to sin. But we both also know homosexuality is a sin and clearly isn't the right lifestyle to live." She sat there. "That incident was just a tactic that the enemy used because Henry wasn't really open to hear what I had to say about the subject. His only purpose was to defend his decision. He just wanted someone to hear him out and see his side. But certainly that wasn't a position that I would take because the bible is clear about homosexuality – it is detestable in the eyes of God. It is an abomination unto God."

She just sat there.

"Not only had the enemy used Henry, but he had also used *you* to come against *me* even though you had no clue that you were being used." Now, I have to say, I anticipated the enemy showing up at any moment and waited for him to manifest himself as I continued. "You said to me,

> 'I think you closed the door. And I think that if he was ready to
> change, he wouldn't come to you. You can be a little harsh;
> sometimes you say things, but you don't say them with love,'

…that was the enemy using you," I said.

In my mind I was thinking, *she had the nerves to say to me that if he was ready to change, he wouldn't come to you (even though I'm the same person that she came to when she was ready to change).* "Basically," I continued, "the enemy used you to try to *dictate* to me how I should handle my *ministry*. In essence, I should've played 'patty-cake' with that *homosexual demon* instead of telling Henry the *truth* (because you know that's a demon, that's not Henry). Henry needed to hear that the Old Testament is just as applicable today as it was then. He needed to hear that marriage equality goes against the Word of God. And He needed to hear that he wasn't born that way. Basically, you said to me that my approach with dealing with that situation was wrong; I didn't handle it in the most effective way. However, the bottom line is clear: if we were on the same page, there would *never* be a time that we wouldn't be in agreement. You would say what I say concerning *ministry*. Not only that, but that just goes to show the level of respect that you have for me and my ministry. Because if I were your spiritual leader, there would be no way that you would *ever* say to me that my approach isn't effective…"

Before I could finish, that devil completely snapped on me, and I was reminded of the Lord saying, 'He was about to expose her.'

"I'm sick and tired of every time I say something you think I'm trying to come up against you! I'm human and I have my own opinions! Every time you say something to me doesn't mean that it's right and that I have to do everything you tell me to do! You are not right all the time and I can say whatever I want to say!"

I sat there, and just as I had anticipated, I watched the enemy use her once again, but I didn't say anything.

"I'm sick of this! You always think your way is the only way and that I'm always coming against you! You don't know me! You don't even spend time with me! You don't know what I think! You don't know how I feel! You don't know anything about me! Because every time I try to say something you're always trying to get me to think like you! Think and do things the way that you do them! I'm my own person! I say what I want to say and do what I want to do! And now you're trying to say the devil is in me."

So, I sat there and watched the enemy have his way with her. That, however, was yet another opportunity for the enemy to entice me to rebuke him. His only tactic was to get me to be disobedient to what the Lord had commanded me to do; *hold my peace.* And yet, he went all out as a last ditch effort to try to get me to respond.

> *'You don't know me! You don't even spend time with me! You*
> *don't know what I think! You don't know how I feel! You don't*
> *know anything about me!*

I could *hear the voice* of the enemy declaring that I didn't know who he was. He was a *spirit of manipulation.* Saying I didn't know him, I didn't know his tricks, and that I didn't know how he operated.

> *Because every time I try to say something you're always trying to*
> *get me to think like you! Think and do things the way that you do*
> *them! I'm my own person! I say what I want to say and do what I*
> *want to do! And now you're trying to say that the devil is in me.'*

He was a *spirit of rebellion*; rebelling against the will of God; refusing to submit to God's authority as he declared he would do what he wanted to do and say whatever he wanted to say.

At this point, I want to point out the fact that it was clear that these were the demons speaking and not Leah because as I said, I could hear the voice of the enemy. Now what we, as Christians, have failed to realize is the fact that demons not only *speak,* but they *have a will,* they *possess knowledge,* and *they have feelings,* which is evident in many of the passages of scripture. Also, there are a number of occasions that they are *referred to as "he," a person with a personality.*

DEMONS SPEAK:

Finally, a spirit came forward, stood before the LORD and said, 'I will entice him.'
"'By what means?' the LORD asked.
"'I will go out and be a lying spirit in the mouths of all his prophets,' he said.
"'You will succeed in enticing him,' said the LORD. 'Go and do it.'
"'So now the LORD has put a lying spirit in the mouths of all these prophets of yours. The LORD has decreed disaster for you."

1 Kings 22:21 – 23 NIV

As the above passage of scriptures clearly indicate:

...a spirit came forward, stood before the LORD, *and spoke.* It also reveals the spirit has a *personality: he* said. He has a *will:* 'I *will* entice him.' He has *knowledge,* a plan, strategy: *'I will go out and be a lying spirit in the mouths of all his prophets,'*

And yet, it is the LORD who determines if the spirit would be *successful:* 'You will succeed in enticing him,' said the LORD.'

And it's also clear that the LORD is the One who gives the *command: 'Go and do it.'*

Now with that being said, again, when the demon used Leah to say, *'You don't know me! You don't even spend time with me! You don't know what I think! You don't know how I feel! You don't know anything about me!'* in essence, he was saying that I didn't know what "type" of demon he was, I didn't know how he operated (I didn't know his tricks and schemes), and I didn't know his character traits; how to identify him.

It wasn't *really* Leah saying that I didn't know *her.*

When the demon said, *'every time I try to say something you're always trying to get me to think like you! Think and do things the way that you do them! I'm my own person; I say what I want to say and do what I want to do!'* that was just him telling me that he wasn't going to submit – not to my authority and not to a holy lifestyle – he was rebellious! So anytime I talked to Leah concerning holiness, he would rebel, which was to keep *her* from living a holy lifestyle. That's also why, anytime we'd have a conversation about her living a holy lifestyle, she'd always say, "I'm my own person. I do what I want to do. I say what I want to say. You can't make me like you." That's the demon speaking – rebelling.

And the one thing I think most of us fail to realize is that these demons are strategic; they're skillful, they have tricks and schemes for accomplishing a specific goal.

Here's another example:

With a shriek, he screamed, <u>"Why are you interfering with me, Jesus, Son of the Most High God? In the name of God, I beg you, don't torture me!</u> For Jesus had already said to the spirit, "Come out of the man, you evil spirit." Then Jesus demanded, "What is your name?" <u>And he replied, "My name is Legion, because there are many of us inside this man."</u>

Mark 5:7 – 9 NLT (emphasis added)

DEMONS HAVE FEELINGS:

The above scripture reference also reveals demons have *feelings:* 'In the name of God, I beg you, *don't torture me!*'

And just as he had said through Leah: '*I'm sick and tired* of every time I say something you think I'm trying to come up against you!'

Here's another example:

You say you have faith, for you believe that there is one God. Good for you! Even the demons believe this, and they <u>tremble in terror.</u>

James 2:19 NLT (emphasis added)

DEMONS HAVE KNOWLEDGE:

I <u>know</u> who you are—the Holy One of God!"

Mark 1:24c NLT (emphasis added)

They know who God is.

A group of Jews was traveling from town to town casting out evil spirits. They tried to use the name of the Lord Jesus in their incantation, saying, "I command you in the name of Jesus, whom Paul preaches, to come out!" Seven sons of Sceva, a leading priest, were doing this. <u>But one time when they tried it, the evil spirit replied, "I know Jesus, and I know Paul, but who are you?"</u>

Acts 19:13 – 15 NLT (emphasis added)

They know Paul. They know Jesus. And they know anyone who comes in the name of Jesus; they know the power and the authority that's in the name of Jesus. But if you try to cast them out in any name other than the name of Jesus, as the above scripture references, they're going to have a problem with you.

Another example of them having knowledge, a plan, strategy? Look at the scripture reference below and you'll see their plan, strategy:

"When an evil spirit leaves a person, it goes into the desert, seeking rest but finding none. Then it says, 'I will return to the person I came from.' So it returns and finds its former home empty, swept, and in order. Then the spirit finds seven other spirits more evil than itself, and they all enter the person and live there. And so that person is worse off than before. That will be the experience of this evil generation."

Matthew 12:43 – 45 NLT

THE PLAN/STRATEGY (IF CAST OUT):

✓ Go into the desert to find rest (find rest means *enter another person);* if there isn't another person, go to plan B)

PLAN B:

✓ Return to the person he came from
  House must be empty, swept, and in order
✓ Find seven other spirits
  More evil than itself
✓ All eight spirits enter the person
  The spirit + seven = eight spirits total
✓ Live there

GOAL:

✓ That person is worse off than before

They're determined; they have a plan and a strategy – to defeat the Christian.

DEMONS HAVE A WILL:

"When an evil spirit leaves a person, it goes into the desert, seeking rest but finding none. Then it says, 'I will return to the person I came from.' So it returns and finds its former home empty, swept, and in order. Then the spirit finds seven other spirits more evil than itself, and they all enter the person and live there. And so that person is worse off than before. That will be the experience of this evil generation."

Matthew 12:43 – 45 NLT (emphasis added)

Clearly, I wanted her to understand that *she* wasn't the devil, but the devil had used her and had influenced her to attack me – there is a difference. However, she grabbed her phone, bible, and keys and was getting ready to walk away, but I grabbed her arm. I had had enough of going around this same mountain.

"You are not going to leave," I said. "We are going to deal with this."

In the garden...

~ MY WATER BROKE ~

We sat there for a few minutes without saying anything to allow her to calm down and the enemy to draw back. He had been exposed. And what was in her heart had been exposed. So, when she had calmed down, I said again, "It's clear that we're not on the same page." But when we realized the time, we started to head back to work. On the way back, I continued, "I shouldn't have to try to convince you that I'm your spiritual leader. By this time, you should already know that the Lord has placed me in your life to help you grow spiritually. There are some things that the Lord reveals to me concerning you that even you're not aware of. That's because I'm here to help you grow."

She looked at me as if I was crazy and said, "Wait a minute. You're telling me that you know something about *me* that even I don't know about myself?"

"Yes."

"Aw, nah, that's not possible! You don't know more about me than I know about myself. There isn't *anyone* who knows more about me than I know about myself. You've got that all wrong!"

"Just like you're your son's mother and you know things about him that he doesn't know about himself, it's the same way with us. I know things about you that you don't know about yourself because the Lord reveals them to me."

And instantly, I felt a **breakthrough** in the spirit.

"Are you serious?" she said with amazement, "Oh, my gosh! Wow! That's a little difficult for me to understand. You've never said it like that before. I think it makes sense even though it's a little hard to grasp – you know more about me than I know about myself."

I was relieved that she had finally gotten it! *Now, we could turn the corner,* I thought. But I was wrong.

"I just want you to know that there is one thing that I think you got wrong," she said.

What!!?? I thought. And without a doubt, I knew the state of confusion was clearly visible on my face. "What do you mean, 'I got wrong'?" I questioned.

"First, I want to clarify what I meant when I said, 'I felt like you were manipulating me with the tithes.' I know the ministry doesn't need anything and that you don't need my money, but what I was saying was that you were trying to manipulate me by telling me that 'if I didn't pay my tithe, that my money would be cursed.' And I just want to say that you discerned that scripture inappropriately."

Completely flabbergasted, I said, "Are you kidding me!? Let me get this straight. When you came to me and said, 'you were tired of struggling financially,' I shared with you the principle of tithing. Am I right? Is that what happened?"

"Yes."

"When I taught you about tithing, I said, 'God wants to bless His people; He wants to bless *you*.' Is that right?"

"Yes."

"Then I explained to you how God informed the people of why they *weren't* prospering. And not only did He tell them why they weren't prospering, but *He gave them the solution as to how they could prosper.* Is that right?"

"Yes."

"And we read the scriptures together; I showed you in the bible the scriptures:

<u>"Should people cheat God? Yet you have cheated me! You have cheated me of the tithes and offerings due to me. You are under a curse, for your whole nation has been cheating me.</u> Bring all the tithes into the storehouse so there will be enough food in my Temple. If you do," says the LORD of Heaven's Armies, "I will open the windows of heaven for you. I will pour out a blessing so great you won't have enough room to take it in! Try it! Put me to the test! Your crops will be abundant, for I will guard them from insects and disease. Your grapes will not fall from the vine before they are ripe," says the LORD of Heaven's Armies. "Then all nations will call you blessed, for your land will be such a delight," says the LORD of Heaven's Armies.**

Malachi 3:8 – 12 NLT (emphasis added)

"So that you would know that I wasn't just saying what *I* wanted to say, but that you saw with your very own eyes the words in the bible that clearly stated: *you are not prospering because you are cheating God.* Is that right?" I continued.

"Yes."

"And I also showed you in the bible that after the Lord told the people that they were cheating Him, the people asked, 'When did we cheat you?' And the Lord said, 'You cheated me of the tithes and offerings due to me.' Is that right?"

"Yes."

"And not only did the Lord say that He wanted to bless His people, but He said *all they had to do was bring the tithes and offerings to the storehouse,* I will open the windows of heaven for you. I will pour out a blessing so great you won't have enough room to take it in! Try it! Put me to the test! Is that right?"

"Yes."

"And I also shared with you that the Lord made it clear that if they *didn't* bring the tithes and offerings to the storehouse that their finances would be cursed. '***You are under a curse, for your whole nation has been cheating me.***' Is that right?"

"Yes."

And immediately, I was reminded of this very teaching: When I was teaching Leah this principle, one of our co-workers, Darnell, came into the classroom, looking deflated and defeated. When we asked what was wrong with him, he shared with us that he was in the process of purchasing a house. However, he'd waited too late and someone else had put a contract on the very house that he wanted. Therefore, he was discouraged. So, since he'd come in while I was teaching on tithing, I said to him, "Clearly, this teaching is also for you." And I shared with him the tithing principle as well. Then specifically instructed him to pay his tithe and watch the Lord move in that situation.

I think it was a week later (if not, two weeks) when Darnell came running back to me and Leah to share with us that while he didn't have the 'tithe, the 10 percent,' he took all the money he had and put it in church. And guess what? The contract that was on the house fell through.

He said, "My real estate agent called me and told me that the contract fell through. And I hurried and put a contract on it and it was accepted – I got the house!" And we were all excited and rejoiced that God had moved on his behalf.

Now, listen to this, shortly after, there was a young lady at work who talked to Leah about tithing, and guess what, she used Darnell's testimony to encourage this young lady to pay her tithe – something that she herself wouldn't do.

But anyway, I continued my conversation with Leah, "So, if that's what's written in the Bible, that's what we read, and that's what I explained to you, how is it that I '*discerned the scripture inappropriately*'?" I questioned.

"At the time you were teaching me about the tithe, you should've been trying to encourage me to pay my tithe and not tell me about the curse."

Oh, my God! I thought. *Only the enemy* would try to undermine the Word of God. I was amazed that this devil was going all out – a fight to the finish.

"Since I'm a babe in Christ," she continued, "you shouldn't have told me about the curse because the curse is what really stuck in my mind and it discouraged me from paying my tithe (instead of encouraged me.) So, because you told me about the curse, this teaching was done at the wrong time."

I just stood there looking at her but not saying anything. Yet, again, that devil was trying to dictate to me what I should and should not teach concerning the Word of God. I just really couldn't believe what I was hearing: *'you shouldn't have told me about the curse…it discouraged me…this teaching was done at the wrong time.'*

So, let me make sure I understood what she was saying: She knew that if she didn't give her tithes and offerings, then her finances would be cursed. However, she was discouraged by the curse so she didn't tithe; thereby, bringing the curse on her finances. Am I right?

Now I know there are many people who don't give tithes because they say, again, 'tithing is in the *Old Testament* not in the *New Testament.*' However, I'd like to just point out that I've come to realize that when someone is trying to justify why they don't want to obey the Word of God, giving tithes in this case, they find it very convenient to say, "Oh, that's in the *Old Testament,* that's not in the *New Testament.*"

Therefore, I'd like to take a look at the New Testament:

"What sorrow awaits you teachers of religious law and you Pharisees. Hypocrites! For you are careful to tithe even the tiniest income from your herb gardens, but you ignore the more important aspects of the law – justice, mercy, and faith. <u>You should tithe, yes,</u> but do not neglect the more important things."

Matthew 23:23 NLT (emphasis added)

And **Luke, chapter eleven, verse forty-two** states the same. So tithing **is** in the New Testament as Jesus points out *the importance of tithing* while not forgetting – justice, mercy, and faith.

However, concerning Leah, I was reminded of *why* she may have been "discouraged." Not only because I told her about the curse (as she said) but I'm sure her friend, Lucia, who used to work with us, influenced her as well:

I remember Leah sharing with me that Lucia, who had been hurt by someone at her church and apparently no longer trusted the church, asked Leah if she tithed to our ministry. Then she asked Leah, 'What are they doing with the money? Are they using the money for their *church house*?'

This all had to be some kind of joke, I thought, so I waited for the punch line.

"It's important," she continued, "that when you're trying to get people to do what you want them to do, you encourage them by telling only the positive things about it."

Before I knew anything, I just started laughing at that devil. Because it was clear he didn't want me teaching her the Word of God. Therefore, he tried to *manipulate* me into only teaching as the Bible says; *what her itching ears wanted to hear* – not the *truth*.

For a time is coming when people will no longer listen to sound and wholesome teaching. They will follow <u>their own desires</u> and will look for teachers <u>who will tell them whatever their itching ears want to hear.</u> They will reject the truth and chase after myths.

2 Timothy 4:3 – 4 NLT *(emphasis added)*

"I've done my research and you discerned that scripture inappropriately," she said again.

Again, as if I were talking to a "four year old child," I said, "Wait a minute! Let me make sure I understand what you just said. So you're telling me that when I taught you about the blessing *and* the curse, that I should've only told you about the blessing. I should've never mentioned anything about the curse. Is that right?"

"Yes."

"And you're saying that because you're a babe in Christ, I should've encouraged you to pay your tithe by only telling you the positive – the blessing. Is that right?"

"Yes."

"And you're saying that because you're a babe in Christ I shouldn't have told you about the curse because it *discouraged* you instead of *encouraged* you. Is that right?"

"Yes."

"Leah, let me tell you something. You don't dictate to me what I am and am not to teach *because* you're a babe in Christ. And for you to try to tell me when and how I should minister the Word of God, you don't even *know* the Word of God. It is my responsibility, as a *minister of the Gospel,* to tell the truth about the Word of God. I would be amiss if I were to only tell you about the blessing and not the curse. It is my responsibility to give you *all* the information so that you would be able to make an intelligent decision. You will *never* be able to say to me that I hadn't taught you what would happen if you *didn't* tithe."

"Well, I did my research and I know *that* scripture doesn't apply to me."

"How is it that the scripture doesn't apply to you?"

"Because it's talking about the leaders and the ministers of the church who were misusing the money and it's not talking about me."

"Well, if that were the case, *nothing* in the bible is talking about you. There's nothing in the bible that specifically says, ***"Leah…,"*** but the principles in the bible are our instructions of how to live a godly and prosperous life. It was Abraham who dedicated the tithe to the Lord, not Leah."

"Well, I don't believe it."

"What don't you believe?"

"I don't believe my money is cursed."

"Well, that's your choice. But just because you don't believe it, doesn't mean that it's not true. Your money is cursed."

"Well, I don't receive that because I don't allow people to say negative things about me. And I choose not to believe that."

"Clearly, that's your choice. Just know that as you continue to go from pay check to pay check, if you miss *a* paycheck, your entire life will be flipped upside down. And if that's how you want to live, then that's on you."

"Well, I just don't see how my money could have a curse on it. Because I know that in the Bible there's a lady that gave only a penny and the Lord blessed her."

"First of all, *that wasn't a tithe,* it was an offering. Secondly, it was her faith, the intent of her heart that she gave *all* that she had. And He blessed her."

"I don't understand why it's such a big deal because I told you that I didn't have the faith to tithe."

"And I understood that. Not only did you say that you didn't have the faith, but you also said that you were working on your faith *in other areas.* And I didn't push the issue. I gave you the solution to prosper, but it's up to you to use it."

"I just don't believe it."

"That's the problem. You don't prosper *because* you don't believe."

For people will love only themselves and their money.

2 Timothy 3:2a NLT

"I told you it's not that I don't want to; it's because I can't afford to."

"The principle of tithing is that you do it in faith and allow the Lord to bless your obedience to His Word."

"I used to tithe before I was saved and it wasn't this difficult. I didn't understand why I was doing it; I just knew I should do it (because the Lord had done so much for me when I was in the world)."

"That's the same reason you should be doing it now! If you know the Lord has done so much for you, then you should be *blessing Him* by giving back to Him what is rightfully His!"

"You don't understand. I can't afford it. I don't have the money. All of the money I make covers my bills and if I pay my tithe, I won't have enough money to pay my bills."

"There's nothing else I can do. I can't give you faith. We've gone over this time and time again. We've had teachings on tithing in bible study and we've had people give their testimony of how they've been blessed as a result of tithing. You know you should be giving tithes and offerings. What else do you want me to do? There's nothing else I can do. I can't give you faith."

"There is something you can do; you can teach me about faith."

Sure. *I* could teach her about faith. There was always something that *I* could've done. Instead of her spending as much time as she had *"researching" why the tithe didn't apply to her,* she should've been *"researching" faith and gave her tithe!* I was done! When I tried teaching her, she said she was exercising her faith in "other areas." But this situation was no different than any of the others – *she accused me* – for her not taking responsibility of committing to learning and growing in the things of God. *'I should teach her faith.' Okay.*

"I just don't understand how there's a curse on my finances and I'm saved."

"Leah," I said exhausted, "the curse on your finances has nothing to do with you being saved. Just because you're saved doesn't automatically cause you to prosper financially. When you were in the world, you weren't in a *covenant* with the Lord – your finances were cursed. And just because you came into the Kingdom, doesn't mean the curse is automatically removed. The only way the curse is removed is by you bringing your tithes and offerings to the storehouse, just as the scripture says. Once you're in a covenant with the Lord, and you start giving your tithes and offerings, then the Lord would remove the curse."

And instantly, I felt a **breakthrough** in my spirit.

"Oh, I didn't know that. You never explained that to me before."

By the time we ended the conversation and went our separate ways, three hours had gone by; three hours of warfare, but the peace of God rested upon me. In my spirit, I felt there was a **breakthrough** – *more mine than Leah's.* I felt something break. Then the Lord revealed:

"Your water broke!"

It took all the strength that I had to endure as the Lord revealed that it was time for ***delivery.*** The tears rolled down my face as I anticipated the pain that the contractions would bring.

I was done!

I had nothing left in me to give.

I was "dog-tired" and could barely hold on as the reality of birthing this ministry had surfaced.

It was time to push!

There was no turning back now. That which the Lord had deposited into my spirit had to be birth forth.

The ***breakthrough,*** forcing my way through to victory *against the resistance* of the enemy during warfare, was short lived, as I quickly anticipated the contractions that were about to come.

I felt the weight of the battle that I'd just been in bearing down on me demanding me to ***push!***

So he went to pray a third time, saying the same things again.

(My Father! If this cup cannot be taken away unless I drink it, your will be done.")

Matthew 26:44 (42) NLT

PART

VI

DELIVERY

~ CHAPTER 1 ~

IT'S TIME TO SHIFT

The next day during my morning devotion, I went before the Lord. Completely exhausted, I laid prostrate before Him. Immediately, the Lord spoke into my spirit, *"You are not Leah's spiritual leader."* Astonished, I sat up quickly. And just as suddenly, I felt a *shift* in my spirit.

The baby had turned. His head was now in the birthing canal and was ready to come forth.

I started to cry as I laid before the Lord because I knew this was going to be the last phase, the last trimester, if you will. I also knew it was going to be *the absolute hardest, most exhausting, and grueling part.* The Lord's anointing rested on me – I knew things would never be the same. His presence gave permission to the tears that were a testament to how desperately I wanted this to be over. And yet, I rejoiced that *finally* the birthing was about to come forth.

When the Lord revealed to me that the shift had taken place, immediately, I knew it was already done in the spirit realm; I was no longer Leah's *spiritual leader.* I was no longer held responsible for her spiritual growth. So the ties that were between us, as leader/layman, had been severed.

Immediately, I was reminded of a prophetic word I received:

I remembered I had come into the place broken, tired, and extremely exhausted, but I had pressed my way because I needed a "word" from God. There was absolutely no way that I could go any further, without a "word" from the Lord. I needed to be strengthened. I stood there as we worshiped the Lord, pleading in my spirit for Him to speak to me. Then the woman of God called me out to minister to me. As I stood before her, the tears rolled down my face as she ministered: *"There are **two people** in particular who don't believe you are who you say you are. But I hear the Lord saying, 'They are going to have to come back and apologize to you for everything that they've done to you."* And immediately, I completely **broke** as the pain that I'd been enduring surfaced; and the tears poured out before Him. *"Mark my words,"* she said. *"They are going to come back and apologize for what they've done."*

And now the Lord was telling me to *shift,* move forward – advance – according to the **breakthrough**. It was time for the birthing, the ministry, the baby to come forth. His head was in the birthing canal; he was in position. He had shifted. So now it was time for me to get into position. It was time for me to shift. And with that came, I had the burden of manifesting this breakthrough in the natural (which was already done in the spirit); I was no longer Leah's spiritual leader.

Then the Lord began to minister to me concerning Lot's wife:

When they were safely out of the city, one of the angels ordered, "Run for your lives! And don't look back or stop anywhere in the valley! Escape to the mountains, or you will be swept away!"

Genesis 19:17 NLT

Lot reached the village just as the sun was rising over the horizon. Then the LORD rained down fire and burning sulfur from the sky on Sodom and Gomorrah. He utterly destroyed them, along with the other cities and villages of the plain, wiping out all the people and every bit of vegetation. But Lot's wife looked back as she was following behind him, and she turned into a pillar of salt.

Genesis 19:23 – 26 NLT

As the Lord continued to minister to me, He revealed that those who put their hands to the plow and look back aren't worthy of the Kingdom. It was time to shift; change my position and direction – leave the place that I was in.

It was time for me to get into position, put my feet in the stirrups, and push!

AND DON'T LOOK BACK.

I have to admit, I struggled with being in this position. And the thought of this thing *really* getting ready to happen sent chills down my spine. I didn't know *how* this was going to happen or *when* it would happen; all I knew was that it *was* going to happen. Consequently, I had to wait on the Lord to reveal His instructions on how He would bring forth this delivery. Then suddenly, I was reminded of the "Prodigal Son."

To illustrate the point further, Jesus told them this story: "A man had two sons. The younger son told his father, 'I want my share of your estate now before you die.' So his father agreed to divide his wealth between his sons.

Luke 15:11 – 12 NLT

I think, for the most part, we're all probably familiar with the story of the *Prodigal Son:* the son got his inheritance, left his father's house, squandered the inheritance, became destitute, then, "came" to himself, and the father rejoiced at the son's return home. However, I had no idea what the Lord was revealing to me. Therefore, He continued to minister to me as I sat contemplating what this *shift* would bring. Unfortunately, I wasn't able to make the connection between what

He was telling me to do and what the prodigal son had to do with it. And as if He had answered my lack of understanding, He prompted me to meditate on the verse:

So his father agreed to divide his wealth between his sons.

So I read it, read again, and read it some more. Then suddenly the Lord spoke into my spirit:

"The *father* agreed."

Immediately, I was enlightened. The father agreed to let the son go. And just as suddenly, I knew in my spirit that *He,* the *Father, agreed* to let Leah go. It was time for her to go; the Lord had released me. And just as suddenly, the contractions started and the tears fell from my eyes as His words pierced my spirit. *I didn't want her to go.* After hours of trying to bring myself to terms with her leaving the ministry, I figured, like Maria and Tiffany had done, she'd come to me and say that she was leaving, so I tried to prepare myself – to let her go.

But in my mind, being pregnant in the spirit was no different than being pregnant in the natural. I wanted it to be over because of the pain and discomfort, but at the same time, I had become accustomed to it (in order to accommodate the growth of the baby; the growth of the ministry). I wanted the birthing to come forth, but somehow, *something* wasn't right. *Even in the natural,* I thought, *when you give birth, you keep the baby.* Immediately, the tears burst forth as the pain of *losing* the baby surfaced. After all that I'd been through, and not get to keep the baby! The thought broke my heart.

"I don't want to lose the baby," I cried out to the Lord. "I can't give the baby up! What was all the pain and suffering for if I don't get to keep the baby?! What was all the *weight* gain; heaviness and pressure of the demonic forces for if I don't get to keep the baby?! Why did I endure the anguish and sorrow, if I don't get to keep the baby?! Why the sleepless nights of prayer and intercession if I don't get to keep the baby?! Lord, how is this possible that she's not staying?!"

"*She* isn't the baby. She's the forceps that I used to bring forth the baby. The *ministry* is the baby *and it's yours,*" He responded.

And still, my heart struggled to let her go as the tears continued to roll down my face. And the pain reverberated throughout my body.

A few days after the Lord had ministered to me, I received a text message from Leah:

Out of respect for your and Pastor's time, I want to let you know in advance I'm going to be absent from bible study on Wednesday. My apologies if it causes a disruption.

Immediately, the pain of separation tore at my heart and my spirit became heavy at the thought of this birthing taking place. My heart was saddened and tears welled up in my eyes; *I did not want to see this happen.*

And yet, the next day, I was in my office when Leah came over and handed me an envelope and just walked away. I looked at the envelope, and of course wondered what was inside. (I had a feeling that it was money). I opened the envelope and there was a letter and wrapped inside was money. The letter turned out to be her *financial declaration* concerning what apparently was her *tithe,* wrapped inside the letter. I was excited to see that she had finally gotten it! So I gave her a note back that pretty much encouraged her that she had done the right thing.

When Randolph picked me up after work, I was excited. I had finally had a breakthrough concerning Leah and her tithe. *Victory* rung out as I shared with him, "Leah gave me her ti..."

"Give it back," he interrupted; causing defeat to silence the voice of my seemingly triumph.

"What?" I asked with amazement.

"Give it back. The tithe is not the issue. The Lord has already revealed that she's not in agreement with this ministry and we cannot walk together unless we're in agreement."

And immediately, I was reminded of the dream:

> **My husband, Randolph, opened the door and said, "I heard all the commotion going on outside."**

Consequently, in obedience to my pastor, I humbled myself before the Lord in prayer. And to my surprise, I couldn't even get in the Lord's presence fast enough before He said, ***"Push!"*** And immediately the labor pains began.

I cried out to the Lord, "Oh, Lord, don't make me do this!" I continued to cry as I felt the tearing away; the separation. "It hurts, Lord. I can't do this! Please help me! Oh, Lord, please help me!"

And as the tears overwhelmed me, and the pain overtook me, He made it clear that I was sadly mistaken; Leah wouldn't be *coming to me* to say she would be leaving the ministry, but rather it was time for *me to uproot her.* Uproot those who opposed the things of God – it was time for me to **become experienced in the wars of Canaan and drive out the enemy.** And there would be no *epidural anesthesia* to get me through this. My tears gave way to the labor pains that confirmed the words He spoke to Lot's wife, 'Don't look back.' It was time to deliver! And as the Lord continued to minister to me, I continued to cry out to Him, and with everything that I had within me, *I pushed!*

The next day, I asked Leah if I could share something with her.

"Do you want to step outside?" She asked.

"Yeah," I answered and we went into the hallway. "First of all," I started, "I want to thank you for everything that you've done for this ministry. You have been very instrumental in the development of this ministry and we appreciate it…"

"Oh, Lord," she interrupted.

"Oh, Lord, what?" I questioned.

"Nothing."

So I continued. "Pastor and I want nothing more than for you to grow and become a mature Christian. However, after much prayer, and based on the things the Lord has revealed to us, this is *not* the ministry for you…"

"You putting me out of the church?!" she interrupted again as she stood there stunned and clearly caught off guard. And just as vulnerable, I found myself in a very difficult position as the breaking of my heart confirmed. She fell against the wall; giving way to the only support that was able to keep her from falling as she said, "I'm hurting so bad right now."

"I know," I said as I was mindful not to *kill her spirit* at the expense of driving out the enemy. "For whatever reason, you're unable to receive from us. Therefore, it's our prayer that you'll connect to a ministry where you are able to receive, so that you can grow and mature in Christ."

She continued to just stare at me in disbelief, but I continued as the contractions kept coming and prepared me to push.

"And with that being said, we want to give you your tithe back." And I reached in my pocket and pulled out the envelope that she had given me.

And with what appeared to be an added shock, she exclaimed, "You have it in your pocket?!" Almost as if to say, *how could you do this to me – like this?* And she stood there as I watched and inwardly prayed that the Lord would enable me to make it through this. Surely, my breathing technique (he, he, who; he, he, who) had failed me. I felt as if I was hyperventilating; my breaths were fast, shallow, and clearly abnormal. I felt as if I was going to faint, pass out right on the spot. It seemed as though I couldn't catch my breath. But there wasn't any time to take any deep breaths that would've allowed me to *inhale,* take it all in; *exhale,* let it all out.

Letting her go had proved to be far more painful than I had even imagined it would be. Standing before me was an immature person, who had undoubtedly been used by the enemy. And yet, I wanted nothing more than to take her in my arms and tell her how sorry I was that it all had come to this – but I couldn't. I was barely able to hold myself up, and visibly on the verge of tears. I knew if I would've taken her in my arms, I would've completely broken down. Because had it not been for the grace of God giving me the strength to stand, surely, I would've been on the floor.

Yet, He enabled me to watch and discern the timing of the contractions.

Therefore, I braced myself in anticipation of the pain that was about to come, and I continued.

"Pastor and I wanted desperately for you to be a part of this ministry and receive the blessings that the Lord had in store for you…"

"I know we've had our differences," she interrupted, "but can't we work them out?" she asked desperately trying to hold on.

"It's not about working out our differences." *It was too late to "work out" our differences.* "It's about us walking in agreement. We aren't on the same page. And therefore, the Lord can't do in you (or in us) what He wants to in order to bless us. So this is what's best for all of us."

"But Daisy, all I'm asking is that you just be a little more patient with me."

"It's no longer about patience. It's about us still struggling with the same issues that we should've overcome in the beginning; I'm still trying to *convince* you that I'm your spiritual leader, you don't trust me, *and* you think I don't know how to discern the scriptures."

"It was just that *one* scripture. I *know* you know how to discern the scriptures."

"It really just comes down to you being in agreement with us; us being on the same page. And the Lord has already revealed what's in your heart from our last encounter…"

"I'm sorry," she interrupted, "I do want to apologize for my behavior because I know I was wrong. And I know that if ever the devil was in me, he was in me *then* because I was already mad and it just happened. I really am sorry. I apologize."

"I accept your apology."

"If you look," she continued, "you'll see I've made some progress and I've come a long way."

"I know you've made progress. Absolutely! And yes, you've come a long way. But we can't walk in disagreement. What goes on inside the house is what also happens outside the house. And we can't have us, as a ministry outside, me saying one thing and you saying something different. The people would see that there is discord in our house and this is what allows the enemy to continue to come in and attack us."

"So, I've been the reason the enemy has been able to come in?"

"Yes. So we've got to be able to move forward so that the Lord can do what he wants to do with this ministry. And we can't move forward if we're not in agreement; two people can't walk together unless they agree. I know you don't think this is what's best because it hurts, but as you continue your relationship with Christ, you'll see, this is the best thing for you."

As difficult as it was for me to have done that, and as if for the slightest reason I may have forgotten *why* it needed to be done, she reminded me.

"But I don't have a problem with Pastor; I only have a problem with you," she said.

I know, Satan, I thought.

"*That's* why this isn't the ministry for you," I said as I stood there and watched Satan try to separate me from my husband. "We are *one.* There is no him or me – it's *us; our* ministry. You've got a problem with *me; he* has a problem with *you!*"

"Well. I guess you heard from the Lord and this is what you have to do. Even though it hurts and I feel like I'm being put out of the church, I guess you may be right. Because this is not a decision I made, so I don't have to worry about if I made the right decision. But rather, the decision was made for me. But I'm not really sure what this means. Does this mean we can't be friends like we were before you started a ministry?"

"It means we have been released as your spiritual leaders; we are no longer responsible for your spiritual development. And you've been released from being a member of this ministry. So now you're able to go and join any church that you like."

She stood there as if she was dazed from the final blow, nothing to say, just staring off. So I asked, "Do you need some time to yourself?"

"Yes. I'm just going to go and sit in the car for a few minutes."

"Okay." And we went our separate ways.

A little while later, I wondered how she was doing because she was on my heart. When I walked past her office, she was there (so I figured, at least she was okay). However, a few minutes later, her office had been cleaned and her light was off as if she was gone for the day. I went to look for her. When I saw her, I could see that she had been crying.

A contraction: my heart completely broke into a million pieces. "Looks like you're headed home," I managed to say through my crackling voice that was under the threat of crying myself.

"Yeah, I'm leaving; this is too much for me to handle."

I hugged her and it took everything within me to let her go.

When I got in the car with Randolph, without any restraint, I completely broke down. I was sobbing because the pain had proved to be far too much for me. I wasn't able to talk because I was overcome by the flood of emotions, tears, and the tearing away; separation as it came rushing forth. It was far more difficult than I had anticipated. *I can't do this!* I thought.

Then I heard the Lord say, **"Push!"**

"It was soooo hard," I said to Randolph while sobbing. However, the tears and the pain kept me from saying anything else. So, I just sat there and cried all the way home. Shortly after somewhat getting myself together, and yet in great distress, I said, "She has no idea what just happened."

Throughout the evening, the enemy bombarded my mind and played on my emotions. I kept hearing Leah say, *'You putting me out of the church?'* And before I knew anything, the tears and the pain would overtake me again as her words played over and over in my mind: *'This hurts so bad.' 'We can work out our differences.' 'Be patient with me.'*

The pain was devastating – excruciating.

But even in the midst of my pain, I knew there was no other way.

Can two people walk together
  without agreeing on the direction?
Does a lion ever roar in a thicket
  without first finding a victim?
Does a young lion growl in its den
  without first catching its prey?
Does a bird ever get caught in a trap
  that has no bait?
Does a trap shut
  when there's nothing to catch?
Does disaster come to a city
  unless the LORD has planned it?

Amos 3:3 – 5; 6b NLT

The reality was, we were not walking in agreement. And her actions had proved time and time again that she had no respect for me, my ministry, or the things of God. Consequently, just as the above passage of scriptures reveal that *when one thing happened, the other was sure to follow.* And consequently, if she wasn't removed from this ministry, it would result in: me being disobedient to the Lord's instructions and the Lord's presence would no longer remain with us. And as long as she was in the ministry, we would be defeated by the enemy.

She had to go.

You see, this situation with Leah was no different than what Joshua had experienced in Joshua, chapter seven. After defeating Jericho, Joshua and the Israelites went up against the city of Ai. And although the city of Ai was smaller than the city of Jericho, Joshua and the Israelites were defeated. Why? One of the men in their assembly disobeyed the Lord's instructions. Yes, you read that right: *as a result of **one man** disobeying the Lord, the **entire assembly** was **defeated.***

That is why the Israelites are running from their enemies in defeat. For now Israel itself has been set apart for destruction. I will not remain with you any longer unless you destroy the things among you that were set apart for destruction.

Joshua 7:12 NLT

Achan replied, "It is true! I have sinned against the LORD, the God of Israel. Among the plunder I saw a beautiful robe from Babylon, 200 silver coins, and a bar of gold weighing more than a pound. I wanted them so much that I took them. They are hidden in the ground beneath my tent, with the silver buried deeper than the rest.

Joshua 7:20 – 21 NLT

The Lord will hold *everyone* accountable for the *disobedience* of *one,* which would result in the Lord not being with them. And ultimately, that meant they would continue to be defeated by the enemy. Therefore, that which had been set apart for destruction had to be removed. So as long as Achan, who disobeyed the Lord, was in Joshua's camp or Leah remained in our ministry, the Lord would remove His presence. So if they wanted the Lord to be with them or *we* wanted the Lord to be with *us,* then they had to destroy Achan and,

Leah had to go.

Then Joshua and all the Israelites took Achan, the silver, the robe, the bar of gold, his sons, daughters, cattle, donkeys, sheep, goats, tent, and everything he had, and they brought them to the valley of Achor. Then Joshua said to Achan, "Why have you brought trouble on us? The LORD will now bring trouble on you." And all the Israelites stoned Achan and his family and burned their bodies.

So the LORD was no longer angry.

Joshua 7:24 – 25; 26c NLT

Now, keep in mind, the importance of the ministry being in agreement is that *everyone* is committed to the cause; possess the land. Otherwise, if one disobeyed, we all disobeyed. Or if one failed, we all failed. Not only that, but if we allowed Leah's disobedience to continue to go unpunished, that would set a precedent with the other members in the ministry – sin spreads. Therefore, it's everyone's responsibility to prevent the enemy from being in the camp by *getting rid of* the undisciplined, disobedient, and that which had been set apart for destruction.

Without God's presence, we're not living; we're merely existing – dead men walking.

~ CHAPTER 2 ~

NO HONOR AMONG FRIENDS

The following days at work proved to be challenging; however, one day after lunch, Leah said, "I have something for you."

"Give me what's mine," I said jokingly. And she gave me a *gift*.

That evening, as I sat in the presence of the Lord, I was reminded of the *gift*, the supposed *"friendship"* we had, and all that we'd been through. And immediately, I *knew* we could no longer be friends.

However, while this was clear in my spirit, it was a little more difficult for my heart to come into agreement. Therefore, I struggled with the realization because I knew it was going to be devastating; not only for her, but for me as well. And to say that the demand was difficult, was an understatement. But there was no mistake, when I looked back over our *"friendship,"* I knew it had to come to an end.

The next morning, I settled in my spirit and concluded that I was going to give the gift back. And as if trying to convince myself wasn't enough, the Lord spoke into my spirit, "If you continue this friendship, the enemy will continue to attack you."

And suddenly, I was reminded of all the pain that I had endured. "Oh, my God!" I cried out, as the pain rung out in my spirit. *I cannot go through that again,* I declared.

"Anyone who isn't with me opposes me, and anyone who isn't working with me is actually working against me."

Matthew 12:30 NLT

"Push!" He encouraged me.

As I was driving to work, I thought about how the demonic forces operate:

For who is powerful enough to enter the house of a strong man like Satan and plunder his goods? Only someone even stronger—someone who could tie him up and then plunder his house.

Matthew 12:29 NLT

A *strong man* represents Satan and his demonic forces, which represents the kingdom of darkness: the rulers, the authorities, the powers of this dark world, and the spiritual forces of evil in the heavenly realms, which is ruled by Satan. The demonic activity that is performed by these demons, fallen angels, embodies spiritual warfare:

So I say, let the Holy Spirit guide your lives. Then you won't be doing what your sinful nature craves. The sinful nature wants to do evil, which is just the opposite of what the Spirit wants. And the Spirit gives us desires that are the opposite of what the sinful nature desires. These two forces are constantly fighting each other, so you are not free to carry out your good intentions.

Galatians 5:16 – 17 NLT

This demonic activity – spiritual warfare – takes place in the spirit realm. Therefore, as the above scriptures indicate in Matthew, chapter twelve, the only way someone is able to defeat a strong man like Satan is someone who is even stronger than he is, and that someone is Jesus.

So while Satan dictates to the demons and associated spirits, their ultimate assignment is to cause an individual to become entangled in sin; any lifestyle that is opposed to God. And the only way that Satan is able to accomplish this goal is by the individual living by what is known as *Works of the Flesh*:

When you follow the desires of your sinful nature, the results are very clear: sexual immorality, impurity, lustful pleasures, idolatry, sorcery, hostility, quarreling, jealousy, outbursts of anger, selfish ambition, dissension, division, envy, drunkenness, wild parties, and other sins like these.

Galatians 5:19 – 21a NLT

So, again, as the Lord stated, "Whoever is not with me is against me, and whoever does not gather with me scatters." But this same God, who is able to defeat Satan (*tie him up and then plunder his house),* commands us to walk by the Spirit and not lust after the flesh. And since we live by the Spirit, let us keep in step with the Spirit by way of the *Fruit of the Spirit.*

But the fruit of the Spirit is love, joy, peace, forbearance, kindness, goodness, faithfulness, ^gentleness *and self-control.*

Galatians 5:22 – 23 NIV

We must be mindful that if we're living by the works of the flesh, it opens the *door* for the strong man, who is powerful enough to enter our house and plunder our goods. What is an open door? An open door is an opportunity for Satan to enter in. In the book of Genesis, as a result of the Lord not accepting Cain's gift, it resulted in Cain being angry and dejected (disappointed). And the Lord said to Cain,

You will be accepted if you do what is right. But if you refuse to do what is right, then watch out! Sin is crouching at the door, eager to control you. But you must subdue it and be its master."

Genesis 4:7 NLT

So, let me point out that anger and disappointment are considered works of the flesh; created by your own desire. And therefore, they open the door or provide an opportunity for Satan to come in. To do what? To *control* you. Notice the scripture states, sin (Satan) is crouching at the door; he's waiting for a chance to enter in. Now keep in mind, *enter in* means *to attack*. And when you live by the **works of the flesh,** it opens the door for him to come in – and again – control you; attack you. And let's not forget that the book of Ephesians, chapter four, verses twenty-six and twenty-seven tells us "don't sin by letting anger control you." Don't let the sun go down while you are still angry, for anger gives a *foothold* to the devil. What is a foothold? It allows the devil to divide us; the body of Christ.

Consequently, the bible also tells us in First Peter, chapter five, verse eight to stay alert! Watch out for your great enemy, the devil. He prowls around like a roaring lion, looking for someone to devour. The only way for us to subdue it and be its master is to walk by the Spirit; live according to the **fruit of the Spirit.** And only the Holy Spirit, Jesus, will be able to master, tie him up and then plunder his house; deliver those who are oppressed by the enemy.

And to reiterate the principle of agreement as Amos stated:

Does a lion ever roar in a thicket
    without first finding a victim?
Does a young lion growl in its den
    without first catching its prey?

As it is with temptation, when one thing happens, the other is sure to follow. And the same holds true for sin – it is progressive – when one thing happens, the other is sure to follow; one thing leads to another. Again, it goes back to that concept: can two walk together except they are in agreement. You and the enemy in agreement equal the works of the flesh, while you and the Holy Spirit in agreement equal the fruit of the Spirit.

Dear children, don't let anyone deceive you about this: When people do what is right, it shows that they are righteous, even as Christ is righteous. But when people keep on sinning, it shows that they belong to the devil, who has been sinning since the beginning. But the Son of God came to destroy the works of the devil.

1 John 3:7 – 8 NLT

So, what am I saying?

Do not bring sorrow to God's Holy Spirit by the way you live.

For when a strong man like Satan is fully armed and guards his palace, his possessions are safe—until someone even stronger attacks and overpowers him, strips him of his weapons, and carries off his belongings. Therefore, we have to close the door that allows Satan to enter in.

And I will give you the keys of the Kingdom of Heaven. Whatever you forbid on earth will be forbidden in heaven, and whatever you permit on earth will be permitted in heaven."

Matthew 16:19 NLT

Once I arrived at work, I waited for the opportune time to give the gift back. And again, I asked Leah if I could share something with her.

"Last night, I thought about the gift that you gave me..."

"You have to give it back?" she interrupted.

"Yes. I have to give it back."

"Oh, my God, Daiz! Don't tell me you have to give it back! Why?"

"Because I have to make sure that I'm not sending the wrong message by accepting the gift."

"What do you mean? How could *you* be sending the wrong message; *I* gave *you* the gift."

"As I thought about the friendship that we've had and all that we've been through, I don't trust you. And in order for us to have a true friendship, I have to be able to trust you. And with that being said, I can't accept the gift because *we can no longer be friends.*"

"Oh, noooo," she cried out. "I don't believe you're doing this. Oh, man! Wait! Wait! Wait! This is too much! Hold on! Give me a minute. Let me take this in," she said as I stood there. "I hear what you're saying," she continued, "and I think I understand what you're saying, but give me a minute to let it all soak in."

So I stood there as she apparently had to come to the realization of what was happening.

"Daisy, I know you may think I should already know the answer to this, but why don't you trust me?"

Are you kidding me? I thought, but I was all the more willing to help her understand. That way, there'd be no mistaking what happened between us. "Leah, throughout our friendship you consistently lied to me, you don't respect me, and then you betrayed me." *Not to mention the many times you attacked me,* I thought but didn't say because she wouldn't have understood. "We can't continue to be friends and you haven't changed; otherwise, you'll continue to do the same things. And just because you're saved doesn't automatically mean you've changed (I added to disprove her thinking once you're saved you're automatically regenerated without effort). The satanic activity that's in your life has to be worked out; you have to be delivered, grow, and mature in those areas. For example," I continued, "you don't just stop being a liar because you're saved. You have to be delivered in that area by making a concentrated effort to change that behavior, and until then – you're still a liar (even though you're saved). And because you're not mature in the areas that we've struggled in, to continue being friends means going right back to square one – dealing with the same stuff we've dealt with since the beginning, over and over again. Therefore, it wouldn't be until you've matured in those areas that we'd ever be able to move past the lying, mistrust, or betrayal." *And even then,* I thought, *we still wouldn't be friends.*

"How did I betray you?"

"You betrayed me…"

"Tiffany. I know," she interrupted.

"Yes. Tiffany." *And, the many times you allowed Satan to use you to attack me,* I thought but didn't say anything. "I told you something in confidence, which was in your best interest to help you grow. Then you not only went back and told Tiffany what I said, but you twisted it and made it out to be malicious, which it wasn't." And all I could think of was, *I was your friend.*

"I know. But I want you to know that I didn't mean to hurt you," she said. "But I have to say, I thought this was about our spiritual relationship, so I don't understand what this has to do with our friendship."

And as if she hadn't heard anything that I had just said, she asked,

"Why can't we be friends like before?"

And immediately, I was reminded of Peter:

Jesus turned and said to Peter, <u>"Get behind me, Satan! You are a stumbling block to me; you do not have in mind the things of God, but the things of men."</u>

Matthew 16:21 – 23 NIV (emphasis added)

Now, what you may or may not know about the above passage of scriptures is, Satan used Peter; it was Satan's attempt to keep Jesus from going to the cross to conquer sin, death, and hell. If Satan could've kept Jesus from getting to the cross, then Satan wouldn't have lost his power; thereby, Jesus wouldn't have accomplished His mission. Therefore, I don't want you to miss the exact same thing was taking place with Leah and me. Even still, the enemy was using Leah to tempt me into remaining friends so I couldn't accomplish my purpose and complete my assignment. And just as Jesus had said to Peter, I thought, *we can't be friends because you are a stumbling block to me; you do not have in mind the things of God, but the things of men.* And it was clear that her assignment was to *stop me from completing my assignment.*

"You've already shown me that you don't have any respect for me or my ministry; therefore, our friendship has been affected by our spiritual relationship; just as our spiritual relationship has been affected by our friendship. You have no respect for me, and I can't be friends with someone who doesn't respect me." I reiterated. "And what you did, friends don't do."

Then they scoffed, "He's just a carpenter, the son of Mary and the brother of James, Joseph, Judas, and Simon. And his sisters live right here among us." They were deeply offended and refused to believe in him.

Then Jesus told them, "A prophet is honored everywhere except in his own hometown and among his relatives and his own family."

And because of their unbelief, he couldn't do any mighty miracles among them except to place his hands on a few sick people and heal them.

And he was amazed at their unbelief.

Mark 6:3 – 6 NLT

"And now," I said, "we have to set boundaries. So going forward our relationship is strictly professional," as I was reminded of the Word of the Lord:

'But if you fail to drive out the people who live in the land, those who remain will be like splinters in your eyes and thorns in your sides. They will harass you in the land where you live. And I will do to you what I had planned to do to them.'

"I have to say," she said, "that I was a little confused because I wasn't sure that since the spiritual relationship had been severed, I didn't know how we were supposed to be friends. I didn't know what we could or couldn't do as friends."

"I know. That's why I'm here to give you clarity. So that we'll have a clear understanding going forward – *we are not friends;* we only have a professional relationship."

"What does that mean?"

"The same way that you interact with the people on the job, that's the way we'll interact. We can't have those *personal* conversations anymore nor can we *hang out* at lunch together anymore…"

"But Daiz!" she interrupted. "You go to lunch with people on the job, and now you're telling me that *we* can't go to lunch anymore? Now all of a sudden you can't have lunch with *me!*"

"Because…"

"I just think that you just don't want to be bothered with me anymore," she interrupted. "That my stuff is too heavy for you to deal with and you're just giving up on me! Why can't you just wait until I mature and then leave?"

Immediately, the pain rung out in my spirit. And anyone with a spiritual eye could see the tears that ran down my face and left their traces of heartache and sorrow. While the enemy had raised the stakes and challenged me, he was tempting me to remain in the *"friendship,"* but it did very little to dissuade me. And immediately, my heart started breaking because it hurt to see her in that position. I wanted nothing more than to have seen her grow and mature in the Lord. I was *mad* that she had allowed the enemy to use her. And now she was the one who would have to suffer the blow at the hand of the enemy. And yet, I did everything that I could to keep my composure as I explained that I couldn't wait for her to mature.

"I don't know what it is," she said, "is it that I'm dragging you down spiritually? Am I a burden for you? What is it?"

I was speechless.

If I said anything, one word out of my mouth, and my defeat was certain – because I would've told her that because I *was* her friend I wanted to stay. I would've told her that I wouldn't have ever *betrayed* her. I would've told her that if I had it my way, I *wouldn't* let her go. And I would've *held her* for as long as I could as the tears streamed down my face.

And immediately, the Lord began to minister to me because my heart was breaking, and I had no words to enlighten her regarding the outcome of our *friendship.* I wanted desperately to tell her how she had allowed the enemy to use her and now she had to suffer the consequences.

I wanted to tell her that everything that we were going through was **the birthing that the Lord hid from the enemy – her, Tiffany, and Maria – until its appointed time, so that they couldn't kill the baby; the ministry or stop it.**

But my words failed me.

Besides, I knew she wouldn't understand. Therefore, I had nothing to say and there was nothing I could do. My heart continued to break as my spirit cried out for God to *do something! Help me!*

"Push!" He responded to my plea for help.

~ CHAPTER 3 ~

DILATED – IT'S TIME TO PUSH

The moment was far greater than what I had anticipated, far greater than what I could handle. Again, as I stood in front of this very same person who had attacked me time and time again, it devastated me to know that she had no idea of what was *really* going on. And yet, my spirit continued to cry out to the Lord because I was burdened. Pleading for Him to help me because I had absolutely nothing to say; my words had failed me. By this time, even if I opened my mouth, surely nothing would've come out.

"Your season is over," the Lord answered.

Strengthened by the words He spoke, and with everything that I had in me, I explained, "It's not that you're dragging me down spiritually or that you're a burden to me, but we only had a set time for God to accomplish His purpose in our lives. The things that He wanted to accomplish in you and the things he wanted to accomplish in me have been accomplished. And now our time together is over; our season has come to an end. However," I said as I had somehow managed to continue, "I have no doubt that one day you'll mature in those areas that you're weak in and I'm excited about that."

"But how are you going to see me when I've matured if you're walking away now. You won't see me."

With every word that came out of her mouth, it caused my heart to break even more, piece by piece, but in my mind, my thoughts were: *I can't stay. I can't wait. I have to go. And you have to let me go.*

"I don't have to *see* you, but I *know* that it's going to happen. Not only that, but we don't know what the Lord has planned – maybe someday I *will* get to see you matured. But I'm telling you now, I don't have to *see* it because I already know that it *will* happen."

"I don't know how much more of this I can take – this hurts," she said as the pain was evident on her face and in her voice.

"I know. But you'll get through it," I assured her.

"I just don't understand it. It seems like this is being forced," she said as it was apparent that she was confused. "I've had friends that I'm not friends with anymore, but it just happened. I didn't have to *tell* the person that we weren't friends; it just happened naturally. I mean, ***I'm trying to pull you to me, but it seems like you're pulling away from me.***"

"That's why it can't happen naturally; you keep trying to pull me to you. ***You have to let me go*** so we can both move on," I said as I pleaded in my spirit, *please, let me go!*

I was weakened by her attempt to hold on and not let go. I had nothing left in me to give that would help either of us get through this. I wanted it to be over!

"Push!" rung out in my spirit.

I continued to cry out in my spirit, *please...let me go.* Then suddenly I was overwhelmed with *the* most excruciating pain as the vision was before me:

In a vision...

I saw the baby's head coming through the birthing canal.

The interpretation...

The baby was being delivered. I was birthing ministry.

The pain was piercing. It was gut-wrenching. And in my spirit, I continued to plead with the Lord as I stood there, *Help me!* And with the last little bit of strength I had left,

I pushed!

"You have to let me go," I demanded.

And as soon as the words were released from my mouth, *"It's over,"* rang out in my spirit.

Going our separate ways, I went into my *secret place* to allow the tears to give way to the birthing pain that had just taken place. And as soon as I made it home, I just laid in the Lord's presence. Every ounce of strength that I had in my body was gone, and all I could do was weep before the Lord.

I was worn out by the lies, deceit, betrayal, and warfare that had brought me to that point; extremely exhausted.

My heart heavy, eyes swollen, mind blank, body completely worn out, and spirit distraught.

I'm done!

~ CHAPTER 4 ~

CUTTING THE UMBILICAL CORD

As a result of our conversation, the text messages, any and all communication (the ministry in particular), as well as us hanging out together ceased immediately. However, the balance between our once *friendship* and now *professional* relationship proved to be more difficult than I had imagined.

And what started out as her asking for my professional assistance slowly turned into familiar conversations, laughing, and socializing again – until little by little we were falling back into our old ways. The conversations went from professional to personal: a little of the baby daddy stuff, what was going on with school, personal stuff, and of course her health.

There were some changes being made on the job and some of the co-workers were being transferred to different departments. And one day Leah asked me about her going to a particular department. She wanted a promotion and was trying to figure out the best way to get the promotion (considering she had missed three or four promotional opportunities). Now I have to say, by this time, we had discussed this same topic I don't know how many times in the past just to hear her say to me, 'You're more concerned about me getting the promotion than you're concerned about me.' However, in the meantime, I had been promoted several times and had received recognition for one of the highest professional achievements in the company. But *this* time, I realized this conversation was no longer about her getting a promotion; *this* was about our friendship.

I struggled within because I wanted nothing more than to be done with the friendship, and her leaving the department would make it one hundred times easier for me to get through this. But I knew the last thing that was on God's mind was "easy;" therefore, I explained to her that it would be best for her to stay in the department because she was getting the support that she needed for the promotion.

"You wouldn't be just saying that so I'll leave the department would you?" she asked as if she had known my heart's desire.

"While I do want you to leave the department, I wouldn't do that," I said.

So she decided to stay in the department.

Then the assistance went from me helping her at work to me helping her with her homework. *She had to let me go.* One time in particular, as she was explaining the assignment to me, I thought, *how am I going to tell her that I'm not going to help her?* Considering in the past, if she had asked, I was there. "I apologize, but time doesn't permit me to assist you with your assignment," I said.

"I already knew that," she responded. "Before I could even finish explaining the assignment, you were already saying, 'I can't help you.' That's okay. I'll get someone else to help me. Thanks, anyway."

In due course, I saw that the *professional* relationship wasn't working either. It was actually preventing me from moving forward (and her letting me go) as well. And for that reason, I became more and more reserved with my assistance and association with her – gradually no longer making myself available to her.

Then I got a call that she was in the hospital.

And needless to say, immediately, I became concerned about her well-being, so I called her to check on her. We talked for a little bit (even though by this time, the conversation felt strained). Now, I have to say that the call was a little emotional, bitter-sweet, because it brought back memories of when she was a part of the ministry and had gotten attacked in her body.

Anyway, after we disconnected the call, I prayed for her. And as I sat there in the garden, the tears rolled down my face as my heart longed to be done with this assignment. I struggled with being able to move forward as the *pull* in the spirit proved to be resilient; a threat to undermine the clarity of our relationship, my assignment, and an outright refusal to let me go.

Leah had taken the rest of the week off in order to focus on her health, so when she came to back work, I was glad to see that she was feeling better (at least enough to come to work). So when I saw her, I hugged her and welcomed her back. However, I have to say *we're no longer friends* was always in the forefront of my mind. So after welcoming her back, I continued to make a conscious effort to remain cordial and distant.

Then the follow up visits and the trips back and forth to the doctor's office resulted in her asking me to pray for her because she just wasn't getting better, and she was in pain.

"You're the only woman of God that I know who has healing hands," she said. "Do you remember that time you prayed for me when I was sick and I got healed?"

"Yes, I remember," I said. "What's wrong? What are the doctors saying?" I asked. And she went on to explain what she was experiencing. "Of course we can pray just let me know when."

We determined we'd pray during lunch, however, when I walked away, the Lord told me to go and pray right then. So I went to the garden area and prayed for her. And immediately, the Lord revealed that it was done. He had healed her. But when I came back, she wasn't around, so I sent her an email. I explained that the Lord had prompted me to pray for her and that it was already done just receive it. However, when I was getting ready to walk away, she walked up and asked if I was ready to go pray.

"I already…"

"You can't pray with me?!" she asked as she interrupted (almost *subconsciously* familiar with what was happening).

"No, no, no," I said for clarity (although that *was* apparently the case). "I already pra…"

"You can't pray without me," she interrupted again.

"I was prompted to go and pray…"

"Noooooo. You can't pray without me. We have to pray together."

"No, we don't. The Lord told me to go pray right then," I continued, "so I went and prayed. And I just want you to know that it's already done. Just receive it."

"Noooooo. We have to pray together. We have to hold hands and I have to hear your voice as you pray."

"No, you don't. What you have to do now is use your faith."

"I knooooow! Now you're going to make me work for my healing instead of us praying together and I just get healed like before."

"That's how faith works. It's already done. Your healing is already done, just receive it." I said as we went our separate ways.

The next day, she was just overjoyed because she felt a thousand times better. It was, "Daisy this, Daisy that, Daisy, Daisy, Daisy…" and it was just too much for me to handle *especially* with the spiritual state that I was in. I couldn't even begin to tell you how burdensome the relationship had become. And just when I thought it couldn't get any worse…

"I have something to show you," she said.

"Okay."

"But I don't have it with me today, remind me and I'll bring it tomorrow."

"Okay."

And as if the battle had somehow intensified, it was just too much for me to handle. There was no doubt that the Lord was *demanding* that I sever the ties that had us bound.

In a dream…

I was in a store getting educational toys for a baby and I noticed the floor was made of sand. When I looked, I saw what appeared to be an alligator/snake; it was a cross of the two. I tried to focus in order to determine what it was, which was a little difficult to make out because it was buried in the sand. It appeared to be fossil-like (dead for a long time). Then it started to move, slowly freeing itself from the sand, then, it slithered away as I watched it.

After it slithered away, I couldn't see where it went, and I became afraid because I didn't know where it went, but I knew it was in the place.

Then I woke up.

The interpretation...

The Lord revealed that getting the educational toys for the baby was a representation of me getting ready to learn a lesson in the ministry.

The floor being made of sand was an indication that my foundation (my relationship with Leah) had not been established; it was not solid.

The cross of the alligator/snake was a reflection of Leah: alligator represents deceit, and a snake represents the enemy; tricks and snares – she couldn't be trusted.

And buried in the sand indicated that the deceit, snare – was hidden.

Fossil – like simply meant that she would not change.

Then she (the alligator/snake) started to move, slowly freeing herself from the sand, which represented her slowly removing the restriction of our relationship.

Slithered away represents – Leviathan, the gliding serpent, the coiling serpent was a reflection of the enemy moving smoothly without being noticed. This was an indication that she was about to do something that wouldn't be that easy to notice.

The coiling serpent revealed the snake was positioned to strike.

I couldn't see where it went indicated I didn't know when or how the attack would come, which revealed my fear.

The next day Leah asked me to come to her office because she wanted to show me something. *The last thing I want to do is go to her office, not to mention see whatever it is that she wants to show me,* I thought. But, reluctantly, I went and immediately I noticed the bible open on her desk. It was not a big deal because she usually had it open. But when she went to grab the bible, I thought, *I know she's not getting ready to show me something in the bible.* And just as quickly as the thought crossed my mind she said, "Look at this," and grabbed the bible. *We're not getting ready to do this,* I thought. *It had already been established that our days of "bible study" were over and had been for a long time now.* So I hesitated because for a quick second I contemplated telling her, "We don't do bible study."

Then I noticed the page referenced homosexuality, and before I knew anything, she had already started sharing what she had to "show me."

> *Then she (the alligator/snake) started to move, slowly freeing herself from the sand, which represented her slowly removing the restrictions of our relationship.*

"When I was reading my bible the other day, I came across this and it gave me some more understanding about homosexuality."

"That's good," I said, although I wasn't really interested and wanted desperately to just walk away.

"Now I know what to say to someone when they say that they were *born* gay. What is it that you say when someone says that they're born gay, again?"

> *Slithered away represents – Leviathan, the gliding serpent, the coiling serpent was a reflection of the enemy moving smoothly without being noticed. This was an indication that she was about to do something that wouldn't be that easy to notice.*
>
> *And buried in the sand indicated that the deceit, snare – was hidden.*

In the past, I had explained *generational curses* to Leah, and how spirits transferred. And in my explanation I used the spirit of homosexuality as an example. And I went on to say that if a person used the excuse, *"I was born this way,"* then being *born that way* would only have been as a result of a generational curse.

You must not bow down to them or worship them, for I, the LORD your God, am a jealous God who will not tolerate your affection for any other gods. I lay the sins of the parents upon their children; the entire family is affected – <u>even children in the third and fourth generations of those who reject me.</u>

Exodus 20:5 NLT (emphasis added)

When someone sins, curses are automatically released upon that person and upon that person's descendants whether already living or yet to be born. Curses are the penalty, or judgment, for sin. Jesus shed His blood on the cross that the power of curses might be broken. However, each one of us must appropriate Christ's finished work on the cross into each area of sin in our lives, *including the effects of the ancestral sins and curses.* This appropriation is not automatic since we must receive it, as well as everything else we receive from God, by faith.

We see it repeated in First John, chapter one, verse nine. God requires us to repent and to be accountable for violating His law.

Our ancestors and parents have sinned. Curses, the consequences of those sins, are passed down through the generations. These curses affect *our* lives. It is possible that the current problem you are dealing with is related to ancestral curses.

"But at last my people will confess their sins <u>and the sins of their ancestors</u> for betraying me and being hostile toward me. When I have turned their hostility back on them and <u>brought them to the land of their enemies,</u> then at last their stubborn hearts will be humbled, and they will pay for their sins.

Leviticus 26:40 – 41 NLT (emphasis added)

The *land of their enemies* is a reflection of the demonic forces that we'd have to contend with as a result of our rebellion, sin, and turning against God.

Against you, and you alone, have I sinned;
*   I have done what is evil in your sight.*
You will be proved right in what you say,
*   and your judgment against me is just.*

Psalm 51:4 NLT

Now, I'd like to point out the fact that while the enemy was moving smoothly and trying not to be noticed, I could see that he was using the Word of God – her sharing the bible with me – to position himself. But I responded, "If a person says to me that they're *born* gay, then I share with them that the only way to be *born* gay is as a result of a generational curse because people aren't *born* gay…"

The coiling serpent revealed the snake was positioned to strike.

"Well, I don't believe that anymore," she interrupted.

Fossil – like simply meant that she would not change.

Immediately, I was able to recognize that the enemy had come to attack just as the Lord had revealed in the dream.

"I think I'm going to say what this person is saying," she said, "and you probably should say the same thing. Now I'm not trying to tell you what to say I'm just saying that if you want to say the same thing then you can."

"No," I said as a matter of fact, "I'm going to *continue* saying what I say."

And I walked away.

And with me, I took the last little bit of strength I had to draw the line.

That day we became adversaries.

THE UMBILICAL CORD HAD BEEN CUT.

And as if the separation had released *the* most intense battle I'd ever known, I found myself fighting for *my* life as I struggled for days, months to free myself from the *stronghold.*

Satan refused to let me go.

> **The ring master raised his whip to instruct the tiger to rise up. When the tiger rose, it appeared to be twelve – fifteen feet tall. I was astonished at how huge the tiger was.**

And as if Satan had taken every weapon that he had, he waged an all out war against me. Consequently, I found myself trying desperately to keep from getting wounded by the blows that he had delivered. I cried out to the Lord, "Help me!" However, the more I cried out to the Lord, the more intense the battle became.

Day in and day out; the battle was constant – never ending.

The demand for me to surrender – give up – was overwhelming. The weight of the demonic attacks weighed on me greatly. The heaviness was so devastating – it forced me to my knees and caused me to collapse. I continued to cry out to the Lord, "Lord, help me!" as the tears fell from my eyes. Desperate; my hands shook severely and trembled relentlessly as I struggled to hold on.

The blows were deadly.

No strength to stand; I lay prostrate before the Lord.

I struggled to make it each day as the warfare caused my soul to be in anguish. I was exhausted by the blows I was being dealt. Wounded; I continued in spite of the great resistance that tried to keep me from going on. But not willing to give up, I continued to call on Jesus. And yet, barely able to stand, the weight was crushing and again had caused my knees to buckle under the pressure of trying to stand. As a result of the intense attack, I had done all that I could do just to keep my soul from spiraling out of control.

With each passing day, and a war waging against me, my heart searched for relief, but no relief came. My heart was faint, and my strength gone. The weight of oppression was overpowering and I couldn't free myself. I couldn't break free from the stronghold – *there was no hedge of protection.* The battle had become more than I could handle. Agony rung out from within as I desperately continued to cry out to the Lord and pleaded with what little strength I had left, "Please, Lord, release me."

No strength to even pray – "Oh, my God! *Free me* from this stronghold!" I continued to cry out.

I was in the fight *of* my life – *for* my life.

Defeat was certain.

There was no more fight left in me; the pressure was too intense, and the pain was too great. I had absolutely nothing left in me; the turmoil went deep. It took everything that I had in me to make it through each day only to collapse at the end of each night. The days were dark and the nights were darker. I'd lie down night after night, not knowing if I would get up again. I lay dying as I agonized over losing the battle.

The bread of tears and the cup of affliction were my portions.

Night after night, late in the midnight hour, and as if I were awakened from the dead, the voice of the Lord answered.

"Prophesy to yourself!"

Pain rung out in my spirit; His Words testified to the realization that I was losing the battle – dead in a valley of dry bones. The battle had worn me down and the pain was a testament to that.

"Speak a prophetic message to these bones and say, 'Dry bones, listen to the word of the LORD!"

But I couldn't speak. My words had become sore to me. I couldn't prophesy.

Then the Lord spoke:

"...Look! I am going to put breath into you and <u>make you</u> live again!"

The tears continued to fall and the pain continued to ring out. "I can't continue. I can't do it!" I whispered as the tears fell from my eyes, as He spoke.

"I will put flesh and muscles on you and cover you with skin. I will put breath into you, and <u>you will</u> come to life. Then <u>you will know</u> that I am the LORD.'"

"Help me, Jesus! Help me!" The pain was so intense that I was barely able to get the words out of my mouth! Every breath was painful, and every thought agonizing. "How much longer, Lord?" I questioned as the tears rolled down my face.

Silence

"Please…Help me," I whispered after the silence.

…*"Speak a prophetic message to the winds…Speak a prophetic message and say, 'This is what the Sovereign LORD says: <u>Come,</u> O breath, from the four winds! <u>Breathe</u> into these dead bodies so they may live again.'"*

Ezekiel 37:4 – 6; 9 NLT (emphasis added)

Come, Lord Jesus…save me; my heart cried.

And yet, night after night, it was the same: as if I were awakened from the dead, the voice of the Lord commanded:

"Prophesy to yourself!"

I was losing the battle. Unable to stand against the enemy as the pain continued to ring out in my spirit. I continued to cry before the Lord, "Help me, Jesus! Strengthen me, Lord to *fight* this battle."

"Prophesy to yourself!" He demanded. His Words pierced my spirit and gave permission for the tears to be released, and allowed the pain to come forth.

So I spoke this prophetic message, just as he told me:

"I speak a prophetic message to these dry bones and say, 'Dry bones, listen to the word of the LORD! This is what the Sovereign LORD says: Look! I am going to put breath into you and make you live again! I will put flesh and muscles on you and cover you with skin. I will put breath into you, and you will come to life. Then you will know that I am the LORD.'"

"I speak a prophetic message to the winds, son of man. Speak a prophetic message and say, 'This is what the Sovereign LORD says: Come, O breath, from the four winds! Breathe into these dead bodies so they may live again.'"

Night after night, after night,

I continued to cry out to the Lord because unlike Ezekiel, there was *no suddenly, no rattling noise, no coming together.* And like Ezekiel, I watched, *and I waited,* but there were *no muscles and flesh – no strength, no skin – no covering, no breath – no life.* "Where are you, Lord?" I asked. And I continued to cry out, even from that dead place as the pain besieged me, and the tears were my only form of relief.

He was there.

And in an ***audible voice,*** He spoke.

"SWORD OF THE SPIRIT!"

The *power* of His voice, His words *SPOKE* to every fiber of my being.

Immediately, *I drew my sword.*

'Dry bones, listen to the word of the LORD! Come, O breath, from the four winds!'

And yet, I struggled as the enemy tried to convince me that *everyone* and *everything* that I had fought for had been lost, as I lie there while he beat my body; relentlessly. My eyes swollen shut from the tears that released some of the pain, the blood, which was evidence that I had been wounded – flowed from the crown of my head to the soles of my feet, the pain rung out as evidence that I had been betrayed, and the hedge of protection removed; handed over to the enemy.

Up against the rope, my only hope was that the Lord would come and save me by allowing me to tap out. *Where are you, Lord?* I wondered. But there was no tag team. There was no tapping out.

I had to fight.

I was desperate for the bell to save me.

As the blows continued to come, they were crushing: my spirit broken, body bruised, and soul battered and worn as anguish overwhelmed me. My tears continued to fall from my eyes.

I continued to prophesy to the dry bones and the four winds.

'Dry bones, listen to the word of the LORD! Come, O breath, from the four winds!'

But still *no suddenly, no rattling noise, no coming together.* I watched, *and I waited,* but still *no muscles and flesh – no strength, no skin – no covering, no breath – no life.*

Immediately, the vision was before me:

In a vision...

I saw the hand of God holding back the four winds.

The interpretation…

The Lord wouldn't release the four winds until my faith was fully developed.

And instantly I was overwhelmed by the vision that bore witness to the pain of knowing *God is in control.* And I cried out to the Lord in distress, "Help me, Lord. Don't let the enemy defeat me! Don't let him win – *I can't lose, Lord. Help me! Please, Lord,"*

I pleaded for the slightest glimpse of hope, "*at least, let me hear the sound of the rattling; the sound of the coming together. Please, Lord, let me hear the sound...the sound from heaven."*

Lord, where are you? I wondered.

"Help me!" I cried out in my great affliction.

He answered.

In the night...

Out of a loud, great, and mighty sound of what I can only describe as lightening clashing...

A Divine Visitation...

...with God Himself, sitting on the throne.

My eyes have seen Him. God revealed Himself to me; a divine visitation, supernatural manifestation of Himself. And all I could say was, "He's alive. I have seen God!"

And for what seemed to be as soon as I laid my head on the pillow, I heard what I can only describe as lightning crashing. It was so loud, and so great and mighty that it caused me to sit straight up in the bed. My heart raced with fear. Instantly I was in the Spirit, in the third heaven. I was before His throne. I saw God sitting on His throne. And so that there would be no mistaking who He was I saw the word *God* before my eyes in a split second.

And when I looked, while I could see Him sitting on the throne, I could not see His face. Because there was light that shone from His face as rays of the sun emanating from Him. I could see there was hair, but I couldn't determine if it was white as wool as John stated because the light was so bright. He had on a white robe as He sat on the throne. And He held the scepter of righteousness in His right hand.

Immediately, I noticed the colors as my eyes searched to take in all of His glory. The colors were absolutely brilliant. Colors I've never seen before. The best way I could describe them were pastel colors made of crystals. I've never seen these colors before – in all their brilliance. The colors sparkled. Now I will say this, they seemed to be the colors of the rainbow. However, the blue seemed to be more prominent. It was absolutely gorgeous. There was peace in His presence. Much needed peace as I had suffered hard and long. And the tears rolled down my face as I felt the peace of being in His presence. It was silent – just His presence. A silence like I've never heard before; as if I were deaf. I mean there wasn't even the slightest bit of sound. I just took it all in.

Immediately, I started crying. I had seen God. God had revealed Himself to me. I had a *revelation* of God Himself. And, as if for the first time, it felt like I had the *indwelling* of the Holy Spirit inside of me as I felt the weight of His glory upon me. It felt like I had expanded to my absolute fullest inside and I was getting ready to explode. My spirit was full; endowed with power.

And every time the thought had crossed my mind, *I have seen God,* my spirit would be overtaken and the tears would just roll down my face.

And just as suddenly, I was reminded of the promise, the assurance as I drank from the cup:

> **Though the Lord gave you adversity for food and suffering for drink, he will still be with you to teach you. You will see your teacher with your own eyes.**
>
> **Isaiah 30:20 NLT**

The tears continued to roll down my face as I was reminded of all that I'd been through – I was tired and my spirit was due for some much needed rest, deliverance. His presence was so soothing and peaceful unlike anything I've experienced before – quite naturally. I don't know if I fell asleep in His presence or if He left and then I went to sleep.

The next morning when I was reminded of being in heaven, again, the only thing I could think to say was "I saw God with my own eyes." And have since come to know that the lightning clashing is significant to God's power and majesty. And then the Lord began to minister to me, revealing *the significance of the color blue* being prominent in His presence:

It was God revealing *I was carrying out His plan and accomplishing His purposes.*

All day long I walked around filled with despair. *How is this possible?* I'd ask myself. *I have seen God.* As the tears fell from my eyes, my heart fainted, and my strength had failed me. I looked for deliverance, but it had not come. I was exhausted by the blows from the enemy.

Another blow, and again, I was crushed! I'd been knocked down as the tears fell from my eyes. I wondered *where is the bell?* Blood, sweat, and tears were evidence that *I* was no match for my opponent. Cries came from my anguished heart. All of my strength was gone.

I didn't know if I was going to make it.

The pain had been unlike anything that I had ever experienced before. I couldn't take another blow; I knew the next blow would surely kill me.

And yet, I longed for the final blow to come.

My soul was crushed to the point of death.

Then all of a sudden the *referee, the Holy Spirit,* stepped in and stopped the fight; **causing the enemy to retreat.**

I lay breaths away from death.

And still, the sound of the bell had not come. However, I was reminded of the vision:

> **I was drinking from a cup. The cup was empty, it had a hole in it, and the water was coming out.**

> **After the third attack, I'd be spiritually empty, and yet the affliction would still cause the anointing to be released.**

Should I pray, 'Father, save me from this hour'? But this is the very reason I came! Father, bring glory to your name."

John 12:27b – 28 NLT

~ CHAPTER 5 ~

THE AFTERBIRTH

Unconscious to what was going on around me; I laid there. I could hear the *referee, the Holy Spirit,* counting to give me a chance to get up. Then in the distance I heard a voice saying, "Get up, and fight!"

"But I don't want to get up," I responded in a worn whisper. ***The ropes of death entangled me.*** I cried out in my spirit as the pain continued to reverberate throughout my body.

Then in a small, still voice the Lord said, "Get up, Daisy, and fight."

The tears continued to fall from my eyes as I continued to cry from the pain that traumatized me, my body; and though broken, battered, and bruised I struggled to get up. And *somehow, someway*, through the tears – in a whisper I declared:

I shall not die, but live, and declare the works of the LORD. The LORD hath chastened me sore: but he hath not given me over unto death.

Psalm 118:17 – 18 KJV

Then the angel of the LORD appeared before me:

In a vision...

The angel of the LORD appeared to me in flames of fire from within coals. And although the coals were on fire, they did not burn.

The interpretation...

"I am here," *He assured me as He answered by fire.*

I didn't know if the final blow had come or not, but immediately I was in the Spirit, in the third heaven; in the presence of God.

I was lying on what appeared to be an operating table. It was clear that I was dead. The Great Physician was performing an operation on me. I heard the voice of the Lord as He explained the purging power of the live coal. It was clear that I was dead in the spirit. But yet, the battle was not over.

Again, I drew my sword.

We are human, but we don't wage war as humans do. We use God's mighty weapons, not worldly weapons, <u>to knock down the strongholds of human reasoning and to destroy false arguments.</u> We destroy every proud obstacle that keeps people from knowing God. We capture <u>their</u> <u>rebellious thoughts</u> and <u>teach them to obey Christ.</u>

2 Corinthians 10:3 – 5 NLT (emphasis added)

So consequently, in addition to prophesying and praying for myself, as Satan waged war against me, *I waged war against Leah – the weapon that he had used against me – cancelling the enemy's assignments.* Let me make one thing clear; this battle was not between me and Leah – this battle was between God and Satan. So we must realize that I wasn't fighting against flesh and blood, but I was fighting against evil rulers and authorities of the unseen world, against mighty powers in this dark world, and against evil spirits in the heavenly places: evil forces of powerful fallen angels led by Satan, who is vicious.

Stay alert! Watch out for your great enemy, the devil. He prowls around like a roaring lion, looking for someone to devour. Stand firm against him, and be strong in your faith. Remember that your Christian brothers and sisters all over the world are going through the same kind of suffering you are.

1 Peter 5:8 – 9 NLT

Leah was always on my heart; therefore, I began to cry out to the Lord on her behalf. I started to war against her *human reasoning* in order to *destroy the false arguments* that had a *stronghold* on her mind, which *kept her from receiving the Word of God.* I warred against *proud obstacles* that *kept her from knowing God;* every time she came against the Word of God that I shared with her, I began to *break the strongholds* that had allowed Satan to *build walls that separated her from God.* Consequently, this is the battle fought when people have *head knowledge of God*, but not a *heart experience or personal relationship with Him*; we try to figure it out instead of walking by faith.

But God's weapons are mighty and powerful to pull down and demolish these strongholds. Just like the enemy used Saul to try to stop David's assignment of becoming King, David played the harp to keep the demonic spirit from oppressing Saul – rebuking the enemy and his assignment against David in the spirit – so that the demonic attack, stronghold, would be defeated.

And whenever the tormenting spirit from God troubled Saul, David would play the harp. Then Saul would feel better, and the tormenting spirit would go away.

1 Samuel 16:23 NLT

So I started to break the power of the enemy by rebuking (binding and loosing) every satanic spirit that the Lord had revealed to me that was a part of this war *(including the spirit of Judas; the spirit of betrayal)* and any and all unhealthy, ungodly soul-ties between us.

"Satan, in the name of Jesus, I break all powers of your satanic hedge that is around and about us and render them powerless. I break the power of all demonic hedges and strongholds that have been formed against us to entangle, entrap, and ensnare us. The blood of Jesus is against you! The Lord God rebukes you!"

"In the name of Jesus, I command you to loose her, and let her go!"

"In the name of Jesus, I command you to loose me, and let me go!"

For three days and nights, I fasted; eating absolutely nothing, and prayed every hour on the hour, declared and decreed that the covenant was broken – as I continued to cry out to the Lord, "Please Lord, break, revoke, cancel, and withdraw me from the covenant agreement that was made with this people; with this nation!"

Then I made a final plea to the Lord:

This is what the L*ORD* my God says: "Shepherd the flock marked for slaughter."

So I shepherded the flock marked for slaughter, particularly the oppressed of the flock. Then I took two staffs and called one Favor and the other Union, and I shepherded the flock…The flock detested me, and I grew weary of them and said, "I will not be your shepherd. Let the dying die, and the perishing perish…"

Then I took my staff called Favor and broke it, revoking the covenant I had made with all the nations.

Zechariah 11:4; 7; 8b – 9b; 10 NIV

"It's broken," the Lord said. And the tears rolled down my face as relief rung out in my spirit.

Leah was transferred to another department the very next day.

LEADERSHIP
ESSENTIAL

~ GOING THROUGH THE FIRE ~

There's one thing that we can be assured of, and that is, for those of us who love God and are called according to His purpose, we're going to *go through the fire*. Go through the fire? Our faith in God, tested. Our calling, proved. Our purpose, solidified. Our beliefs and core values, established. Our thoughts, examined. Our hearts, revealed. Our character, pressured. Our patience, prolonged. Our endurance, developed. Our perseverance, challenged.

God Himself will be present through it all.

When God begins to take us to the next level in Him, you know, the "promotion" we're always desiring, we must be mindful that along with the promotion comes…persecution; betrayal. And it isn't a "quick work" either; you'll have to endure; patiently endure.

Everything concerning every fiber of our being will be tried by the fire – by the Lord – in the refining process that we must go through:

I will bring that group through the fire
  and make them pure.
I will refine them like silver
  and purify them like gold.
They will call on my name,
  and I will answer them.
I will say, 'These are my people,'
  and they will say, 'The LORD is our God.'"

Zechariah 13:9 NLT

In the process of refining metals (silver and gold), the raw metal is heated with fire until it melts. The impurities are separated from the raw materials and rise to the surface. They are removed, which then leaves the pure metal. Without this refining process (heating and melting), there could be no purifying.

Now, just as the refining process is done, the same holds true for us concerning the *spiritual* refining process:

- ✓ The raw metal represents – us, the believer.
- ✓ Heated and melted with fire represents – the trials and tribulations that we endure under the fire until it melts us, develops us.
- ✓ The impurities in this process represent – anything that is not like God; the areas in which the Lord is developing.

The impurities are separated, removed (developed and matured) as a result of the work that the Lord does in and through us – leaving only the pure metal; mature Christian.

So if you didn't know, now you know; with promotion comes persecution. There is…

No power without pain.

I have refined you, but not as silver is refined. Rather, I have refined you in the furnace of suffering.

Isaiah 48:10 NLT

I have no doubt that everybody wants "promotion." And while it's clear that God uses suffering to bring forth spiritual growth, I know everybody isn't willing to go through what it takes to get that promotion. If that were the case, we'd have many more mature Christians and many more developed gifts in the body of Christ.

A part of going through the fire, as I mentioned above, is having our faith in God tested to see if we'll remain faithful (and obedient) to Him and His Word (all while under the distress of being persecuted and afflicted by Satan). So going through the fire is a tool that the Lord uses to determine if we'll **hold our peace,** if you will, as He instructed; be obedient.

Are we committed to His ways enough to go through the fire even though the heat would be turned up? Do we trust Him enough to know that even though we'd go through the fire, we wouldn't get burned? When your friends walk away, turn their backs on you, come up against you, and then betray you, do you *know that you know that you know* that He'll be there for you? Or do you fear that He'll forsake you as well? Would it all be worth it in the end?

I knew my ministry would go to another level. God had promotion on His mind concerning me, which He revealed to me in the beginning, before the trial, test came. But, there were times when I didn't know if I would make it. I didn't know if it would all be worth it. I wasn't sure if I would be able to strengthen my brothers and sisters in Christ if I myself didn't go through the fire. There were times when I wasn't sure if God's purpose for me, my life would be fulfilled. I didn't think I would be in a position to advance the Kingdom of God. Often times I even wondered if I would get the anointing, power, and authority that came with the next level that He promised *if I didn't go through the fire.*

The *only* way to get the next level of anointing, power, and authority is by going through the fire. He shows us the reward in the beginning, but He doesn't tell us what we have to go through to get the reward, (ask Joseph about his experience from the pit to the palace). But the only way to *"get to"* is to *"go through."* There were a number of times I had to remind myself, *this isn't even about me. This is about the lives that will be affected as a result of the ministry that the Lord was birthing in me; this is about the ministry that the Lord has entrusted me with.*

This was his eternal plan, which he carried out through Christ Jesus our Lord.

Ephesians 3:11 NLT

Though I struggled, the one thing I knew was to call on God. I knew that He was the *only* One who'd be able to deliver me from the fire; *from the hands of the enemy.*

He was there. God was present. Even though there were times when I couldn't hear Him or see Him; He was there. There's a saying that's often said: *The Teacher is always silent during the test.* It reflects the analogy of a student in school preparing for a test. The teacher provides the student with the knowledge that he needs in order to prepare him/her for the test. The test would determine if the student is prepared to go to the next level. Wait! Let me say that again, *the test would determine if the student is prepared to go to the next level.* You see, the teacher had taken the time that was needed, had given the instructions that were needed, had given the materials that were needed (or weapons in our case) – BEFORE THE TEST CAME.

Therefore, while taking the test, the teacher is silent.

Now the one thing that I'd like to point out in this scenario is, not only is the teacher silent, but *He's watching closely,* I might add, *to see if you're prepared.* Did you pay attention? Did you do your homework? Are you ready? Another thing I noticed in this analogy is, there *isn't* an opportunity for you to cheat. Either you're prepared or you're not! There is no "turn to your neighbor," looking to see what your neighbor would do. You see, no matter how hard it gets there's no one there to help you, BUT GOD.

He was watching me – while I was looking for Him to give me the answers that He'd already given me. I was stuck. "Lord, what do I do?" I asked. Somehow, I didn't feel prepared to take the test – my anxiety built, the uncertainty mounted. I was sure there were times when I should've been listening, but wasn't. There *was* that one assignment that I didn't turn in. I wanted to cry. I wanted to just get up and walk away. I would've settled for a zero, but then I would've had to go back through the persecution and betrayal, and *then* be tested again. "What's the answer, Lord?" I asked.

I know this, I told myself, *calm down; you got this!* "Where are you, Lord?" I asked. *Oh, my God, I can't do this,* I told myself as doubt presented itself. *He has already given me the answer. I know that. But I can't seem to figure it out.* My mind raced frantically to try and remember the answer – I cannot get this wrong. *I know this! I know this!* I continued to encourage myself. I know He told me to *'Hold my peace,'* but I couldn't seem to figure out *why.*

He was silent.

But by His grace, I was reminded:

Then Jesus was led by the Spirit into the wilderness to be tempted there by the devil.
For forty days and forty nights he fasted and became very hungry.
During that time the devil came and said to him, "If you are the Son of God, tell these stones to become loaves of bread."
But Jesus told him, "No! The Scriptures say,
　'People do not live by bread alone,
　　but by every word that comes from the mouth of God.'"

Then the devil took him to the holy city, Jerusalem, to the highest point of the Temple, and said, "If you are the Son of God, jump off! For the Scriptures say,
　'He will order his angels to protect you.
　And they will hold you up with their hands
　　so you won't even hurt your foot on a stone.'"

Jesus responded, "The Scriptures also say, 'You must not test the Lord your God.'"
Next the devil took him to the peak of a very high mountain and showed him all the kingdoms of the world and their glory. "I will give it all to you," he said, "if you will kneel down and worship me."
"Get out of here, Satan," Jesus told him. "For the Scriptures say,
'You must worship the Lord your God
and serve only him.'"

Then the devil went away, and angels came and took care of Jesus.

Matthew 4:1 – 11 NLT

Now, for the most part, we're probably already familiar with this passage of scriptures. And I have to share with you that initially, I couldn't understand what Jesus being tempted in the wilderness had to do with me being attacked by my *so-called friends*. Of course, I understood that with Jesus being tempted, all bets were off for the Christians – *we would also be tempted*. Clearly, I understood *that* and did not have a problem with that. But I have to say, my frustration went further than just being tempted by the enemy or attacked continuously.

I could not understand *why* the Lord wouldn't just allow me to rebuke that devil and be done.

There was never a doubt in my mind that this devil was already defeated; I have power over the enemy. However, I struggled to remember *why* I couldn't use this power. I was starting to think that maybe I didn't have the power to rebuke the enemy and somehow, unbeknownst to me, the Lord was actually sparing *me* from getting rebuked by the enemy. My mind was tormented. *At what point do I give up?* I wondered.

Now, I have to say, the thing that I noticed was, not only did the enemy tempt Jesus, but He tempted Him in the areas that He had power and authority in. Now these may have also been areas that he *appeared* to be weak in, but these were the very areas that He was actually strong in. Clearly, Satan had to know Jesus, the Son of God, has power and authority, right? Of course he knew Jesus had power and authority. He remembered Jesus from when they used to live together – in heaven – before he was kicked out like lightning.

So, does this mean the areas that Satan tempts *us in* are areas that we already have power and authority in? So is this test about power and authority that we already have, but aren't aware that we have? I mean after all, the Lord revealed that I had *a new level of power and authority before the test began.* Or is the test about something else? Clearly, Satan knows that we have the power and the authority, that's why he tempts us in these *very* areas, but do *we* know that? I mean, when I think about Job, the enemy tempted him *because* he was a faithful, righteous man of God. He thought that because God had blessed Job with all of the material blessings *that* was the only reason that Job was so faithful to God. Therefore, God had to *"prove"* him; allowed Job to be *tested*. But again, I say, the enemy came *because Job was faithful.*

Okay, I think I have the answer now, Discipline. But wait, it's a two-part answer. "Oh, Lord, Help me!" Okay, wait, let me think. One important factor of our faith and walk with Christ is that we're striving to do the will of the Father; to remain in the center of His will and not doing things in our own strength.

For example, Christ turning the stone into bread wouldn't be a bad thing because he was hungry, right? Nevertheless, what we fail to realize is that He wouldn't be *just* turning the stone into bread. But rather, He'd be satisfying *His* desire for food at the expense of his *purpose and destiny.* In other words, Satan was trying to get Jesus to **sacrifice his discipline.**

Now, I have to say, and we all probably already know this, but this temptation wasn't *really* about Jesus being hungry – it was about Him being **obedient** to what He had come to do. He wasn't led to the wilderness to eat – He was led to the wilderness to fast; to discipline His flesh so that He could carry out the plan of salvation. You see, He knew that on His way to the cross, he was going to have to bear the weight of His physical body being crucified.

And the same held true for me.

Each and every time the enemy came up against me, accusing me: ***"You're judging me." "Your methods aren't effective." "You don't know if I've been delivered." "You let me down."*** and ***"You didn't prepare me for the right battle."*** all I could do was stand there and bear the blows of the demonic attacks. You see, Satan was trying to get me to satisfy *my* desire to rebuke him. But by doing so, it would've been at the expense of my *purpose and destiny.* The attacks weren't about me exercising my power and authority, but rather they were about me *disciplining* my power and authority; being **obedient** to the Father; to see if I would obey, *hold my peace.* Otherwise, I would've sacrificed my discipline.

What is discipline? The Webster's New World Dictionary indicates discipline is training that develops self-control, efficiency; strict control to enforce obedience, orderly conduct, and a system of rules.

Consequently, just as Jesus wasn't in the wilderness to eat, but to fast; I wasn't called to rebuke the demonic forces, but I was called to hold my peace. Did I have power and authority over the enemy? Absolutely! But this wasn't about me exercising my power and authority; this was about me bringing my flesh under subjection to the will of the Father by exercising obedience, self-control. Therefore, Jesus' temptation wasn't about turning stones into bread, and my temptation wasn't about rebuking demonic forces – the temptation was about **being obedient, disciplined.**

Ultimately, this is how Satan works. He tries to persuade us to take action, but for the wrong reason or at the wrong time. Surely, I wanted nothing more desperately than I wanted to rebuke the demonic forces, but *not as much as* I wanted to be obedient to the Father.

The fact that it is the Lord's desire (and mine) to see anyone who's being used or bound by the enemy – delivered, proves there's nothing wrong with having the desire to *want* to rebuke the demons. However, I would've been *sinning* by being disobedient to what the Lord instructed me to do. Obedience allowed me to remain in the center of His will for my life, which gave me the strength and the power to endure the attacks.

So let me put it this way: Not only does Satan tempt us because of our weaknesses, but in the areas of our strength as well. Why is that? Because it is his desire to get us to use our power without considering its purpose. We know Jesus had power over the stone. We know He had power over the kingdoms of the world. And we know He had power over the angels. And I know I had power over the enemy, which was revealed at the beginning of this book.

Oh, wait! I got it! I got the answer! Obedience. That's what this test was about *Discipline and Obedience.*

And yet, at the expense of being disciplined and obedient to obtain the prize of the high calling in Christ Jesus – new levels of anointing, power, and authority; I endured.

But not without wondering, *when do I let go?*

And he said unto me, My grace is sufficient for thee: for my strength is made perfect in weakness. Most gladly therefore will I rather glory in my infirmities, that the power of Christ may rest upon me.

2 Corinthians 12:9 KJV

Grace. The Lord's unmerited favor, the Lord's power, presence in exchange for my weakness.

And while it was clear that the Lord wasn't going to deliver me from the temptation until His appointed time, it would become clear that He would demonstrate His power in this trial. When God is taking you to new levels in Him, He wants to first see if He can trust you; *are you going to be obedient and remain faithful.* Therefore, we must understand that the trials, the tests, have come to make us strong. They have come to develop, mature, and discipline us! And the very areas which you're being *promoted* in are the very areas that you're tempted or tried in. And while it *appears* to be areas of weaknesses *to the enemy,* they're actually areas of strength *in training to develop self-control* to prepare you for the next level.

The greater the levels of anointing, power, and authority results in the greater the discipline, development, and maturing. The greater the persecution, weakness, and limitation results in the greater dependence on God and *the greater the grace.*

Through it all…He's there.

And while it's understood that there is no other way but *to go through,* the anguish, torment, and pain is overwhelming, but it demonstrates our love for Him. It may not be clear at the time, but it is certainly true; the hours, days, and months may bring what appears to be defeat but ultimately turns into an experience of His power.

Our
eyes
will
weep
Our
hearts
will
ache
Our mouths are silent Our hands will shake
Our knees will kneel Our strength is gone
Our
pain
is
real
but
we
hold
on

Unfortunately, not before the many nights that you'll cry, all night long, for days, with no end in sight. And certainly not before you're awakened out of your sleep, every night, for days, in the midnight-hour and demanded to fight. And most definitely not before you're on the verge of losing your mind from all of the demonic attacks on your character, integrity, ministry, and faith in God. And let me tell you this, if that doesn't do it, there is absolutely no way you're coming out before the grenade goes off and you're closed up in the warfare chamber – and you have to take your mask off.

Clearly your cry won't necessarily be a cry not to drink from the bitter cup, but a cry for His help; a cry for comfort in a place of darkness and seeming abandonment.

My God, my God, why have you abandoned me? Why are you so far away when I groan for help? Every day I call to you, my God, but you do not answer. Every night you hear my voice, but I find no relief.

Psalm 22:1 – 2 NLT

Who is this God who has demanded you to be obedient to His instructions? Who is this God that has asked you to trust Him? Who is He that He has not rescued you from the hand of the enemy? You'll wonder as the tears roll down your face.

Where is God – while the enemy taunts you all day long saying, "Where is your God now? Where is this God that you say is 'your God'? Where is this God that you praise and worship?" The enemy will taunt you as the pain rings out in your soul.

"Where is this God that you love and adore – this God that you believe sits on the throne with all power and authority in His hands?" Your mind will be tormented.

*"Where is your God…A God you serve **but have never seen?"***

HE'S IN THE FIRE.

But he knoweth the way that I take: when he hath tried me, I shall come forth as gold. My foot hath held his steps, his way have I kept, and not declined. Neither have I gone back from the commandment of his lips;

Job 23:10 – 12a KJV

While it was clear, and I never had any doubts that the only way that I was going to make it through was that God, and God alone, would be the One to bring me through. I never lost faith in Him or His ability to save me from the hands of the enemy. Now, whether He would or not, I didn't know, but I knew He was able. And I knew that if He didn't do it, *it could not be done.*

Even though Jesus was God's Son, he learned obedience from the things he suffered.

Hebrews 5:8 NLT

Now, there will be times when you'll find yourself crying out to God because the attacks are so great that your faith *will* be shaken. *Where are you, God? When is it going to end? Will I possess the promise?* You'll wonder. And there won't be any speaking to the storm, "Peace. Be still." But you can rest assured that God will be right there – in the storm with you.

Not only so, but we also glory in our sufferings, because we know that suffering produces perseverance; perseverance, character; and character, hope. And hope does not put us to shame, because God's love has been poured out into our hearts through the Holy Spirit, who has been given to us.

Romans 5:3 NIV

Without the trials, tests, tribulations, we'll never know who we really are. We'll never know what we're made of. And we'll never know that we're able to overcome until we've overcome.

The attacks, accusations, and betrayal are a part of God's plan to get us to depend on Him, and for Him to discipline us, develop us, and get us to our destiny. Therefore, the trials only come to make us strong and to mature us. So let's continue to praise Him as we suffer. Not *because* we suffer, but because we *know* that God is doing a mighty work in us. The refining process is needed so that in the end we'll come forth as pure gold. Suffer not the enemy's attacks, for God has allowed it to produce perseverance, which in turn produces our character. And our character produces hope; hope without shame. In the midst of the afflictions, it's His grace that enables us to become triumphant.

Trials and tribulations are crucial so that we may get to see the God we serve *with our own eyes.*

Now, I'd like to point out that while I shared some of the revelation about the dream in the beginning, what may not have been so obvious is the fact that the *ring master* is *the Lord Jesus,* and *the tiger in the cage* is *Satan.*

And while the Lord had given Satan the authority to launch the attacks, what wasn't revealed was the fact that Satan was subject to the Lord's command. If you notice, the attacks weren't launched until the ring master, the Lord Jesus, gave the command; he raised his whip to instruct Satan to rise up. It was clear that the attacks were orchestrated by the Lord.

> *In a dream...*
>
> *I saw what appeared to be a circus; where the ring master and a tiger were in a cage. The ring master raised his whip to instruct the tiger to rise up. When the tiger rose, it appeared to be twelve – fifteen feet tall. I was astonished at how huge the tiger was.*

The cage itself revealed that Satan was limited to what he could and couldn't do. He was not at liberty to do to me whatever he wanted to do. He didn't have the authority, power, or the ability to act independently of the Lord. He could only do what the Lord had allowed him to do. Ultimately, he was powerless; subject to the Lord. He was confined, restricted to do only what the Lord allowed him to do. The cage was also an indication that Satan would be defeated – he was bound.

Immediately, I was reminded of Job.

Satan replied to the LORD, "Yes, but Job has good reason to fear God. You have always put a wall of protection around him and his home and his property. You have made him prosper in everything he does. Look how rich he is! But reach out and take away everything he has, and he will surely curse you to your face!"

"All right, you may test him," the LORD said to Satan. "Do whatever you want with everything he possesses, but don't harm him physically." So Satan left the LORD's presence.

Job 1:9 – 12 NLT

Now the Bible is clear that Satan attacked Job because of his motives; his reasons for serving God and for being faithful. He indicated that Job was blameless and had integrity *only* because God had a wall of protection around him and he prospered. So Satan wanted to prove that Job was only faithful to God because he prospered *not* because Job loved God. And needless to say, God allowed Satan to *"test"* Job.

Satan replied to the LORD, "Skin for skin! A man will give up everything he has to save his life. But reach out and take away his health, and he will surely curse you to your face!"

"All right, do with him as you please," the LORD said to Satan. "But spare his life." So Satan left the LORD's presence, and he struck Job with terrible boils from head to foot.

Job 2:4 – 7 NLT

And again, as I mentioned, Satan was limited to what he could do to Job; each time he attacked Job, he had to get permission from the Lord. So while Satan had the authority to torment and persecute Job, he was still limited; he couldn't take his life. And the same held true for me; while Satan had the opportunity to attack, torment, and persecute me, he was limited to what he could do to me, which was evident in the Holy Spirit stepping in as I laid breaths away from death.

And consequently, as He had done with Job, the Lord removed the hedge of protection from around me so that He could *"teach"* or *"test"* me to *"prove my obedience unto Him."*

So while I had been placed in a *hostile environment;* in *a large-scale fight between armed forces,* I was mindful that ultimately, the battle belonged to the Lord.

"You have no experience in a hostile environment," He said.

Now, what I'd like to point out is the fact that, as always, with God, things aren't always as they seem. While it may be clear, as I've shared with you already, the attacks were deliberately launched against me, but what wasn't as clear is the fact that the *battle* wasn't about me. Nor was the battle about the land; *the battle is about the people.*

The battle was against the demonic forces *on behalf* of the people. The *battle* was about a fight *for* the people.

The war is against their human reasoning in order to destroy the false arguments that have a stronghold on their minds, which keeps them from receiving the Word of God. The war is against proud obstacles that keep them from knowing God; any time they don't receive the Word of God that is shared with them, it became a test for me to break the strongholds that allowed Satan to build walls that separated them from God. *Hence Leah.*

Let the wicked change their ways
  and banish the very thought of doing wrong.
Let them turn to the LORD that he may have mercy on them.
  Yes, turn to our God, for he will forgive generously.

Isaiah 55:7 NLT

And while I had no experience in fighting against the enemy in *battle* where the demonic forces would *oppose me – come up against me – and fight back; creating a hostile environment,* the hostile environment was created to determine if I would give up. Would I give up in spite of the hostile environment? Would I give up and stop fighting *for* the people in spite of the seemingly defeat? So while the enemy was fighting against me to keep me from getting to the next level, I was fighting so the people could obtain the promises of God. The fight was never about me and the individual. Again, we must realize that the battle isn't against flesh and blood, but against evil rulers and authorities of the unseen world, against mighty powers in this dark world, and against evil spirits in the heavenly places: evil forces of powerful fallen angels led by Satan.

So consequently, as Satan waged war against me, *I waged war against the weapons that he used against me – cancelling the enemy's assignments.*

MY WEAPON OF WARFARE – *hold my peace.*

Demonic attacks came against me to **teach** and **test** me in order for me (like the Israelites) to "possess" the "promise" that the Lord had given me. Again, there was no mistaking it; He had given me the promise – the promise was mine. However, He revealed, I, like the Israelites, had to **"possess"** the promise. "You have to have power over the promise," He said. In other words, when the enemy came up against me or opposed me, I had to have *"power over"* the enemy; defeating the enemy and *"taking"* the promise. Holding my peace was power over the enemy!

"You have no experience in driving the people out," He continued.

Therefore, I had to fight, battle, and *drive them out.*

In the midst of the test, trial, I found myself in unfamiliar territory and needless to say, burdened with uncertainties and seemingly unprepared.

While the Lord made it clear that He would use the nations in order to **"teach," "test," "prove my obedience unto Him,"** to become experienced in the wars of Canaan, I'd like to point out what this *experience* was all about…**a shift.** What shift? *A shift or significant change in my thought process.* But let me first of all make mention that any time there's a spiritual battle or warfare, the battle/warfare takes place *in the mind.* Therefore, what God was revealing or what He was concerned about was the way I *thought* didn't line up with the way *He thinks.*

The way I thought didn't line up with His plan, purpose, and destiny for my life. So, my thought process was being challenged. It was time for me *to shift.* It was time for a significant change in the way I thought about those who opposed God; His will, His way.

You see, I've always *thought,* believed, in fact, the church is the place people go to in order to develop spiritually and to get that much needed help to become victorious. I never thought that it was okay to *put someone out of the church.* No matter what! It didn't matter the sin or how many times they sinned, the church was a place that you go to in order to get delivered. My thought was simply – you don't put people out of the church. It wasn't "spiritual" or "scriptural."

But I learned that was not the case.

"My thoughts are nothing like your thoughts," says the LORD.
 "And my ways are far beyond anything you could imagine.
For just as the heavens are higher than the earth,
  so my ways are higher than your ways
  and my thoughts higher than your thoughts."

Isaiah 55:8 – 9 NLT

So, when the Lord demanded that I *drive out* the nations, it was a direct conflict with my thought process, which speaks to the difficulty I faced when He instructed me to release Leah from the ministry – resulting in a significant change; shift – in the way I thought.

Now, in this experience, what was also happening in the process of the Lord significantly changing my mind, I was getting to know Him in a way that I'd never known Him before. I got to see Him in a way that I'd never seen Him before, and I got to experience Him in a way that I'd never experienced Him before. Consequently, the process or experience was not only about me being attacked, tormented, or persecuted, but it was also about me getting to *know* Him (in the fellowship of His suffering). Well, to say that I was getting to know Him would only be half-true. The other side of that coin was *I* was also getting to *know* myself. That's right. I was getting to know myself. Ultimately, the Lord was revealing a side of me – to me – that I didn't even know existed.

I didn't know that I'd be able to withstand the attacks, torment, or persecution of the enemy. I didn't know that I'd fight, and continue to fight until the battle had been won – in spite of the hostile environment. Nor did I know that I'd be able to *hold my peace* in the process. And I most certainly had no idea that I'd be able to "drive out the nations," release someone from our ministry. And while in my mind, I was "barely fighting the demons on the level I was on," there was absolutely no way I thought I'd be able to defeat demons on a higher level; tigers – devils I had never contended with – defeated.

"What? Another level? Wait! But I have no experience!"

Who does that? Only God would do something like that; the God who knows your *end* in the *beginning.* Of course God who knows more about you than you know about yourself. The God who reveals to you a side of you that *you* don't even know exists. Therefore, when being tested, tried, the Lord is saying,

For I know the plans I have for you," says the LORD. "They are plans for good and not for disaster, to give you a future and a hope.

Jeremiah 29:11 NLT

Faced with my own uncertainty, timidity and apprehension of not being prepared or experienced – I was trying to figure it all out – as He took me step by step and showed me the way to accomplish what He had purposed for me. Not only was He revealing *me to the tigers,* He was also revealing *the tigers to me;* demonic forces disguised as my friends. So, now *they* know who I am, and I know *the spirit* in which *they* come.

NEW LEVELS – NEW DEVILS

This means that God's holy people must endure persecution patiently and remain faithful.

Revelation 13:10c NLT

PART

VII

RECOVERY

BREAKTHROUGH – RECOVER ALL

After all that the Lord had done, I was constantly reminded of my spiritual state as I lie dead in the spirit. I had become desperate; I needed to *recover* – I needed a breakthrough. I still hadn't had a **breakthrough.**

The *"man of God"* was scheduled to come to town; however, I wasn't excited about going. As a matter of fact, I was almost dreading the idea of going because I knew there were going to be so many people, and I just wasn't up for the crowd. But I went anyway because I needed a breakthrough. Besides, I reasoned with myself, I hadn't seen him minister in years, and I knew the Word was going to be good. So I went.

When Randolph and I arrived at the church, the parking lot was pretty much full. So right away, I knew we were going to have to stand in line, which no doubt would be around the corner and down several blocks. However, I got out of the car, puzzled, because I didn't see the line of people. *The people must be going in another door that would obviously be more accommodating for the large number that would be attending,* I thought.

As soon as I got out of the car, I took off running; telling Randolph to hurry (because just as we were pulling up, there were other people pulling up, too.) The closer I got to the church I could see that the front door, the main entrance was open. The usher was standing with the door open to let the people in. *Wait a minute, there's no crowd; no line wrapped around the corner*, I thought. Instantly, I was deflated as I thought the usher was there to let us know, as a courtesy, that there weren't any more seats available.

We got to the door, was greeted, and ushered in; lead to the sanctuary. Immediately, I was confused. *What is going on? How early are we that there aren't any lines and the sanctuary isn't jam packed?* I wondered. We went in and got our seats. We sat close to the back. *The big screen monitors would serve their purpose*, I thought. I started to get excited as my expectations started to rise in anticipation of hearing from the man of God. I couldn't wait to hear the Word; I already knew *it* was going to speak to me and give me life – allowing me to get up off that operating table. There were even a couple of empty seats next to me, so I had plenty of room in case the Lord wanted to *slap me down on my face.*

Then the service started. The praise team came out and started to sing as the congregation joined in the praise and gave God glory. I stood there; nothing. I looked around and wondered, *What am I missing? What is this? Is this the praise and worship? Really?* I struggled to get in the Lord's presence. There was no doubt, the anointing was present, but something was amiss. I continued to press, but struggled.

NOTHING!

Oh, my God, I thought, but decided I'd just wait for the Word and let the Lord have His way. The man of God came out and we welcomed him. He returned the love and appreciation. My spirit man got excited; I could hardly wait for the Word – I needed it! Then we prepared for the Word as he started with prayer.

Immediately, my heart sank. I had just heard him preach this same message the week before. *Okay,* I thought, *obviously, there's something he said last week that I didn't get, so here he is to say it again. It must be something important – or else the Lord wouldn't have sent him with the same message.* (Because of course, he had come to give *me* the Word, which was going to help me recover; get a breakthrough.)

I struggled to get past the message that I'd already heard but somehow needed to hear again. *I continued to press.* There was *something* in that place for me, and I had come to get it. So if I had to sit through this sermon that I had already heard (and pretty sure I hadn't missed anything), then, so be it. I wasn't leaving that place empty; the same way I came. God was going to do something on my behalf. I was expecting.

Get it together, I kept telling myself. *God has something for you. And if you don't get it together you're going to miss it.* So I was very attentive to the Word of God. However, true to his teaching, the man of God didn't stray from the message that he'd spoken the week before. "Lord, what are you saying?" I asked.

And still nothing.

There were a couple of things that he'd ministered that I hadn't remembered him saying, and the Lord ministered to me as I sat quietly crying. And yet, it wasn't the **Word** I had come to get. It wasn't the **breakthrough** that I was looking for and needed. It was good, and it ministered to me, but that wasn't it.

Nothing!

Where are you, Lord? I wondered. I needed a breakthrough. I couldn't shake the vision of me lying dead in the spirit or the tears that continued to bear witness to the pain.

The service ended.

And still...nothing!

I didn't know what was going on, but something was amiss. Randolph and I had already decided that because we were at the conference we would get some of the teaching material to add to our library. So after the service, we went to purchase some products; I knew exactly what I wanted. I knew there was a "word" for me. Now whether it was on one of the DVDs or CDs, I didn't know, but I was expecting a "word" from the Lord.

I fasted, prayed, meditated on the Word of God, and declared and decreed my breakthrough.

The very next day I was watching *with expectation* the DVDs that I had purchased. I watched the first DVD; *nothing.* I watched the second DVD; *nothing.*

"Lord, I know you have a "word" for me. And if I have to watch every single DVD the man of God has, I will! I need you to move mightily on my behalf," I cried out.

As the man of God continued to minister, the Lord *spoke* into my spirit, *"That old man is dead,"* which gave me understanding of me lying dead on the table; the *old me* was dead. I rejoiced!

And immediately, my spirit was quickened, as the vision was before me:

In a vision…

I saw myself get up off the operating table.

The Interpretation...

I had been raised with another level of anointing, power, and authority.

Our bodies are buried in brokenness, but they will be raised in glory. They are buried in weakness, but they will be raised in strength [power]. They are buried as natural human bodies, but they will be raised as spiritual bodies.

1 Corinthians 15:43 – 44a NLT (emphasis added)

The God of our ancestors raised Jesus from the dead after you killed him by hanging him on a cross.

Acts 5:30 NLT

The old man was dead.

And just as suddenly, I was reminded of the vision:

> **Consequently, just as suddenly as I had seen the tigers, I knew I had been given another level of anointing, power, and authority.**

My God! I was amazed that the victory had been won. The battle had been won. And to think, the weapon He used to win the battle; HOLD YOUR PEACE – it was mind blowing. And I was reminded of just how significant that was for me – **the old me** wouldn't have held my peace. I would've rebuked that devil had he come up against me. There wouldn't have been me just standing there as he accused and attacked me time and time again. Surely, I would've hit back if he had hit. And I definitely wouldn't have had anything to do with anyone if they betrayed me – **that went without saying.** You would've been cut off with the quickness!

But that was the *old me.* I don't wage war as the world does. The weapons I fight with are not the weapons of the world. On the contrary, they have divine power to demolish strongholds. I demolish arguments and every pretension that sets itself up against the knowledge of God, and I take captive every thought to make it obedient to Christ.

I GOT THE VICTORY!

Jesus replied, "Now the time has come for the Son of Man to enter into his glory. I tell you the truth, unless a kernel of wheat is planted in the soil and dies, it remains alone. But its death will produce many new kernels—a plentiful harvest of new lives. Those who love their life in this world will lose it. Those who care nothing for their life in this world will keep it for eternity.

John 12:23 – 25 NLT

And still…that wasn't it.

SOMETHING WAS MISSING.

I needed a breakthrough!

When suddenly, I realized the victory had come, the breakthrough had come – *in the spirit.* And while I understood *it was going to come to pass* because it was already done, I also understood *it had to manifest in the natural.* Therefore, I had the burden of manifesting this **victory, breakthrough** in the natural. So I had to continue to force my way through to victory *against the resistance* of the enemy to **receive** the breakthrough.

Consequently, I continued to meditate on the Word of God and stayed in His presence.

Then I noticed that the *woman of God* was coming to town and immediately felt led to go. Of course, I thought it was odd because I hadn't watched her ministry in years. But being obedient to the Lord, I went.

I went to see the woman of God with the expectation that God would move mightily on my behalf. So, when I arrived, I expected the praise & worship to just usher me into the presence of God. Therefore, I already knew, before I got there, that the anointing would be so great that I wouldn't be able to stand. I just knew I was going to be stretched out in the floor from the power of the Holy Spirit – just slain in the spirit.

I got there, and went right in (it wasn't that crowded because it was still early). I went right to the front because I saw some empty seats, only to get up there and they were all RESERVED. So, I turned around and started looking for a seat when a young lady saw me and waved me over to the empty seat next to her, which was right behind the RESERVED seats. And right away, I knew it was a set up! God had *something* for me and *He* was going to *make sure* I got it. I was excited because I had *come to get* whatever He had *for me.*

The conference started with praise and worship. Lo and behold, *nothing! Okay,* I thought, *no big deal it's praise – just to warm the people up; get us ready to shake the cares of the job off. Wait,* I encouraged myself, *the worship is going to start and the anointing is going to just slap me down on my face. I'll be doubled over in a minute.* I was so excited in my spirit that I could hardly wait until the Lord showed up. This was going to be it. This was going to be the break-through that I'd been waiting for. God was going to do this thing – no doubt.

And…nothing.

I sat through the Word convinced that I was at the wrong conference. The woman of God was talking about God's grace!!!??? *What? What is this?!* I questioned. *I need a breakthrough!*

"God, is tonight the night? Should I have waited until tomorrow night?" I asked. "Surely, either You've missed it or I've missed it – somehow – we're not on the same page." Convinced, either He wasn't there or I was in the flesh. Something wasn't right. I was glad, in fact, had rejoiced that the woman of God had only ministered for what seemed to be thirty minutes. I couldn't wait to get out of there.

Nonetheless, throughout the night my spirit was disturbed. *What happened?* I wondered.

"I was expecting you, Lord. You didn't show up! Today was the day; we had an appointment. You didn't tell me that the appointment was cancelled; I didn't get an email that it was cancelled, no text message – nothing! Where were you, Lord," I asked.

SILENCE

I went to bed dead set – I mean, I could hardly wait until our 3 a.m. time together because I knew He was going to explain, *"Something came up and I just couldn't make it."* In spite of Him not showing up, I was expecting Him more now than before because this was the exact same thing that had happened at the woman of God's conference I attended in 2000. So, I *knew* He was waiting for *me* to show up, and it was going to be on! As a result of His visitation, I knew I was going to have to get in my usual corner in the house (to keep my husband and son from hearing me wailing and from seeing all of my snot tissues), but I was ready!

Nothing!

Three a.m. came and went…and nothing.

I had become like Job:

"I go east, but he is not there.
   I go west, but I cannot find him.
I do not see him in the north, for he is hidden.
   I look to the south, but he is concealed."

Job 23:8 – 9 NLT

I prayed.

I knew He would answer. He *had* to answer. "Say something, Lord. Please, I need to hear from you."

And immediately He responded:

In a vision...

I was carrying a huge cross on my back. It was heavy.

The interpretation…

No interpretation was needed.

Immediately, the tears came forth as the pain and realization of my calling was before me. And suddenly I understood the message of grace that the woman of God ministered. But that didn't stop the tears from falling from my eyes as I sat before Him.

What is this that I've I longed for; suffered for; carried the cross for? I wondered.

SILENCE

Randolph and I got ready for work and headed out. I was still *eating* the Word of God. We were listening to the man of God minister in the car. I was still expecting a breakthrough. My spirit was expecting, my soul was anticipating, and my heart was rejoicing – *something* was getting ready to happen. *Something had* to happen!

The Word was good, but I was half listening because I was still wondering, *Where are you, Jesus?* The light was yellow; cautioning me to yield to His Spirit. Then the Word started to get really good. He was in my lane, coming down my street. I was right there – red light – waiting; allowing Him the right of way; *to have His way.*

My expectation was building. I knew the *light* was about to change!

There was no need to *look to your neighbor.* There was no need to *look both ways* before crossing. There was no need to *look to the left or look to the right.* The pathway had already been made clear.

Then the Lord spoke,

"IT SHALL BE RELEASED!"

And His words reverberate throughout my spirit, "IT SHALL BE RELEASED! IT SHALL BE RELEASED! IT SHALL BE RELEASED!" ***Then suddenly…***

GREEN LIGHT; GO!

And the Spirit of the Lord came upon me.

And in that very instant, I cried out with everything that was within me – completely broken in His presence – the Spirit of the Lord overtook me.

I could hear Bishop T.D. Jakes' voice, "GET READY! GET READY! GET READY!" ring out in my spirit as the "word" of the Lord was confirmed.

My ***BREAKTHROUGH*** had finally come.

And as a result of the outpouring of His Spirit, the anointing was so heavy. I was unable to control the tears; I wept.

Suddenly! The *stronghold* had been broken! The barricades had been removed! And there was an explosion in my spirit. I had broken through the enemy's defense:

These are the nations that the LORD left in the land to test those Israelites who had not experienced the wars of Canaan.

Judges 3:1 NLT

The walls of the kingdom of darkness had been penetrated, and the enemy had been defeated. And in an instant, *everything* that had been trying to hold me back from advancing – had been loosed! All barriers that had been set up to keep me from my purpose, my destiny, had been demolished! And as if a military movement had taken place, the Lord's army was at my defense; suddenly, advancing, rendering all nations – powerless!

And just like in the natural, this *birthing, delivery* gave way to the *joy of the Lord,* which overshadowed the heartache, pain, anguish, sorrow, suffering, and betrayal that I had endured throughout this birthing process.

Every time I thought about what the Lord had done for me, the tears would fall from my eyes as His anointing rested upon me.

I WAS DONE! *THE BATTLE HAD BEEN WON!*

ANOINTING, POWER, AND AUTHORITY – RECOVERED!

Spiritually, physically, mentally, and emotionally drained; I was **completely** wiped out.

However, the next morning, I got a wakeup call at 2 a.m., but had convinced myself that I just "woke up," not that the Lord was calling me and inviting me into His presence. Then the wakeup call came again at about 4:15 a.m. Therefore, I decided I'd get up and see what the Lord was saying.

I was sooo exhausted!

Barely able to keep my eyes open; I laid prostrate before Him. But, it wasn't long before I dosed off.

And immediately, I was awakened by the *sound of the bell.*

My eyes popped open, and I stared into the darkness as I tried to figure out what had just happened. *What was that?* I questioned in my spirit as my eyes searched the darkness. And just as suddenly as I had heard the sound of the bell, the vision of the bell was before me. Then I realized that while the sound of the bell had come, it wasn't the *ding, ding, ding* that I had longed for – that was to stop the fight.

But rather, it was *BONG, BONG, BONG* – *the sound of the church.*

Then four years later...

One day my phone rang. I didn't recognize the number, but I answered the call anyway. The voice on the line asked, "May I speak to Daisy?"

"This is Daisy," I responded, but didn't recognize the voice.

"Hi, Ms. Daisy. This is Tiffany." And ***immediately,*** I was reminded of the prophetic word that the woman of God spoke: *"There are **two people** in particular who don't believe you are who you say you are. But I hear the Lord saying, 'They are going to have to come back and apologize to you for everything that they've done to you."*

"Hi, Tiffany," I responded as the tears welled up in my eyes; the Lord was true to His word.

"Ms. Daisy, I was calling to apologize to you for everything that happened," she said as the nervousness in her voice was apparent. "I just wanted to let you know that I'm sorry and that you were right about everything that you said about me. You *did* hear from God when you said I was to be the praise leader. My pastors said the same thing that you said, that the Lord wants me in a place of praise and worship." I just sat and listened, waiting for her to pause so that I could accept her apology, but she continued. "I went through deliverance with my pastors; I was delivered from a ***spirit of rebellion.*** So now that I've been delivered I'm able to see that everything that I was going through with you, I was going through with *my* pastors. And now I can see that I was wrong and I needed to apologize to you, I'm sorry."

"I accept your apology, Love." I said as my heart went out to her. I couldn't help but think *four years of that **same demon**; spirit of rebellion* and she hadn't prospered. I thought of her pastors, and her doing the same things to them as she had done to me; same demon, different ministry.

And then, a few months after speaking with Tiffany, I got a text from Leah saying how she had been thinking a lot about me lately and wanted to know if everything was okay.

"All is well. What have you been thinking?" I responded.

"Just thinking about how we don't talk anymore like we used to, and to be honest, I was thinking about all the stuff that I put you though. And I want you to know that I am so sorry. I know that I put you through a lot. And you're going to get a great reward just for putting up with me. You know I didn't mean to put you through all of that. I appreciate everything that you've done for me. I wouldn't be where I am today if it hadn't been for you. Thank you for putting up with me."

"I know, Love, you're welcome." Like Tiffany, my heart went out to Leah. She hadn't prospered in the four years either. She was still struggling financially, still not tithing, and still hadn't gotten a promotion. She was practically the ***only one*** in the company that hadn't been promoted. And she ended up joining the same church that Tiffany belonged to.

This is what they do. They're trained.

PROPHETIC WORD OF ENCOURAGEMENT

"I had a dream...

You had a beautiful baby boy. He was a good baby."

Prophetess, Dr. Sharon D. Dominguez

God's purpose in all this was to use the church to display his wisdom in its rich variety to all the unseen rulers and authorities in the heavenly places.

Ephesians 3:10 NLT

ABOUT DAISY S. DANIELS

Daisy S. Daniels has been married to Randolph E. Daniels, Sr. for 23 years. They have three children: Ronald, DaiSha, and Randolph, Jr. Daisy is Pastor of The Embassy of Grace (co-laborer with Senior Pastor, Randolph Daniels). She is an anointed woman of God who operates in the apostolic five-fold ministry in the body of Christ; under a prophetic mantle.

Prophetess Daisy's leadership, motivational, and transformational expertise encourages, inspires, and empowers the body of Christ. She ministers prophetic deliverance to women. She's proficient and flows in the prophetic anointing as well as the ministry of healing and deliverance.

She is founder and CEO of Daisy S. Daniels Ministries; a ministry that empowers women to increase in mind, body, soul and spirit into new levels, realms and dimensions; new regions and territories to break spiritual, physical, psychological, emotional, and sexual strongholds.

She is President and CEO of The Writing on the Wall Publishing Services; a full-service Christian publishing house that is committed to excellence in Christian-theme publications that enables you to write and publish the books of your dreams.

She received her M.B.A. in International Business from Keller Graduate School of Management in 2011.

TO CONTACT THE AUTHOR

Write: Daisy S. Daniels
P.O. BOX 621194
Orlando, FL 32862
Telephone: (708) 704-6117
Email: daisysdaniels@aol.com
Website: www.daisysdaniels.wix.com/ministry

ALSO BY DAISY S. DANIELS

THE TIES THAT BIND

BREAD FROM HEAVEN

YOUR FAITH IS ON TRIAL

INCREASE!

21-DAY FAITH FAST

THE WRITING ON THE WALL PUBLISHING SERVICES

The Writing on the Wall Publishing Services is a Christian publishing house that is committed to excellence in Christian-theme publications.

While every Christian believer is called to be a minister of the gospel of Jesus Christ, everyone is not called to minister from the pulpit. Therefore, our mission is to spread the gospel of Jesus Christ through Christian publication; the written word, which is interpreted prophetically.

The Writing on the Wall Publishing Services' goal is to equip you with the tools needed to successfully write, publish, and print your intellectual property, which will allow you to minister to the nations and advance the Kingdom of God. Our services include:

- MANUSCRIPT REVIEW
- EDITING
  - CONTENT EDITING
  - COPY EDITING
  - PROOFREADING
- MANUSCRIPT DEVELOPMENT / CONSULTING
- PAGE DESIGN AND LAYOUT
- COVER DESIGN
- ISBN NUMBER / BOOKLAND EAN BARCODE
- PRINTING
- COPYRIGHT

For more information, contact us:

Write: The Writing on the Wall Publishing Services
        P.O. BOX 621194
        Orlando, FL 32862 – 1433
Telephone: (708) 704-6117
Website: www.thewritingonthewal.wix.com/daisysdaniels
Email: thewritingonthewall@aol.com

www.ingramcontent.com/pod-product-compliance
Lightning Source LLC
Chambersburg PA
CBHW062033090426
42740CB00016B/2896